ORWELL:
THE TRANSFORMATION

ORWELL:
THE TRANS

FORMATION

Peter Stansky and William Abrahams

 Alfred A. Knopf   New York   1980

THIS IS A BORZOI BOOK
PUBLISHED BY ALFRED A. KNOPF, INC.

Library of Congress Cataloging in Publication Data

Stansky, Peter.
  Orwell, the transformation.

  The second part of Orwell's biography, begun with The
unknown Orwell.
  Bibliography: p.
  Includes index.
  1. Orwell, George, 1903–1950. 2. Authors, English—
20th century—Biography. I. Abrahams, William Miller,
joint author. II. Title.
PR6029.R8Z7898   828'.9'1209 [B]   79–3490
ISBN 0–394–47394–9

Manufactured in the United States of America
FIRST AMERICAN EDITION

For Ruth
and in memory of Mark

CONTENTS

ILLUSTRATIONS

ACKNOWLEDGMENTS

THIS STUDY HAS BEEN BASED ON ORWELL'S PUBLICATIONS, manuscript collections, and interviews with those who knew him. We are intensely grateful to those who were kind enough to see us, most of whom are mentioned in the text. Without them, this book could not have been written.

We are extremely grateful for the use of Orwell material in the Berg Collection, the New York Public Library; the Humanities Research Center, the University of Texas; the Library, the University of California at Los Angeles; the British Library; as well as material in private hands.

William Allan of the Stanford University Library gave great help in acquiring needed material. And we would like to express our thanks to the Rockefeller Foundation for providing time at the Villa Serbelloni where we were looked after so well by Bill and Betsy Olson, and to Pasquale Vuilleumier of the Hotel Palumbo, Ravello. In Bellagio and Ravello, most of this study was written.

Following *Journey to the Frontier*, whose subject was John Cornford and Julian Bell, the publication of this book about George Orwell, along with its predecessor, *The Unknown Orwell*, completes our original purpose: a study of three British writers of the 1930's, and the reasons for their involvement in the Spanish Civil War.

P.S.
W.A.

BEGINNING AS ORWELL

ONE

On MONDAY, JANUARY 9, 1933, THE OFFICIAL PUB-
lication day of *Down and Out in Paris and London,* he entered literary history as George Orwell. Not that he, or any
one else at the time, would have thought of the event in
such grandiose terms, though as it now appears they do
precisely sum up the case. Ordinarily, one would be the
same person on the ninth of January that one had been
on the eighth. What gave his situation its little peculiarity,
set it apart from that of the general run of authors bringing
out a first book, was that on the eighth he was Eric Blair,
and on the ninth he was George Orwell—or so it stated on
the title page of his book. And if, as we will see, the reviewers were much taken, relatively speaking, with this hitherto
unknown writer George Orwell for the first week or two
of his new existence (thereafter forgetting him until his
next book would appear), his family and friends—those
among them who had been told of the pseudonym—were
not. To them, as to himself, he was still and only Eric
Blair. So that on January 9, 1933, a day we now recognize
as having some consequence in literary history, the difference between being Blair and being Orwell was as slight, as
imperceptible, as the difference between Sunday the
eighth and Monday the ninth of January: another day
torn from the calendar.

After all, two months earlier the name itself hadn't existed. Blair had cautioned his agent, Leonard Moore, in April 1932 that if the book were accepted (which it was, by Victor Gollancz, in July), he would want it published pseudonymously, as he was "not proud of it." But in spite of repeated requests from agent and publisher, he did nothing to resolve the question of the pseudonym until November, the last possible moment, when the book was already in galleys with a title improvised by Gollancz, *Confessions of a Down and Outer,* and its authorship attributed simply to "X."

Even then there was a curious degree of equivocation. On the nineteenth of November he finally sent off to Gollancz (via Moore) not one but four possible pseudonyms, among them "George Orwell," which he admitted he "rather favoured." But the choice was left to Gollancz. Never once did Blair say "I *want* George Orwell," and there is reason to believe that if Gollancz had insisted on Eric Blair as the name for his author, Eric Blair it would have been: he would have resigned himself to it. Ever since his career as a schoolboy cynic, which had been launched at St. Cyprian's, his prep school, and had flourished when he was in College at Eton, he had come to accept as a matter of course—in *his* life anyway—life's ironies and disappointments: it would have been no more than the expected thing that the pseudonym he favored would not be the one to be chosen. In the event, however, his preference was followed: Gollancz made him Orwell.

Yet there is a further possible irony: that Blair may actually have preferred his own name to his chosen (or conferred) pseudonym. It seems worth pointing out in this connection that even after the publication of *Down and Out,* and in 1934 of his first and second novels, *Burmese*

Days and *A Clergyman's Daughter*, all three as by George Orwell, he was still making professional use of his own name. During 1934 he appeared several times in the *Adelphi*, as a poet and as a reviewer, and his contributions were always signed Eric Blair or E.A.B., never George Orwell.

The question of the pseudonym and its possible significance must continue to run its way like a thread in a carpet through any biographical study of Orwell in the 1930's. Some years ago, Samuel Hynes in the *Times Literary Supplement* brought up the question of pseudonyms, their uses, and as it were their unintended revelations and self-disclosures. "When a writer chooses another name for his writing self, he is doing more than inventing a pseudonym: he is naming, and in a sense creating, his imaginative identity." Hynes's subject, Rebecca West, had been born Cicily Fairfield—"a name that in itself seems almost too good an example of English gentility"—and she chose for her pseudonym, with marvelous aptness as it turned out, the name of the rebellious young heroine of Ibsen's *Rosmersholm*. Then, as though to reinforce the point, Hynes brought up the case of Orwell, and what is in fact a story of considerable complexity was drastically simplified: "Hence, George Orwell—a commonplace Christian name and an English river—together name the plain-speaking Englishman that Eric Blair *chose to be* in his work." It is all phrased in so straightforward, plain-speaking a way, with such an absence of bothersome qualification, that one can only wish it were true: one of the more exemplary cases of name-changing and self-transformation in literary history. And indeed, if one follows the thread as we intend to do in the present volume, it seems inarguable that by 1938—after his return from Spain and the writing of *Homage to Catalonia*—the consonance between George

Orwell in his work and his life, the "creation of his imaginative identity," had been virtually completed. But it had not been achieved without struggle, nor was it a matter simply of a change of name. That in itself was a first step—by which "the essential second self was set free"—and what followed was a slow, arduous process of transformation.

TWO

T HE PUBLICATION IN HIS THIRTIETH YEAR OF *Down and Out in Paris and London* marked not only the beginning of the literary career of George Orwell, but also the end of the literary apprenticeship of Eric Blair. When Blair, in the summer of 1927, returned to England from Burma and resigned his commission in the Indian Imperial Police, he was not prompted by some vague literary-romantic yearning. He knew, in the most ruthless and determined way, that he wanted to be a writer; in retrospect it seemed to him he had always wanted to be a writer, since his earliest childhood. He also knew that he had a lot to learn, and that he was starting out comparatively late, an unknown novice at an age when Cyril Connolly, his friend and contemporary at St. Cyprian's and at Eton, was already a conspicuous figure in the London literary scene. If he was a little envious and too proud to revive the friendship with Connolly during these years of obscurity, envy and pride helped to strengthen his determination. Wherever he happened to be living—in bed-sitters around London, in a shabby hotel in Paris, but most often in a room that was his by sufferance in his parents' house in Southwold—he wrote. Between 1927 and 1932 he would not take a regular job—he lived to write, a state made possible only by the generosity of his mother and his aunt Nellie Adam, who kept him in funds. It was an arduous apprenticeship, and his success in those five years was minimal. Still, it seems worth emphasizing—along with Blair's sense of literary vocation, which was fierce (however diffident he might seem) and unwavering—that he did enjoy some small degree of recognition. His was not an utterly hopeless cause, though at times it may have felt so to him and seemed so to his parents.

As Eric Blair he published a number of journalistic and literary pieces in the Paris weeklies during the year and some months he was living there. When he returned to England in 1931, he began to publish reviews, verse, and essays in the *Adelphi*, the *New Statesman and Nation*, and the *New English Weekly*, always in his own name. As Eric Blair he wrote and submitted to publishers two versions of the book we know as *Down and Out in Paris and London*. (Both were rejected by the firm of Jonathan Cape; the second and final version was also rejected by Faber & Faber upon the advice of their reader, T. S. Eliot.*)

For almost seven years he had been steadily writing and infrequently publishing as Eric Blair. It was only in April 1932, when Leonard Moore was ready to send off the manuscript of *Days in Paris and London* (the first title), that Blair raised the question of taking a new name as an author. His mention of a pseudonym in a letter to Moore (April 26) and in several further letters to him over the

---

* It was Eliot again, some years later, who advised Fabers against publishing *Animal Farm*. Orwell, not unmindful of these snubs, eventually got his own back with some adverse, not wholly unjustified or philistine, strictures on Eliot's poetry. Official relations between the two, however, were always cordial, and Eliot, at Orwell's request, would broadcast for the BBC Indian Service during the Second World War.

next seven months, culminating in the letter of November 19 when he finally and belatedly submitted a choice of four names for Gollancz—these constitute the only written contemporary evidence we know of a subject that has come to assume legendary, even mystical proportions in later commentaries. (The significance read into that plain Christian name, George—so working-class, to those who wish to think of it thus; so classless, to others; so rural or so royal— after all, six sovereigns have borne it; so *English*, from whatever stance. And then, that river, the Orwell—flowing through Suffolk out to the sea at Harwich—so plumbed by literary historians and critics for its symbolic yield.)

That summer of 1932, in Southwold, Blair told his sister Avril that he would be publishing his book under the pseudonym because he was afraid it would shock their parents. Avril replied with the directness characteristic of her that she felt he was overly concerned: their parents were more sophisticated than he seemed willing to admit, although their father, getting on in years, *was* something of the Victorian in his views on proper language. But of course, she concluded, with the diffidence that was very much a Blair characteristic, if Eric wanted to use a pen name for the book, that was his affair. His argument might have been more persuasive if he had not already published "The Spike" under his own name in the *Adelphi* (and would make it into two chapters of *Down and Out*); and "Hop Picking" and "Common Lodging Houses" in the *New Statesman and Nation* (also under his own name); and the three pieces together (which the elder Blairs seem to have taken in stride) gave a fair enough notion of what to expect in the book.

The one logical argument that he might have made, but which he did not make then or later, was that *Down and*

Out, presented as an autobiographic account of an author about whom nothing was known would carry much more weight, given its proletarian subject matter, than as the work of Eric Blair, an Old Etonian.

In any event, before the end of November, Victor Gollancz had decided that Eric Blair was to be George Orwell, and his book *Down and Out in Paris and London.* Then, with a celerity that must seem astonishing in the light of the difficulties that beset present-day publishing, the book was brought into being in a matter of weeks. Two days before Christmas, Blair, who was spending the holiday with his parents in Southwold, received a parcel from Leonard Moore: advance copies of the book, each bearing on the jacket the helpful, commercial phrase "A recommendation of the Book Society." So there it was at last, visible proof of his identity as an author, the book itself: to be weighed, examined, considered, approved, the size of it marveled at.

The advance copies could hardly have arrived at a more opportune moment: Christmas gifts for certain close friends of his in Southwold—Brenda Salkeld, who taught at St. Felix School on the edge of town, and Eleanor Jaques, who had been a pupil of Brenda's, and Dennis Collings, Eric's closest friend there, who was presently to marry Eleanor, although their engagement was not yet "official"— all of whom had been allowed to know that he was gathering material for a book about the lower depths. And copies too to the family, which meant there were none left over to send to such close friends in London as the Fierzes or Richard Rees.

Mabel Fierz had, of course, read the book in typescript, and it was she who brought it to Leonard Moore at a time when Eric himself had given up on it completely. She would now behave with the generosity that was typical of her: when the book was officially published three weeks later, she went to a bookshop and actually bought a copy— not all authors are so fortunate in their friends. Mabel's generosity went still further. At about this time she and her husband, Francis, went off for a weekend in Ostend. Knowing Eric's fondness for French books, she asked if there was anything she might buy for him there. "Yes," he said, "Joyce's *Ulysses*," for although he had already read a friend's copy, smuggled in from Paris—the novel still couldn't be published in England—he wanted one of his own. Mrs. Fierz, once again, was able to serve.

Avril and the elder Blairs seem to have read *Down and Out* with a good deal less shock or outrage than Eric had anticipated. Indeed, there is some question as to whether or not Mr. Blair ever did actually read it, though none at all that he heard about it at tiresome length from his Anglo-Indian cronies; the secret of the pseudonym was soon out in Southwold. Father and son continued to be estranged, as they had been ever since Eric had thrown up his commission to become a "writer." Now they were on a pretense of civil terms—after all, the son had been living, and intermittently would continue to live, under the father's roof—but their reconciliation, such as it was, was for the future. Mrs. Blair, like any mother, was distressed at the life Eric described himself as having lived in Paris—about which he had told her nothing—and so different from the accounts she had received from her sister Nellie: those reassuring, bourgeois evenings *chez* Adam, when Nellie and her husband, the professor of Esperanto, would entertain Eric at dinner. But, as any mother would, she rose above the mere subject matter of her son's book. After so many years of hearing him at the typewriter, the very existence of the book pleased her: did it not prove that Eric wasn't pursuing a will-o'-the-wisp? that he might do what he set out to do? Still, if the family were pleased with the book, for whatever reasons, they were not fervent in their enthusiasm: it would not have been their style to be so, any more than it was Eric's (or George's) style. Fervent enthusiasm he had already had from Mabel; if there was to be more of that, it would have to come from the reviewers.

THREE

AT THIS TIME ERIC WAS ON HOLIDAY FROM HIS JOB AS a schoolmaster at Evelyn's, a drab little private school in Hayes, outside London, where he had been teaching since the previous April. He disliked the job intensely—the first he had held since coming back from Burma—and looked forward to the day when he might be able to support himself as a full-time writer: would it happen with *Down and Out?* Meanwhile he took advantage of his holiday in Southwold to work away at his next book, a novel to be called *Burmese Days,* and he wrote to Moore that he "hoped to polish up a chunk" to show him when he was back in London. This was very much Orwell the professional writer, just as he had intended to be from the beginning, though he signed the letter Eric A. Blair: first book about to come out, and second already on the stocks.

It was all very well, even admirable, to write with such confidence of one's future plans. But the period between the arrival of advance copies and the official publication day of a book, especially for the author of a first book, is often a kind of limbo, wherein he alternates between euphoria and anxiety. For Blair it was a matter of eighteen days, which he filled with hours at the typewriter, long gossips with his mother, and much visiting to and fro between the Blairs' house, the Jaqueses' and the Collingses'. "It was a happy time," Dennis Collings would recall, long afterwards, "much freer, no standing on ceremony, everybody knew everybody else. Southwold was a nice place to be—I know that Eric enjoyed himself there."

A conviction of Orwell's—which at certain moments in his life was to rise to the level of paranoia—was that there was a literary racket in full-scale operation which determined the future of a book and its author. To be out of favor (a posture in which he had perennially liked to see himself ever since his time at St. Cyprian's) doomed one to failure. The members of the racket, *mafiosi* to a man, so to speak, were those "gilded young beasts," usually down from Cambridge, against whom he would rail in *Keep the Aspidistra Flying;* the literary editors of the weeklies (he was eventually to become one himself for some years at *Tribune*); Old Etonians; clubmen—a whole network of the charming, effete, unprincipled, and successful, who opened and closed the essential doors, making a Hell in Heaven's despite, or vice versa.

That this version of "the literary racket" had more to do with fantasy than with reality was to be proved by the widespread, highly favorable reception of *Down and Out,* though Orwell himself never drew the appropriate inference from it. In fact, he was eventually to have his experience with the racket, but it was the political not the literary racket—and even in the most celebrated instance, the rejection of *Animal Farm* by so many publishers in wartime England for what seemed to be valid political reasons, when it was finally brought out by the not unknown and perfectly respectable firm of Secker & Warburg, it proved to be a literary as well as a financial success: Orwell's most popular book.

We have no wish to explore here the racket as it actually is (very different, let it be said, from Orwell's fantasy of it), but one strategic point can't be overlooked: that a book from a publisher of established reputation, such as Gollancz, is more likely to be reviewed, though even that should not be considered an inflexible rule, than a book from a publisher who is unknown. The review itself may be highly unfavorable, but the book will at least have been noticed, and sent on its way to oblivion with a few cruel or patronizing epithets. To that degree, consciously or not, there is a literary racket: the book that is unnoticed might for all practical purposes never have been written. That was not to be Orwell's fate, at any point in his career, from his first book to his last.

Punctually on the first day of publication, and continuing generously thereafter, came the reviews of *Down and Out in Paris and London*. Gollancz had done its work efficiently, as one would expect, even to securing that recommendation from the Book Society. Of course, in England at the beginning of 1933, still deep in the Depression, a first-hand account of poverty and life among the unemployed would be almost certain to attract attention; and the fact that the author was unknown, might not even be a "writer" at all, would add to the "authenticity" of his book. Victor Gollancz himself, at the beginning of his relationship with Blair, seems not to have understood that he was dealing with a professional author. Hence his proposal that the book be signed "X." This Blair indignantly rejected—"X" would be of no use to him for all those books he intended to write in the future.

On the whole, the reviews were favorable and discriminating. Orwell was not one of those luckless writers who have to wait years for recognition and appreciation. Once published, after the ordeal of his two rejections, he was understood from the first, and the only serious particular in which past and present judgments differ is that no one in 1933 thought to describe his prose as Orwellian.

First came the daily papers, and the first of these was the *Manchester Guardian* on January 9. Its reviewer, M.H. (the initials of a woman named Muriel Harris), is deserving of a place in literary history, not only because she wrote the first review of George Orwell, but because she was also the first to recognize certain qualities that were to distinguish him as an author all through his career:

> Mr. George Orwell tells of things which to most people are horrible in a quiet, level tone which enables him also to use a vocabulary suited to his subject. No one . . . can fail to be deeply moved by the truth which is evident in every sentence. He has, in short, so much to say in that quiet, level voice of his that he has written a book which might work a revolution in the minds of those who are totally unable to look on down-and-outs as other than something entirely unlike themselves.

The next day came the *Morning Post*. The editor of the book page, E. B. Osborne, did the review himself, and it was something of a letdown. For the most part, his judgment was favorable, but Osborne (as Brenda Salkeld, Ruth Pitter, Jack Common, and others of Blair's friends had done at the time, and as many of Orwell's critics have done since) seized upon the problem that would dog him through all his down-and-out experiences: that he had put himself into a somewhat "false" or "inauthentic" predicament—he was not trapped in his situation as his fellow tramps were. "Because there was always a way out for him," Osborne wrote, "Mr. Orwell never felt the extreme misery of helpless, hopeless poverty." This was a severe if accurate observation; and the laudatory, even flowery sentence that followed it, however quotable from a publisher's point of view, must have been small consolation to a vulnerable young man not given to deceiving himself: "But his picturesque book touches several problems of the modern underworld with a finger of light."

Two days later, the big guns of middlebrow reviewing were heard from: J. B. Priestley in the *Evening Standard,* and Compton Mackenzie in the *Daily Mail.* It was perhaps just as well for Orwell that Priestley did not know him in his true identity, for Blair, as Blair, had earlier described him in the *Adelphi* as "blatantly second rate" and shrugged off his generally admired, best-selling *Angel Pavement* in standard reviewerese: ". . . excellent holiday novel . . . gay . . . pleasant . . . a good bulk of reading. . . ." For Priestley, *Down and Out* was "uncommonly good reading, and a social document of some value. It is, indeed, the best book of its kind that I have read in a long time." But Priestley was virtually mute in contrast to Compton Mackenzie, who let loose with a volley of praise. True, *Down and Out* came third in his column, after *A Passionate Prodigality* by Guy Chapman and *Pocahontas* by David Garnett. But when he finally arrived at Orwell's "immensely interesting book," Mackenzie summed it up as "a genuine human document, which at the same time is written with so much artistic force that, in spite of the squalor and degradation thus unfolded, the result is curiously beautiful with the beauty of an accomplished etching on copper. The account of a casual ward in this country horrifies like some scene of inexplicable misery in Dante."

It is not our intention here to supply either a history or

critique of book-reviewing in England, but it seems worthwhile—if only to correct the myth of a neglected Orwell and
to suggest the amount of attention paid to him at the very
start of his career—to note that yet another well-known
writer of the period, H. E. Bates, reviewed *Down and Out*
in the *New Clarion* and found it "fascinating but terrible
reading." Even the *Tatler*, of all places, allowed room for a
highly favorable review. That curious publication, then as
now dedicated to recording the doings of society week after
week, included an intelligent column on books by Richard
King. (Some years later, the column would be taken over
by Elizabeth Bowen.) King, rather adroitly, attuned his review to the magazine's preoccupations, quite as though
Orwell were reporting on another "set" in society, albeit
an unimportant one: "This terribly interesting but uncomfortable book will open up a new world—a world that has
its customs, its prejudices, even its social sets, equally pronounced as in the world which passing it by and regarding
its inhabitants is filled either with contempt, horror, or
self-superiority, and occasionally pity."

Three other reviews deserve mention: those in the *New
Statesman and Nation,* the *Adelphi,* and the *Times Literary
Supplement.* Ordinarily, the review in the *New Statesman*
of March 18 might be passed over in silence, for it has slight
literary or political interest. But as a part of Orwell's checkered history with that publication, climaxing in an unhappy
altercation during the Spanish Civil War, it has its place.
The literary editor of the *Statesmen* at the time, David Garnett (author among many other works of *Pocahontas*) had
had what he must have thought an inspired idea: to assign
Down and Out for review to W. H. Davies, the poet and
professional tramp. But Davies seemed to have a disdain
for deadlines, and it was not until the middle of March that
his review appeared. When it did, it proved to be just the

sort of review that an author (quite understandably) dis-
likes most: a kindly sentence or two wherein, if he is lucky,
the title of the book and his name are given (not always
accurately), and the greater part of the precious space used
for a potted essay in which the reviewer serves up notions
of his own, or, more commonly still, serves up the author's
notions as though they were *his*, with a knowing allusion to
further work in the field already being done. (Further work,
let it be said, is always being done: that is a basic law of
literary life.) In the case of *Down and Out*, it was perfectly
clear that its chief interest for Davies was the light it shed
for him on his own experiences as a super-tramp.

With C. Day Lewis in the *Adelphi*, the situation was very
different, in respect to both the review and the reviewer.
W. H. Davies was in his sixty-third year, his reputation as
a poet was in decline; most of his memorable lyrics had
been written years before, as a pre-Georgian. In a representative anthology of modern British poetry, one finds him
preceded by Charlotte Mew and Hilaire Belloc, and followed by J. M. Synge and Ralph Hodgson. Day Lewis, a
year younger than Orwell, was already famous as a poet,
and growing each day more famous as a member of the
triumvirate of the young literary Left, whose other members were W. H. Auden and Stephen Spender. For many
years Orwell would resent the triumvirate, and the writers
associated with them, stigmatizing them as "the pansy
Left" and singling out Auden as "a gutless Kipling." Eventually, certainly by the time of *Animal Farm*, fame had done
its equalizing work, and Orwell, having met and grown to
like some of them, Spender in particular, revised his contemptuous judgments. But it has to be said that the "quiet,
level tone" we so value could at times rise virtually to a
shriek and it is not a pleasant sound to hear.

Day Lewis was not only a poet, he was also a Marxist,

and, as was not uncommon among poets who were Marxists
in 1933, he was also briefly a member of the Communist
party—which is to say that he was politically committed in
a way that would have been incomprehensible to Orwell
at that time. One has no wish to patronize the author of
Down and Out by saying that politics were above him,
beneath him, or beyond him; it is closer to the truth to say
that in January 1933 his political consciousness, insofar as
it existed at all, was in a dormant state; and one of the
themes of the present work is to trace the movements of its
awakening. What this meant in practical terms is that while
Day Lewis read *Down and Out* appreciatively, the thoughts
it called to his mind had little to do with Dante or "the
beauty of an accomplished etching on copper." He was
taken with "the facts" that Orwell revealed; they "should
shake the complacence of twentieth century civilisation if
anything could; they are 'sensational' yet presented without
sensationalism. He [the narrator] has no illusions about the
extremely poor; he finds the effects of hunger and poverty
upon himself and the rest compelling shame, lying, self-pity,
bestial fatalism." But for Day Lewis, these facts, so unsen-
sationally and convincingly presented, are not the stopping
but the starting point. As a writer who is conscious of politics he goes on to ask, as Orwell himself never does, what
the facts mean, and what inferences we are to draw from
them. A curious and, considering its subject, an unexpected
aspect of *Down and Out* is brought into focus: what a non-
didactic and apolitical book it is. (Paradoxically, that may
help to explain its continuing vitality and interest: tracts
for the times seldom survive the times they were tracted
for.) In part, of course, it is the effect and indeed the
effectiveness of Orwell's quality (or trick, or technique) of
understatement, but there does not even appear to be any

crusading zest under the surface of the text; there is little feeling that the world that has excruciated these down-and-outers as its victims must somehow be remade. Life among the victims is terrible—a fact to be passively accepted and impassively recorded. The book is oddly static in its concept of the life it describes, as if nothing in it will ever significantly change, despite the patronizing and inadequate character of private charity, the boredom and ugliness of public assistance, all those devices that society invents to cover up its wounds, rather than to cure them.

Like Orwell, and unlike Day Lewis, the anonymous reviewer in the *Times Literary Supplement* refused to impose any social point on the narrative. "One lays down his book wondering why men living in such conditions do not commit suicide, but Mr. Orwell conveys the impression that they are too depressed and hopeless for such a final and definitive effort as self-inflicted death."

One would rather have liked a comment from Orwell himself on this chilling conclusion, but his attention was diverted by a letter to the *Times,* responding to the review, from one Humbert Possenti. Writing from the Hotel Splendide, London, Monsieur Possenti was moved to claim, "as a *restaurateur* and *hôtelier* of 40 years' experience," that the state of French hotel kitchens as described by Orwell and accepted by the reviewer in the *TLS* was "inconceivable," and added that in all good hotels customers can see over the kitchens at any time they wish.

Orwell, offended by the tone of the letter, decided to reply to it, and in doing so, made use of a well-known trick of schoolboy debaters. He was not referring to "Paris hotels in general," but to one in particular. Since Monsieur Possenti had no way of knowing which hotel the author had in mind, he had no way of verifying or contradicting his description of it. "So," Orwell concluded, ". . . in spite of his 40 years' experience, my evidence in this case is worth more than his."

Judged strictly in debating terms, there is no question that Orwell was the winner, but the habit of making generalizations, often outrageous and unprovable, was endemic with him throughout his lifetime, and they turn up even in *Down and Out*. It is difficult to imagine a reader, fresh from the pages of the book with its horrendous accounts of squalor in the scullery, who would not hesitate at least an hour or two before crossing the threshold of even a three-star establishment in Paris.

Meanwhile, like many such correspondences in the *Times*, this one led to a subsidiary point, with the book that had inspired it rather lost from sight. On February 17, Sir St. Clair Thomson wrote to suggest that there should be notices posted in restaurants inviting inspection by guests. A week later, Possenti, now transformed from Humbert to Umberto, announced that such a notice would indeed be posted at the Splendide. Orwell himself did not feel called upon to comment, and the correspondence languished.

FOUR

Blair had signed his letter to the *Times* "george Orwell," and those quotation marks around the name tell a story of their own. He was not yet at ease with the pseudonym. On the title page of his book, and in the reviews, he was George Orwell, but in the ordinary world where he lived he was still Eric Blair. The modest little fame that might have trailed in his wake as the author of a very well-received first book was denied to him, since he had made up his mind to deny his true identity. There were none of those congratulatory letters from absent or neglected or neglectful friends he might otherwise have counted on. In fact, it would be another two years before even such an Old Etonian friend as Cyril Connolly would learn that George Orwell was none other than Eric Blair. And by 1937, when new friends began to enter his life who had never heard of Eric Blair, the pseudonym no longer applied: to them he was George Orwell without quotation marks.

On January 17, the day before he was to return to his hated job at Evelyn's, he wrote to Leonard Moore. Diffident about his identity Blair might be, and diffident in his nature he certainly was, but he was also an author, and like any author he was anxious to know if the favorable reviews of the book were affecting its sales. More than that, he thought of himself as an author whose intention was to live by what he wrote: the sooner the royalties accumulated sufficiently for him to give up his job as a teacher, the better. But before raising the fateful question, he remarked that the notices were better than he'd expected, and that he was pleased no libel actions had been threatened. (This latter risk would be an obsessive concern of his, and with good reason, throughout his career.) Then, approaching the point that specially interested him, he noted that the *Sunday Express* had listed the book among the best sellers of the week, but he realized (and here the question was implicit) that it would be some time (would it not?) before Moore had the sales figures. To which the immediate answer was Yes.

But looking into the future, which was Blair's implicit concern at that moment, one can say that between a critical success, as *Down and Out* had undoubtedly been, and a popular success there is an enormous gap. Gollancz had ordered a first impression of 1500 copies, a second of 500 copies at the end of January, and later in the year an impression of 1000 copies. In the eyes of a novelist such as Hugh Walpole, to evoke one of Orwell's *bêtes noires* of the 1930's, a sale of 3000 copies might count for nothing, but it represented in less exalted company a promising launching of a literary career, and Gollancz, Moore, and Blair (perhaps in that order) had every reason to be pleased, the more so as the author was already at work on his second book, and was contemplating his third. What it did not mean was that he could give up his work as a schoolmaster.

The next day he went up to London from Southwold. He had spent his holiday profitably, for in his bag he was carrying the revised first hundred pages of his novel *Burmese Days*, which he meant to send on to Moore as soon as he had a chance to read them once more and judge their effect. In London there was a pleasant lunch with Mabel Fierz, which he insisted upon paying for on the strength of future royalties, and a pleasant pause with Mabel before a window of a shop in which his book was impressively displayed, and pleasant plans were made, as they were so often in those years, that he should count on spending the weekend with the Fierzes at their house in Golders Green. Then it was time to say goodbye, and off to the train at Paddington, and back to darkest Hayes.

His room in The Hawthorns, that genteel rooming house in Church Road, was just as he had left it in mid-December as Eric Blair, but returning to it as George Orwell, it must have seemed even damper, colder, and more dismal. His being Orwell was, of course, a secret not to be shared, certainly not with Mr. Evelyn, the headmaster and proprietor of the school, who had no notion that his staff now included the well-known young author of *Down and Out in Paris and London;* not even with the only friend Blair had made since coming to Hayes, an earnest young Church of England clergyman.

Fortunately for his novel in progress, schoolmastering demanded less of him now than it had in the autumn, when, in addition to his usual teaching he had taken on, or been given, the responsibility of writing, producing, and even making the costumes (suits of armor) for the end-of-term play. The costumes (cut from sheets of brown wrapping paper and glued together) were a particular nuisance from which, as he put it, he suffered "untold agonies." It was an experience he was presently to reproduce in exact, agonizing detail in his novel *A Clergyman's Daughter,* so from a literary point of view, it was not wholly wasted experience. Similarly, with his painting and gilding a cigarette box for the church bazaar, a task he had undertaken at the behest of his friend, the curate of St. Mary's, for whose sake also he felt he would ultimately have to take Holy Communion, something he hadn't done in years. Evidently in Hayes, Blair was a fairly regular churchgoer, more (it would seem) for social than religious reasons, and he feared that his curate friend would "think it funny if I always go to Church but never communicate." This, too, he would put to literary use, and it has to be said of Orwell that he was one of those writers who are remarkably thrifty with their experiences. Somehow, one way or another, they manage to get them into whatever they write; indeed, within a year, Blair would be in danger of cannibalizing his experience as it was taking place, or, to put it another way, having the experience for the sake of having something to write about.

But *Burmese Days*, which had been simmering in his mind for a long time, and upon which he resumed work immediately upon his return to Evelyn's, was meant to be a distillation of his five years in Burma. Beyond his routine schoolmastering, and the occasional church service for friendship's sake, there was nothing in Hayes to distract him from his purpose. The preceding September he had written to Brenda Salkeld that he'd spent a day reading through the rough draft of the novel and that it depressed him terribly. A month later the news to Eleanor Jaques was that he was making a little progress, but that he would have much to do when the rough draft was finished. In November he was writing to Moore to say that he preferred not to promise to have the book in final form by summer. In December, as we have seen, he planned to use the Christmas holiday in Southwold to "polish up a fair chunk."

A few days after returning to Hayes, he read over the hundred revised pages and was sufficiently pleased by them to send them to Moore. Then he tried patiently to wait for the verdict. Days passed, he heard nothing. Disconsolately he set out for Golders Green, where he was to spend the weekend with the Fierzes. Encouraged by Mabel—one got nowhere without *go,* of which Eric had deplorably little, she felt—he rang up Moore at his office. As it was a Saturday, Moore, not surprisingly, was not there. A partner in the considerable firm of Christy & Moore, he represented not only the newcomer George Orwell but a great many better-known clients whose manuscripts also had to be read—though not, usually, on weekends, which were consecrated to cricket—but no writer really ever understands this, and even if he does in theory, in practice he feels that his is the manuscript that should be read first.

The days of silence continued. On the thirty-first of January, with the publication of the indignant letter from Possenti, Blair had a legitimate pretext to write to Moore: he enclosed a copy of his letter of reply to the *Times.* The tone to his agent was diffident, as it usually was, even a little timid—in marked contrast to the assured manner of his letter to the *Times*—and as usual, the crucial questions, the real reasons for writing, were reserved for the last. (If one were attempting a psychoanalytic study, Moore would be an obvious candidate for a "father figure." Their correspondence, of which only a portion has been published, is of great interest in this and other respects.) What, came the belated, painful question, did Moore think of the first hundred pages? Characteristically, Blair was quick to admit they were "fearful from a literary point of view." But supposing various revisions were made, was this "the sort of thing people want to read about?" As though to provide Moore with the answer that he, Blair, was eager to hear (for he had no intention of being dissuaded from going on), he ventured to think that the fact of its being one of the very few novels about Burma might make up for its meager action and excessive description. (Later he would think of the description as the novel's sole redeeming feature.) Too proud to be assertive, Eric had written just the sort of letter that would make Mabel despair—obviously she hadn't been consulted on the writing of it: where was the go?—and even when he brought himself to admit that towards the end of the novel there would be a murder and a suicide, he felt constrained to add the dispiriting news that they would "play rather a subsidiary part."

To this bleak, wistful letter Moore replied in his own good time—the middle of the next month—with measured encouragement: he had read the hundred pages and liked them and looked forward to reading more. As to what people wanted, who could say? The vagaries of public taste are unpredictable; if they were not, all publishers would be rich, and the number of published authors drastically, sensibly curtailed. Clearly Moore had no intention of speculating in the future: his interest was in the present and there he had good news to report—he had made an arrangement with Harpers' for an American edition of *Down and Out,* a pleasant reminder to Blair, coughing and hacking in the damp gloom of The Hawthorns, that he was indeed the writer George Orwell.

His first reaction was simply pleasure; by mid-March, returning the signed contract, he was a little apprehensive because he could not remember if there was anything said in the book about Americans that they might find offensive and he should therefore cut out. (In fact, there is a contemptuous paragraph set at the unidentified luxury hotel —actually the Lotti—about the inability of Americans to know good food, but criticism of this sort coming from an

Englishman would only amuse Americans, and there are no textual differences between the two editions.) One has a sense at this time of some equivocation about the pseudonym: how stringently it was to be observed, how much to reveal, how much to conceal—he had heard of the way American publishers were supposed to misuse biographical details. It is not at all clear, though, what he had in mind, unless he feared that his being an Old Etonian and a former member of the Indian police (facts still unrevealed in England) might be exploited to his disadvantage. In any event, he had decided against sending a photograph: it would not be a good advertisement, he felt, perhaps too modestly.

It seems permissible at this point to jump forward in time a few months to conclude the brief, not especially happy history of the American publication of *Down and Out in Paris and London*. On June 30, 1933, the book was brought out by Harpers' in an edition of 1750 copies. Perhaps on Blair's assumption that nobody in America would know him anyway, and that since the book had been successful in England there was no need, after all, to be ashamed of it, perhaps feeling that the news of its true authorship ought to begin to be disseminated—whatever the reason, the copyright notice was in the name of Eric Blair, and the observant reader could make of that what he wished. (The English edition did not contain a copyright notice; such usage did not come into standard practice in Britain until after the Second World War.)

Reviews were slow in arriving—the first was in the *Herald Tribune Books* on July 30—and were relatively few and scattered thereafter. One of the last was by James T. Farrell in the *New Republic* five months after publication, who described it as "genuine, unexaggerated and intelligent."

Generally the reviews, such as they were, were favorable: the most enthusiastic being the first, by Fred T. Marsh; the most interesting by Herbert Gorman in the *New York Times Book Review*. Gorman, a well-thought-of novelist and critic, and an early biographer of James Joyce, was able to single out those qualities that explain as well as any why writers so dissimilar as Henry Miller and Mary McCarthy should have spoken of *Down and Out* as the book by Orwell they like best: "He possesses a keen eye for character and a rough-and-ready styleless style that plunges along and makes the reader see what the author wants him to see." Gorman regarded the author himself—that is, as he figures in the text—with a slightly jaundiced eye, and was perceptive about Orwell's tendency to arrange facts. In this first book the contrivance is apparent to any careful reader, and Gorman found the narrative not altogether unvarnished. It occurred to him that the author's imagination had "colored the facts a trifle," and although he does not specifically say so, one suspects that the "down there on a visit" element in Orwell's approach bothered him a little: "One reads on with a sort of horrid fascination happy in the suspicion (eventually verified) that this existence in the gutter is but the temporary condition of a man who rather enjoys being down and out." But it is the initial singling out of "the styleless style," which in fact is anything but artless, that distinguishes Gorman's review; and Orwell, along with Christopher Isherwood (and their common literary ancestor, Somerset Maugham), was to bring that antithesis of Mandarinism to its highest levels of achievement in the decade that followed.

Favorable though the American reviews had generally been, they were too few and sporadic to make any impact upon book-buying readers. By October, Moore was conveying the disappointing news to Blair that Harpers' hadn't been able to sell more than 1100 copies—not as lamentable a sale then as it would seem now, and Harpers' was sufficiently pleased and optimistic to take Orwell's next book when, in accordance with the option clause of the contract, it was offered to them, but it was a good deal less than was needed to liberate him from Evelyn's.

In February 1934, nine months after publication, the type was distributed, and 383 copies were remaindered. Upon which melancholy note, we return to the winter of 1933.

FIVE

"**M**ELANCHOLY" MIGHT ALSO SERVE AS A WORD TO sum up the winter of 1933 itself: for Blair at Evelyn's, teaching; for Orwell in the evenings at The Hawthorns, writing his novel; and indeed (to make a ludicrous-seeming leap beyond the scale of our narrative thus far) for the Western world—it was on the thirtieth of January in that year that Adolf Hitler became Chancellor of Germany. But having made the leap, we draw back. We are not writing "history," using Orwell as an exemplary or typical figure (he was neither); nor do we intend to introduce snippets of history (clues and cues to great events in the world outside) in an effort to make a biographical study such as we are writing "historical," when all the evidence suggests that it could not be so. The truth is, in this winter of 1933, Blair had little interest in anything that did not directly concern himself— his teaching, the garden he had begun in a patch of ground behind The Hawthorns, letters to friends, a pubcrawl with Mabel Fierz through the East End one evening, in which, as she remembers, he was much less at ease in the public bars than he had led her to believe—and what would concern him most, through that melancholy winter and for several months beyond it, his novel *Burmese Days.*

Of all his books it was the one which he would think about longest—it can even be said that the period of gesta-

tion extended back to 1927—and the one on which he
would work the hardest. In June, when he was two-thirds
through the rough draft, he complained to Brenda Salkeld,
to whom he had sent the manuscript, that he had to revise
continually, and he added, "I wish I were one of those people who can . . . fling off a novel in about four days."
Ironically, in the future he was to develop just that sort
of facility, in and out of fiction, and some of his best, most
characteristic pieces resulted from it, for journalism, which
later came to occupy him increasingly, simply doesn't allow
time for the sort of revisions that he was suffering through
with *Burmese Days,* and it taught him to think and say
what he had to say as soon as he sat down to write. Deadlines have a way of shortening the quest for *le mot juste.*
Part of the difficulty now, however, came from the fact that
this was his first novel; and since he was determined that
it was to be very much a novelistic novel—not journalism
tricked out as fiction—replete with all the traditional in-
gredients of the form (character, setting, theme, plot), it
meant that he had to master, or at least to learn in a rudimentary way, a number of skills that he hadn't been
called upon to exercise before. What he was attempting was
something very different from the documentary reportage
of *Down and Out,* the genre in which his gifts could most
naturally develop and flourish.

To judge from the finished product, his aim seems to have
been to write a well-made, dramatic, satiric, romantic,
multicharactered novel in exotic settings that would have
something of the narrative ingenuity and worldliness of
Somerset Maugham, something of the ironic and sympathetic understanding of misunderstandings between East
and West of E. M. Forster, something of the poetic de-
scriptive power of D. H. Lawrence, something of his own,
Eric Blair's, experience of Burma, and something of "the

sort of thing people want to read about." A genius of pastiche might just conceivably have reconciled such disparate objectives; and the surprising thing is not that *Burmese Days* falls short of being the masterpiece one wishes it might have been, but that it should have turned out so good a novel as it is.

Perhaps he ought to have trusted more to his gift for writing about his own experience—what he had heard, seen, done, felt, and smelled—as in *Down and Out*. *Burmese Days* is far different from the autobiographical outpouring—from cradle to university—that is the expected first novel of a literary young man; almost a pity, in Orwell's case, that it should not have been, for the peculiarity of his passage from Eton to Burma was potentially so much more interesting than the passage from Eton to Oxbridge of the usual literary young man. And when he did come to write of it, in *The Road to Wigan Pier* in 1936, he was in the process of being politicized, and the material was exploited, albeit highly effectively, for its political, didactic value—how an Imperialist becomes a Socialist.

Much of the strength of *Burmese Days* does derive from its autobiographical detail—one knows that Orwell is writing from direct observation of a milieu he disliked intensely —but it is not autobiography in the guise of fiction and should not be read as such. If the eye is Orwell's throughout, the "I" is only seldom present, and not merely because the story is told in the third person—indeed, a great portion of his own Burmese experience has been excluded. Paradoxically, one is most aware of him—that is, of "I," the author—when he is most invisible, in the clear *de haut en bas* tone of the novel, which is not so much Maughamian as Etonian. Characters (in many instances drawn or caricatured from "real life") are scored off time and again for their commonness, their middle-classness, their vulgarity:

the ghastly Lackersteens and their husband-hunting niece Elizabeth, with her aversion to culture; the denizens of the Club, with their cartoon-like attitudes towards race and Empire; even Verrall, the polo-playing officer who is Flory's rival for the affections of Elizabeth—to both aunt and niece the blond young lieutenant is the epitome of upper-class *chic*—is revealed as having attended a *third-rate* public school. One does have the sense, especially in those portions of the novel revolving around the Club, of five years of accumulated grievances being paid off. At the same time, much that had happened to him during those five years (his own life, his own interior life, so different from the clichés of the novelist) he left untapped: the whole painful experience of his time in the Delta, for example. Perhaps the decision to write a "well-made" novel determined him to confine himself to Katha (the Kyauktada of the novel), even though he had been stationed there only during his final three months in Burma.

True, Katha was particularly vivid in his memory, with its hot pinks and flaming scarlets and smoldering purples —so different from the acid wastes of the Delta—and it is vivid in the novel, too. Kyauktada is a feat of evocation that may owe something to Orwell's having written it in the bleak, colorless setting of Hayes, that it was winter and he had a beastly cold, that smoke from the stacks of the H.M.V. Gramophone factory on the outskirts of the town had soured the fields and killed off the wildflowers that once had grown there.

Three years later, writing to Henry Miller, Orwell mentioned *Burmese Days* as the only one of his books he was pleased with—not as a novel, he hastened typically to say, but the descriptions of Burma weren't bad, he admitted, which is perhaps carrying diffidence too far.

SIX

ORWELL WAS NEVER VERY SPECIFIC ABOUT HIS DIF-
ficulties with the novel—it was prolix, too long, "broken
backed" . . . beyond that he doesn't go. One suspects,
though, that it was the fictional elements in *Burmese Days*
that made the greatest trouble for him, beginning with the
need to invent a biography for Flory that would put him
at a remove from himself—for whom, at the same time,
Flory serves as a spokesman: the man who sees clearly the
awfulness of things as they are.

Very likely Flory, as a character, had his roots in Captain
Robinson, the cashiered ex-officer whom Blair had met in
Mandalay—with his opium-smoking and his native women,
Robinson was already a stereotype waiting to enter somebody's novel. But his deepest roots are traceable to fiction,
in a range from Conrad's Lord Jim through all those Eng-
lishmen gone to seed in the East that are one of Maugham's
better-known specialties. Even the friendship of Flory with
the Indian Dr. Veraswami, convincing though it is, has its
stronger fictional counterpart in the friendship of Fielding
with Dr. Aziz in Forster's *A Passage to India*. But the love
story that Orwell invents for him with the ineffable Elizabeth is surely the weakest element in the novel, predictable
in each of its turnings. However deeply felt, it comes out

seeming false: in G. M. Young's phrase, "the gush of popular fiction." Perhaps Orwell thought this was "the sort of thing people wanted to read about." On the evidence here it was not the sort of thing he was able to write about best, and one reads *Burmese Days* for the accuracy of its reportage, its feeling for colonial and native life at several levels, its biting characterization, and the vividness of its settings.

Not that the "love story" as such is so badly done; it is written with sufficient skill to open an alarming prospect, that if Orwell had *really* wanted to be a popular novelist, in the middlebrow, best-selling sense of the term—as, until 1936, he intermittently thought he did—he might have brought it off, ending up as a kind of James Hilton *manqué*, with *1984* as his *Lost Horizon*.

Orwell himself would never again attempt so "romantic" and novelistic a plot as he had burdened himself with in *Burmese Days,* nor would the women characters in his future novels be quite so uniformly unpleasant. But then, "unpleasant" is a word that might be applied to almost all of the characters in *Burmese Days,* whatever their sex or nationality.

Misogynistic he was not. He was a late starter, but from the time of his return from Burma women would always be necessary to him. During these years he had a number of casual affairs, two quite considerably more than that. But he would be truly happy, and happily in love, for the first time in his life only after he married Eileen O'Shaughnessy in 1936. And yet, perhaps because he came to know women relatively late, he seems never to have been entirely at ease with them, or, as many of them thought, to understand them. The sentimental fantasy of his friendship with Eleanor Jaques, in which his feelings were deeply engaged and whose progress in letters—for he wrote to her more often than he saw her—can be traced in a telltale graph from Dear Eleanor to My Dearest Eleanor, foundered on a crucial misunderstanding: she was fond of Eric, but was in love with Dennis Collings, and intended to marry him, and did, in 1934.* "I don't think he really liked women," Brenda Salkeld says flatly. And another woman who knew him intimately at this period in his life offered as her considered opinion years later: "I don't believe he understood women, or had much interest in understanding them." She smiles in a reminiscent way; obviously she could tell more than she intends to tell. "They were ready to bed with him; therefore, what was there to understand? And of course they did—married women around Southwold—bed with him, I mean. He had quite a few little *affaires* that didn't count for anything. One or two that did. But all this talk of the ascetic Orwell! Not Eric! I do think he tended to be contemptuous of women—just a little. Until Eileen came along. That was a different story, of course."

---

* The eleven letters from Blair to Eleanor Jaques included in *The Collected Essays, Journalism and Letters* provide material enough for a novel on the scale of *Adolphe*. It is striking how many are concerned with suggestions for meetings that never occur. And how many more are recapitulations of the pitifully few meetings that actually did take place. Again, it is striking to notice that she did not respond when he asked where she would be at a particular time—his holiday in Southwold—and so, after a fortnight's interval, waiting vainly to hear, he wrote again, asking for the same information. Did she reply? It is the last of the published letters. None of which is surprising, considering, as we have said, that Eleanor was in love with Dennis Collings—a fact that Blair, in his loneliness, chose not to acknowledge, or at least not to admit into his fantasy.

SEVEN

O RWELL'S LIFE IN THE EARLY MONTHS OF 1933, AFTER
the publication of *Down and Out* and his return to his job
at Evelyn's School, provides a clearcut illustration of the difference between the quotidian and the creative existence
of the writer. There was the tedium of his external, day-
by-day routine: the teaching, the gardening—that pump-
kin, would it or would it not survive?—the occasional letter
received and in due course replied to (How nice to hear
from . . . Forgive me for not . . .). There was, exacer-
bated no doubt by the tedium, an irruption of a slightly
bogus-sounding world-weariness—"A few years ago I
thought it rather fun to reflect that our civilization is
doomed, but now it fills me above all else with boredom to
think of the horrors that will be happening within ten
years"—a remark that might have been made with perfect
consistency by a character in *Point Counterpoint*, or some
fifteen years earlier by the Young Cynic at Eton; but coming from Blair in 1933 it suggests the distance he would
have to go before he truly became George Orwell.

The only excitement of these months was inward. He was
a writer in full creative flow who happened to be "living
and partly living" in Hayes, but his important life was being lived in recollections of Katha and restored to the page
as Kyauktada.

Then the real world of 1933—of the Depression, Hunger
Marches, and Unemployment, the stuff of headlines that
counted for less than the look of a particular bird remembered from Katha—rudely intruded. In the spring, poor Mr.
Evelyn had the disagreeable task of informing his staff that
the school was collapsing. Despite its "very good reputation" as an independent preparatory boarding school, it
simply wasn't attracting enough pupils for him to pay the
bills, and this would be the final term. For Blair it meant
that he would soon be joining the ranks of the unemployed.

The news of the approaching demise of Evelyn's School
was relayed along the academic bush telegraph, and in
May, Mr. John Bennett, the owner, founder, and headmaster of Frays College in nearby Uxbridge, a much larger
and more affluent school, came over one afternoon to see
what of its portable effects—desks, chairs, bookcases, etc.—
he might buy. (The building that housed the school was
presently to be taken over by Hillingdon Hospital for staff
accommodation, and the name itself, with permission of
the hapless Mr. Evelyn, was bestowed upon a county school
which is now, some forty years later, a flourishing compre-
hensive mixed school, situated quite near the site of the
original Evelyn's.)

On the afternoon of his visit, apart from acquiring some
useful supplies at bargain prices, Mr. Bennett was introduced to Eric Blair, and acquired him as well. By a happy
coincidence, there was a vacancy coming up on the staff of
Frays that he seemed particularly qualified to fill. A certain Monsieur Souchard, who took the boys in French, had
just been called up for military service in France, and
would be leaving Frays in a few weeks. The only disadvantage from Blair's point of view was that Mr. Bennett would
want him as a holiday tutor in mid-August to give private

tutoring to the eight French boys who were living at the school. He had been looking forward to a long holiday in Southwold, in part because he could accelerate, perhaps even finish, the writing of *Burmese Days,* in part because he would have a chance to spend time with the friends he saw too seldom—Eleanor, Brenda, Dennis, not to mention his mother and his sister Avril; and the Fierzes, as was their custom, would be taking a house there for the month of August. But one did not quibble over details of jobs at a time when jobs were in short supply, and he speedily accepted it.

Freed from the worry of having to look for another post, which might have slowed him down intolerably, he hurried along with the novel. In May, three-quarters of it was in rough draft, and he sent off that much of the manuscript to Leonard Moore. In June he could report to Brenda Salkeld that Moore was quite "enthusiastic," though he added with that note of deprecation one comes to expect from him wherever this novel is concerned, "which is more than I am." Still, he was sufficiently pleased with it to send it to her to read, reassuring her that the final version would not be as misshapen as it might now seem. Early in July, while still at Evelyn's, he wrote to Eleanor Jaques to ask her holiday plans, and mentioned that he expected to have the novel finished by the end of the month. This good news he qualified (of course!) by saying that he disliked much of it and would spend months revising it. Two weeks later, writing to Eleanor again, he could announce that the novel was done. "But there are wads of it that I simply hate and am going to change." This was not so different in tone and strategy from what he'd written Brenda as long ago as the previous September, and from what he'd let fall in conversation with Mabel in the months ever since, that he'd been reading over what he had written and found it, each time, a depressing experience. The crucial difference now was that at last he had a *finished* novel, however much revision might still be needed, and in his letters to Moore that summer cheerfulness keeps breaking in. He could go off to his new job in a better frame of mind than when he had left his old one.

Frays College, where he took up his duties in August, had had its beginning in 1926, when John Bennett, unhappy about the education his children were receiving at their schools, decided to found his own—the Uxbridge High School—where he might put his more liberal teaching principles into practice. A short time later he changed its name to Frays College, after the Frays River, a rather narrow stream—too broad, however, for jumping—that flowed past the school property, and under that name it continued to thrive into the 1970's.

Uxbridge, like Hayes, is just outside London in Middlesex and, with its multileveled car park and other accouterments of the "outer city," has been thoroughly suburbanized. But in the 1930's it was still something of a country town. Frays, only a short walk from the center, had as its aim the preparation of students for the civil service, the universities, and the professions. It was coeducational and took children from the ages of five to fifteen or sixteen. At the time that Blair was there, from August through December 1933, there were about 180 students, some 30 of whom, 15 boys and 15 girls, were boarders. Blair had originally been taken on only as a "holiday tutor," but Mr. Bennett was soon satisfied that he was qualified to replace the departed Souchard, and engaged him formally to join the staff of 16. As an assistant master his chief responsibility was teaching French, but he was also expected to take

classes in other subjects, English among them, and to super-
vise hockey and cricket. It was a full day of activity, and it
meant, in practical terms, that work on the novel had to
be put off until evenings, a repetition of his experience at
Evelyn's, save that here he was spared the genteel dingi-
ness and loneliness, as well as the expense, of The Hawthorns. The school occupied a large, rambling Edwardian
villa, with a garden behind, extending in terraces down to
the river. There was a series of small bedrooms, known
familiarly as "the horse-boxes," assigned to members of the
staff, and in one of these Blair lived and Orwell worked. At
night, from behind his closed door, would be heard the
sound of the typewriter: he was completing the revisions
and typing the final draft of *Burmese Days*.

To judge from the recollections of those who knew him
at Frays, he would seem to have been a successful master,
popular with his students and on cordial terms with his colleagues, although he was still, as he had been in the past
and would continue to be in the future, "somewhat aloof"
—not unfriendly, but determined to go his own way and to
use his time for himself. In the evenings he would not sit
for long in the Masters' Common Room, but presently
would slip away to his horse-box and his waiting typewriter. At meals, which the staff took at their own table
apart from the students, he was always perfectly amiable,
although he was more likely to respond to conversation
than to initiate it. But he was not shy, and the other
members of the staff were impressed by his courage, as a
new master, in persisting in smoking at table (generally
frowned upon), the more so as he made his cigarettes from
very strong and odorous French tobacco. (It was thought
to be quite a feat that he should roll his own, when it was
extremely uncommon to do so, with one hand.) On one

occasion, when a dance was held for the thirty boarders to the music of a wind-up Gramophone, he dutifully appeared, and even seemed to enjoy himself. Tall to the point of ungainliness, he made a memorable picture—memorable enough to be recalled forty years later—dancing with an older and extremely short mistress who rather terrified many of her colleagues.

There were two members of the staff with whom he was on relatively close terms: the Stapleys, a young couple, recently married, who had been given a larger suite of rooms in honor of their married state. With them in their sitting room, which Mrs. Stapley had done her best to de-institutionalize, he spent pleasant times, chatting and drinking cup after cup of strong coffee. To them—as to no one else at the school—he entrusted the secret of his second identity; he presented them with a copy of the American edition of *Down and Out;* he told them how much he had hated his time in Burma and allowed them to infer that that was to be the subject of his next book.

It was characteristic of him that his principal recreations at this time—as the Stapleys recall them—were solitary in nature: to fish; and to drive about the countryside on his newly acquired second-hand motorcycle, something he hadn't done since he and Roger Beadon, his fellow police officer, drove recklessly through the streets of Mandalay. Fishing, of course, was an abiding interest, which had had its beginnings in his boyhood in Henley-on-Thames, and he would spend a good deal of such free time as he had fishing in the river at the foot of the garden for trout, roach, and gudgeon. Mrs. Stapley has a clear memory of him one day coming in dripping from the river and handing her a mess of fish, which she rapidly transferred to the cook for dinner.

As these inconsequent but evocative details will suggest, the Stapleys—Mr. Stapley eventually became headmaster of Frays—have kept pleasant memories of him, and he gave them no indication during those months, when they were seeing him virtually every day, that he was unhappy at the school; on the other hand, he never pretended that teaching was anything but a stopgap career for him, to be given up at the first feasible moment. And like so many of his friends and acquaintances, once he had passed from their ken, they would never see or hear from him again.

There was one other person at Frays upon whom he made a strong impression, and that was Graham Bennett, the son of the headmaster, who was not at the school as a pupil but was living there with his parents. Blair, as an older man of wide and unusual experience, had great fascination for a boy in his late teens. Bennett found him likable, witty, quizzical, and unpatronizing; they would chatter away about "anything and everything"—although it seems worth pointing out that Blair never bothered to tell Bennett that he was in the process of writing a novel or that he had already published a book under another name. Even so, Bennett found him slightly "mysterious," which only added to his interest: he was "some sort of Socialist," in the sense, one gathers, that Sir William Harcourt's *bon mot* of the 1880's, "We are all socialists now," might have served as the motto for the 1930's. And of course his appearance was unforgettable, very different from the neatness and trimness that the schoolmaster of the day affected. Blair, in his thirty-first year, had the looks that he would keep for the rest of his life. He had lost the robustness and weight of the time when he was playing in the Wall Game at Eton, and the spruceness and firmness of the young officer in his first year in Burma. Those years in the Delta had taken their toll, as had ill health and the years of living on the cheap since his return. He was tall and weedy, and his style of dress, which was permanently decided upon by this time, helped to create an effect not easily forgotten. Graham Bennett still remembers a certain shabbiness: Blair in bags—trousers with wide cuffs—a frayed sports jacket, and checked shirt. He would be dressed much the same a year later when Rayner Heppenstall met him: "He wore baggy grey flannel trousers and a leather-elbowed sports coat, with a khaki or dark-green shirt, and a pale, hairy tie. He continued to favour this style of attire in the days of his prosperity." Years later, in the early 1940's, when T. R. Fyvel knew him, he still dressed like this, to Fyvel's mind a mixture of the seedy sahib and a French workman. Perhaps it would be simplest to say that in 1933 he had begun to dress as George Orwell: a transformative process that would work from the outside in.

Towards the end of November he wrote to Leonard Moore to say that the novel was finished, truly finished as far as he was concerned—"I am sick of the sight of it"—and he asked if he might bring it over to Moore's house in Gerrard's Cross the following Sunday, December 3. On the Sunday, with a characteristic disregard for the realities of the wintry weather, Blair went off on his motor bike, carrying the manuscript, and wearing his usual sports coat and flapping trousers, without even a scarf or pullover, despite the urgings of the Bennetts and the Stapleys. This was how he had dressed since coming back from Paris, how he would continue to dress, whether dashing about on the motor bike or walking through the streets of London or visiting his sister Marjorie in the North, not wearing a topcoat even on the coldest days of winter, as Ruth Pitter had begged him to do two years before in a vain attempt to make him take care of himself.

The result was predictable. In the middle of December, while out on his motor bike, he was caught in an icy rainstorm, got thoroughly drenched, and came down with a terrible chill—Graham Bennett remembers him being blue with cold. At first he was nursed at the school by Mrs. Bennett and the matron. But the chill developed into pneumonia; with his weak chest his condition worsened perceptibly; and at the advice of Dr. Bennet-Coles, whom the headmaster had called in, he was transferred to the Uxbridge Cottage Hospital, just up from the school on Harefield Road.

He was terribly ill; in fact, it was thought almost certain that he would die, and the Bennetts sent for Mrs. Blair from Southwold. Avril drove her down, but by the time they arrived in Uxbridge, the crisis had passed and the chances of his recovery had notably improved.

Avril remembers the nurse telling her that when Eric had been delirious, he had talked incessantly about money: one of the obsessions of his life emerging, as it were, from the unconscious and demanding to be heard. Now, as she and Mrs. Blair sat by his bedside, "We reassured him that everything was all right, and he needn't worry about money. But it turned out that it wasn't actually his situation in life as regards money that he was worrying about, it was actual cash—he felt that he wanted cash sort of under his pillow."

Dr. Bennet-Coles recommended that he must have at least six months' rest once he was discharged from the hospital, so there was no question of his continuing with his job at Frays. He took the doctor's recommendation one dramatic step further in a letter to Moore at the end of December: obviously he couldn't be back at the school at the beginning of term; therefore he had decided to chuck teaching, imprudent though that might be. Out of every misfortune a blessing, however; for now, without the dis-

tractions of having to teach, he would be free to work un-
interruptedly at his next novel—that would be *A Clergyman's Daughter*—and with the enthusiasm of a prisoner on
the point of liberation, felt he would have it finished within
six months. Meanwhile, in the last sentence of his letter,
where he usually tended to raise such questions, he ventured to hope that all would go well at Gollancz with
Burmese Days.

That was on the twenty-eighth of December. A week
later (January 4, 1934) he wrote to Moore that he was
leaving the hospital and would spend a few days at a hotel
in Ealing until he felt strong enough to travel, then go
straight down to Southwold to his parents' house. There he
would simultaneously convalesce and create. His career as
a schoolmaster, which had never provided him with much
satisfaction and which he would deal with in the future
with more ferocity than accuracy, was at an end.

EIGHT

H E RETURNED TO SOUTHWOLD IN A MOOD OF HIGH elation, to which his release from teaching, his escape from the threat of death, perhaps something of the flushed excitement symptomatic of TB, perhaps the child-like pleasure of being looked after by his mother and his sister Avril, all contributed. His mind was teeming with literary schemes and projects, enough to occupy him, if he wrote unceasingly, for the next several months. Surely, though, this was not the "complete rest" that Dr. Bennet-Coles had recommended?

He signified to Rees that he was ready to do reviews again for the *Adelphi*. He wrote to Moore about the possibility of his doing a translation from the French of Paul Gille's *Esquisse d'une philosophie de la dignité humaine*, which his Aunt Nellie's husband, under his professional name of R. Lanti, was busily translating into Esperanto in Paris (nothing came of this). In early February he proposed that he might undertake a short life of Mark Twain for a biographical series that was being published by Chatto & Windus (nothing came of this). And, of course, there was to be the new novel. That, indeed, did come into being at a much faster rate than its predecessor, which had proved such arduous work that, coupled with his schoolteaching, it may have contributed to his physical debilitation over the many months of its writing and revision.

Although the early news of *Burmese Days* was discouraging, Blair's mood remained high: he was confident that all would go well with it. By mid-January Gollancz had read the manuscript and admired it, but consulted his solicitor and then rejected it, fearful of its potentially libelous content, which seemed to be taken from Blair's own experience—a notion that Blair himself did nothing to discourage. Granting that a solicitor's advice to a publisher in such circumstances tends to be overly cautious, it was not unlikely that Gollancz might indeed be sued for libel if Blair had indeed drawn some of his characters, which again would not have been unlikely, directly from life. The most unexpected people have been known to read a novel as though it were a mirror; Roger Beadon remembers hearing that the Principal of the Police College in Mandalay, whom Blair thought an oaf, threatened to horsewhip the author when he read *Burmese Days*. So if someone had chosen to recognize himself in the text, publisher, author, and printer might well have been sued for damages.

Before the end of the month, Heinemann's, to whom Moore sent the manuscript next, had also rejected it, and for the same reason. It is possible that Orwell was the victim now of the reputation he had won with *Down and Out in Paris and London*. No one had questioned his veracity then as a faithful reporter of life as he had observed it, and it would be a logical assumption that his next book, though labeled a novel, would also draw in large part upon what he had experienced at first hand, faithfully described.

But even this news of a second rejection did not unduly depress him: he still had no doubt that the novel would be published. It helped to sustain his mood to learn from Moore that Eugene Saxton, the editor in chief of his American publishers, Harpers', who had an option for his next two books after *Down and Out,* happened to be in London at the very moment Heinemann's sent back the manuscript to Moore. Moore dispatched it immediately to Saxton at his hotel, and Saxton, in the fashion of American publishers in London on a "buying trip," read it in an evening, liked it, and was anxious to talk with the author about it. On Wednesday, the seventh of February, Orwell took the train from Southwold to meet with Saxton in London that afternoon. It proved to be an editorial rather than a legal conference: questions of libel didn't arise.

Rather surprisingly, considering that at the time he was writing *Burmese Days* he was very closely rereading Joyce's *Ulysses* (Mabel's gift from Ostend), and writing admiring didactic letters about it to Brenda, he was wholly uninfluenced (then) by that landmark of experimental fiction. He was thoroughly committed to straightforward, even old-fashioned, storytelling, and Saxton in a mild sort of way objected to the old-fashioned last chapter, after Flory's suicide, when the later careers and lives of the characters are taken beyond the proper confines of the story, much as in a fairy tale we are reassured that "they all lived happily ever after." Blair couldn't have disagreed more: "I hate a novel," he wrote to Moore the next day, "in which the principal characters are not disposed of at the end." Still, he would be willing to cut out the offending pages if he must—that is, if Saxton insisted; but he did not, and the tidying-up remains in the text. The chief result of this meeting between author and editor was that Orwell agreed to remove the offending phrase "It now remains to tell" from the beginning of the chapter, and it appeared that, so far as American publication was concerned, all problems had been resolved.

But in March the specter of libel again raised its head. The contract for the book was negotiated by Harpers' agent in London, Hamish Hamilton. Difficulties arose because it was known that two English publishers had already rejected *Burmese Days,* and it was surmised that they had been moved to do so out of fear of libel. A special clause was inserted in the contract, stating that Orwell would withdraw such material as Harpers' advisors might consider libelous; or if the publishers considered the material too libelous to be published, the book would be withdrawn and the contract annulled. The threat of libel sufficiently worried Orwell himself that he added a stipulation of his own: that a statement should be inserted in the book saying that all characters were fictitious, and this was done.

The contract was signed in March 1934. At the end of the month, Harpers' sent the manuscript to their lawyer in New York to be vetted for libel. A few days later he reported to them that he felt, despite the author's disclaimer, that quite a few characters were drawn from life, particularly Flory, and that the book did libel several people, although it was unlikely they would bother to sue. Still, there was some risk. Harpers' decided to take the matter further. In April their lawyer wrote to a solicitor in London to inquire if Harpers' as an American firm could be sued in England. Apparently the reply was equivocal enough to be reassuring; Harpers' decided to go ahead and publish, and in the autumn sent the agreed-to advance, payable on publication, of fifty pounds.

Once again for the sake of clarity we ignore chronology and leap forward to deal with the history of *Burmese Days,* first in America, correctly as Orwell's first novel, and then, in England, where it was published as his second novel, having been preceded there by some months by *A Clergyman's Daughter*. Harpers' brought out *Burmese Days* on October 25, 1934, in an edition of two thousand copies, far more, as it turned out, than would ever be needed. Again, although the book was by George Orwell, it was copyright by Eric Blair. This time, however, a certain amount of publicity material was forthcoming—enough, it was hoped, to tantalize prospective readers: that the book itself couldn't be published in England for fear of libel; and that the author had served in the Indian Imperial Police in Burma, resigning, in the words of the reviewer for the *New York Times Book Review*, because "he disliked putting people in prison for doing the same thing which he should have done in their circumstances." The most conspicuous of the American reviews, and the only one that Blair himself saw, was in the *New York Herald Tribune Books*. It had been given pride of place, first among the fiction of the week and prominently headlined, but it was quite unfavorable. The reviewer, Margaret Carson Hubbard, found that all of Orwell's sympathies were with the natives, which does not suggest a very careful reading of the text, and that "as a result, the only characters that seem real are U Po Kyin and the native doctor Veraswami. The trouble with this novel is that the ax Mr. Orwell is grinding is so vastly important to him that it has chopped to pieces all interest in the very situation he most wants to expose. The ghastly vulgarity of the third-rate characters who endure the heat and talk and nausea of the glorious days of the British Raj, when fifteen lashes settled any native insolence, is such that they kill all interest in their doings." Not, as a publisher might say, "a selling review," though Blair consoled himself, in a note to Moore, with the thought that it had been given big headlines, "which I suppose is what counts."

The reviewer for the *New York Times Book Review* was the same Fred T. Marsh who had written so favorably of *Down and Out* the year before in the *Herald Tribune,* and he was a good deal more discriminating than Mrs. Carson Hubbard. But the most discerning American review appeared in December, in the high-toned and gentlemanly *Boston Evening Transcript,* a newspaper long since defunct that survives, so to speak, as the subject and title of a minor poem by T. S. Eliot. The anonymous reviewer for the *Transcript,* noticing that the book had been refused publication in England, admitted to some bafflement on the point, for it was hardly a book which painted the English as all black—*pace* Mrs. Carson Hubbard—and the natives as all white: Burmese, Indians, Eurasians, and English are made equally to appear silly and mean. If Orwell disliked the English more than the others, it was simply that they happened to be the most powerful: "Virulent as at times are Mr. Orwell's strictures, he visualizes as candidly those native—well, racial—idiosyncrasies against whose passive resistance all the power of Western Empire repeatedly proves unavailing." The central figure was thought to be "analyzed with rare insight and unprejudiced if inexorable justice," and the entire book was praised as full of "realities faithfully and unflinchingly realized." But kind words in Boston were not enough to save a hopeless situation, and before long, Harpers' gave up on the book entirely: in February 1935, just four months after publication, the type was distributed, and 976 copies were remaindered.

Blair himself, though dissatisfied with the book, was not at all ashamed of it, and there was no reason that he should have been. But he was sufficiently concerned that a complete record be kept of his literary output that in December 1934, he personally presented, and inscribed as George Orwell, a copy of the American edition of *Burmese Days* to the British Museum, which had not automatically received the book, as it would have done if it were an English publication.

But in fact, perhaps because no libel actions had ensued from the American edition, English publishers picked up courage. In September 1934 Jonathan Cape expressed interest in the book. Blair's first reaction was skeptical. He told Moore he thought there was little point in showing it to them, as Cape had the same libel lawyer as Gollancz—which has the sound of an improvised reason; quite possibly he just did not want the book to go to Cape, for they were the publishers, it will be remembered (Blair certainly hadn't forgotten), who had twice rejected *Down and Out*. But then he had a second thought. After all, they had *asked* to see it; perhaps they would be the ones brave enough to accept it. In October he reminded Moore that Cape had published *The Best Poems of 1934*, in which a poem by Blair as Blair had been included, and perhaps this should be called to Cape's attention when he was shown *Burmese Days*—a rather naïve misunderstanding of the realities of publishing. But his third and final thought was realistic enough—that Cape would not want the book; and when they were sent the manuscript, that proved to be the case.

Then, in February 1935, Victor Gollancz, who would be publishing *A Clergyman's Daughter* in March, decided to reconsider *Burmese Days*. This time his response was enthusiastic. Whether Gollancz himself hadn't done more than glance at the manuscript the first time around, or whether the political overtones and implications of the novel, its caustic picture of the Raj in action, now made a special appeal to him, one can't say for certain. But he did want to publish it; and although Blair would tell Henry Miller in 1936 the fanciful story that his publisher had been afraid the India Office would try to suppress the book, all that actually stood in the way was the libel problem— still existing, of course, but for which a solution would somehow be found. Towards that end, even while the same lawyers who had originally recommended against publication were giving the book another microscopic reading, it was arranged that Blair should come to the Gollancz office to discuss the problem with Norman Collins, deputy chairman of the firm. Their meeting, certainly as recalled by Collins long afterwards, had its elements of comedy; perhaps only Orwell's friend of his later years, Anthony Powell, could do justice to its more subtle ramifications.

Collins, four years younger than Orwell, had become a director of Gollancz in 1934. From 1929 to 1931 he had been assistant literary editor of the *News Chronicle*. Then in 1932 he had begun his own career as a writer with *The Facts of English Fiction,* and in 1934 had followed it with a novel, *Penang Appointment.* (A decade later he was to have an immense international success with his novel *England Belongs to Me.*) He was a trim, elegant figure who personified, inadvertently as it were, the rewards and privileges of the literary life that for Blair were equivalent to the shades of the prison house. This has to be kept in mind to savor the comedy that followed.

Collins hadn't met Blair before, but he had read his books, and *Down and Out* had prepared him for a writer out of the usual run. Even so, he was taken aback at the entrance of a tall, painfully thin figure, shabbily dressed, wearing a jacket whose sleeves were much too short for him, with a ravaged face that looked, Collins thought, as though it belonged to an El Greco saint.

There was an attempt at social conversation before getting down to the serious business of the day. Tea, always a useful tactic for getting over initial awkwardness, was sent for. Blair spoke. Collins had no difficulty in recognizing that Etonian accent, which doubtless became more noticeable as the interview progressed, and which explained the shabbiness as a form of eccentricity.

Collins arrived at the problem of libel itself. In a general way he made it clear—he was really being very helpful—what sort of answers were required from Blair; once given, they would simplify everything for everyone. But Blair, despite his El Greco face, was in a puckish rather than a saintly mood, and was not yet ready to cooperate.

"How much of *Burmese Days* is actually based on fact?" asked Collins.

"All of it," said Blair.

"All of it?"

"All of it."

Pause.

"Now then, about the characters. Would you say they are drawn from life?"

"Yes."

"Well, one or two, or how many?"

"All of them."

"All?"

"All."

Pause.

Collins had never had an experience with an author quite like this one before. "But surely you've changed their names for the novel?"

"Oh no."

"You mean that you've used their actual names?"

"Oh yes."

"How many?"

"All of them."

It was Blair in a mood and style that would not have been unfamiliar to friends, acquaintances, and masters who had known him at Eton.

Eventually, however—if not that afternoon—he accepted the seriousness of the problem as it was put to him. He did, after all, want his novel published in England, and Gollancz agreed to publish it if certain changes were made.

In the light of Blair's sweeping claims to Collins, it comes as something of an anticlimax to discover that the changes were only three in number, a matter of new names for certain characters: most importantly, the evil Burmese magistrate U Po Kyin became U Po Sing, and Dr. Veraswami became Dr. Murkhaswami.*

* In later editions of *Burmese Days*, beginning with the Penguin edition of 1944, the names of the characters were restored, and the American and English editions have since that time been identical.

NINE

A Clergyman's Daughter WAS PUBLISHED IN MARCH 1935, but to give it its proper place in Orwell's history, one must go backwards in time to its inception. It will be remembered that at the end of December 1933, even before Blair had left the hospital in Uxbridge, he was writing to Leonard Moore that one advantage of his giving up teaching was that he would be able to write his next novel in six months.

In January he was in Southwold, convalescing in his parents' house, and already at work. In April he was able to report to Moore that the novel was not going badly, and that he had made even more progress on it than he had anticipated, though it was still in very rough form. By now Blair really saw himself as a professional man of letters: one or two novels a year . . . reviews, essays . . . a typewriter never silent. *Down and Out* had been published in England and America, and contracts for French and Czechoslovakian editions were being drawn up. Arrangements had been completed for the American publication of *Burmese Days;* there was no reason to doubt that eventually it would find an English publisher.

The difficulty that faced him, although he was still unable to recognize it—the significant difficulty any author of Orwell's bent would find himself having to face—was that his literary capital was drying up; some of the experience that went into the new novels was not sufficiently digested; and his power of imagination was deficient—whole areas of life eluded him, especially where women were concerned. For his best, most persuasive work he had to draw upon what he had himself experienced. Burma had had a long time to ripen and formulate in his mind, and the same would be true of *Animal Farm* and *1984*. *Coming Up for Air* in 1939, written after a break from fiction of four years, drew upon the milieu and recollections of his childhood in Henley-on-Thames. But *A Clergyman's Daughter* in 1935 and *Keep the Aspidistra Flying* in 1936, the novels he wrote in immediate succession to *Burmese Days*, industriously and with hardly a pause to think or invent between them, are generally thought to be his weakest. So Orwell himself came to feel: he gave instructions that they were not to be reprinted, and during his lifetime they were not.

The lessons to be learned from the writing of *Down and Out* and *Burmese Days* Blair was as yet unable to accept: that his gift was for reportage rather than the invention of plot, that his depictions of women were drawn less from life than from the stereotypes of fiction. Although his books were best when they were truest, he was determined to prove himself an authentic novelist of a traditional kind, capable of a full-dress, traditional, imaginative characterization. How better to prove it than to write from the point of view of a central character who would bear no relation to himself—not even tangentially, or as a spokesman, as with Flory—and what better way to prove *that* than to make his central character a woman? Hence: Dorothy Hare, the luckless heroine of *A Clergyman's Daughter*, whose last name is borrowed from Blair's paternal grandmother, and whose pathetic adventures are meant to be fictional but all too soon and too recognizably are drawn from Blair's own.

It is a classic case of an author misjudging his talent and his material.

Orwell himself never explained why he should have chosen to write about this particular character or the crisis in her life—her loss of faith as a believing communicant of the Church of England—that provides the novel with its thematic spine. In 1934 it couldn't be claimed that the plight of the genteel spinster daughter hadn't already been explored in some depth by earlier writers, perhaps less often in the novel than the story, a genre to which it seems peculiarly suited: by Katherine Mansfield, for instance, in "The Daughters of the Late Colonel"; and by D. H. Lawrence in "The Daughters of the Vicar." As for the loss of faith, that hallmark of the postwar age, it had been a "resource" all through the 1920's, along a spectrum in time and quality that would range from Joyce's *Ulysses* in 1922 to Noel Coward's "Twentieth Century Blues" ("they're getting me down") in 1931. The best justification for Blair's entering such well-mapped territory—apart from his wish and his need "to write a novel"—would have been if he had felt deeply enough for Dorothy to bring her to life on the page: not as life observed, but as life lived. Orwell, in Herbert Read's phrase "the last great English journalist in the line that begins with Defoe," would acknowledge in a piece in *Tribune* in 1945 that a major difference between himself and Lawrence (and in fact what made the latter a genius) was that Lawrence was able to know imaginatively what he could not know by observation. The particular work of Lawrence's to which he refers in this piece is "The Daughters of the Vicar," a long story whose theme of the genteel spinster he doubts Lawrence could have dealt with successfully in a full-length novel. Perhaps this was Orwell's own way of admitting that he hadn't been up to the task either.

And yet, he had begun very well, and one can understand his cheerful tone when he wrote to Moore in April. The opening portions of *A Clergyman's Daughter* are in the best traditions of English social fiction. Its setting, the village of Knype Hill, is precisely evoked, with a shrewd eye for its awful and all too credible social discriminations —not for nothing had Eric been strolling the streets of Southwold, or dropping in at the tea shop that Avril and a friend were managing at this time off the High Street, or engaging in long conversations and gossips with his mother at home. Dorothy herself is much more sympathetically rendered than Elizabeth in *Burmese Days*. Poor thing, she is instantly recognizable as one of life's victims, and her victimship is compounded by her particular circumstance: as the only and devoted daughter of an altogether selfish man, the vicar of St. Margaret's (C. of E.), in whom are united snobbish intellect, un-Christian spirit, and insufficient income, and to whom Dorothy ministers in the multiple role of daughter, quasi-wife—the actual spouse, Dorothy's mother, having wisely deceased years before— and housekeeper and bookkeeper. The last is a particular source of anguish to her, for the Hares are the embodiment of gentility at the end of its tether, piling up bills with the local tradesmen which they can never entirely pay.

Dorothy's long day's journey into night provides the substance for the long, excellent first chapter. It begins with her enduring, for the good of her spirit, an ice-cold bath; and then in lonely attendance, for the good of her spirit also, at early morning service, over which her father presides with weary disdain. Thriftily, Blair could make use of all that he had observed at St. Mary's in Hayes, and his friendship with the curate there now paid handsome dividends. Once or twice the tone does go slightly off, when certain Orwellian obsessions with what is physically noisome and disgusting are foisted upon Dorothy: as she takes the communion cup from a slobbering old lady, she forces herself to drink from the cup precisely where the slimy mouthprint still lingers. But on the whole, the air of truth envelops it all, whether at the vicarage or in the streets of Knype Hill: Dorothy dutifully calling upon aged and infirm parishioners; her humiliation at the butcher shop as she attempts to stretch credit past the breaking point; even her visit that evening with the slightly louche but not unamiable Mr. Warburton. He is the one man she knows who offers her a possible escape from the limitless tedium and bleakness that extend before her, but it is an escape she cannot take, since, in addition to being one of life's victims, she is also one of its pathological virgins. At an attempted pass from Mr. Warburton, she flees down the road from his house, back to the vicarage, the tyranny of her father, and her joyless, self-lacerating faith in God.

It is at this point that Blair's difficulties with the novel began. By July his early optimism had given way to despair. "I am so miserable," he confessed to Brenda Salkeld, "struggling in the entrails of that dreadful book . . . loathing the sight of what I have done." This was neither diffidence nor panache, but a true cry from the heart.

Sometimes an author will know, as it were by instinct, when he has plumbed his material to its proper depth, when he has discovered the formal structure that will show it to its best advantage; this would happen only once in Orwell's career, with *Animal Farm*.

In *A Clergyman's Daughter*, having written at length and

with copious persuasive detail of a day and a night in the life of Dorothy Hare, Blair discovered that he had told all that there was genuinely to tell about her, the character he had *imagined*. The end, which in the novel comes after another two hundred pages, was already suggested at the very beginning of the first chapter, and might have been left for the perceptive reader to conclude for himself at the chapter's end, as Dorothy disappears down the road from Mr. Warburton's house, on her way back to the vicarage: one of those pathetic figures who lose their faith and yet, if they are to survive at all, must go on with the forms of the faith in which they no longer believe.

Blair had written what he failed to recognize: a long story of considerable power, firmly rooted in the realistic tradition. But he had intended to write, and was still determined to write, a full-length novel. In practical terms this meant that he somehow, some way, had to find a further narrative for her; and he found it, as one might expect, by returning to his own experience. Ostensibly Dorothy continues as the heroine of the novel, but his true subject, his inevitable model, was himself in disguise. The result, artistically, must count among his failures, as he himself recognized; but for a biographical study such as this, it has its peculiar interest.

His powers of imagination seem to have deserted him completely. What will happen next? is the primitive, essential question any novelist must ask of himself. In the case of Dorothy Hare, considered as a character in her own right, the question would have been complicated for Blair by the very skill with which he suggested the likelihood that hers was a life in which *nothing* would happen next: that was the whole sad scarifying point of her story. But once he was determined to go on with it, and make a novel of Dorothy's story, certain suppositions of a novelistic kind might have been considered—supposing *this* were to happen, *then* she might in turn do thus and so—suppositions not wholly inconsistent with her character as it had been so clearly, so convincingly drawn in that opening chapter. To the question What will happen to her next? Blair answered that this clergyman's daughter would go down and out, even as he had done at various moments in the years before he became "George Orwell."

There is a significant difference, of course, between the situations of Eric Blair and Dorothy Hare. Blair chose voluntarily to go down and out as a writer in search of material and experience: the last such descent into the lower depths he had made three years earlier in August to October 1931, when he went to pick hops in Kent as soon as he had finished the final version of *Down and Out*. For Dorothy there was no logical, or underlying psychological, motive for this particular experience, nor was she to have the choice (as he had had) of returning from the depths to ordinary normal life whenever it pleased her to do so. Like a ballet dancer performing the choreography of someone else's invention, she is simply to undergo a number of the experiences that were Blair's own—many, one discovers, are taken quite unchanged, even as to phrases, turns of speech, and emotional responses, from his hop-picking diary. The crucial difference—one is tempted to say, the fatal difference—from the point of view of fiction, is that what had happened to him is now to happen to her.

All that had to be invented was a fictitious device for getting her there—down into the lower depths. By no stretch of the imagination can we persuade ourselves that a girl like Dorothy would ever have voluntarily chosen such a fate—as unlikely, almost, as her emerging naked from a pie at a church bazaar. Therefore the fate must be imposed upon her, and Blair's device is a massive, prolonged attack of amnesia, brought on (we are left to conclude, for it is left unexplained) by the traumatic effect of Mr. Warburton's pass—in any event, this is the last night that she will be in Knype Hill for months to come. There is a period of five days and nights that are never accounted for, long enough for her to get to London, and to have had experiences of some sort that are never to be described. Then she re-emerges, her memory and her wardrobe totally gone. When we next see her—it is indeed Dorothy—she is wearing a scruffy version of a tart's costume, soiled satin dress and black mesh stockings. Remarkably, her virginity appears to have remained intact, and continues so to the end of the novel: the transforming, apocalyptic sexual experience a Lawrence might have had in mind for her, Orwell will have none of.

What he had in mind for Dorothy was that she should re-experience, while still in her amnesiac state, something of his own experience as a hop-picker in Kent—and he had his hop-picking diary, kept faithfully from August 25 to October 8, 1931, to draw upon for that. Then, having recovered her memory, she shall reexperience something of the poverty he had known in his down-and-out explorations of London, descending to ever more disgusting and filthy lodgings, until she is literally penniless and homeless, and must spend a night in Trafalgar Square, one among the many shivering derelicts huddled together for warmth—and for that he could draw upon his memories, as well as *Down and Out* itself, where they had already figured. Finally, she will reexperience a kind of grotesque, luridly exaggerated version of his own experience as a teacher in a private school: he could draw equally upon his memories of Evelyn's and his nightmares of St. Cyprian's for that.

From even this cursory summary it will be evident how rapidly Blair was using up his literary capital. After all, he had chucked teaching only a few months before, and here, in however distorted a form, was the material already being used: no matter that the teacher in question was Miss Hare rather than Mr. Blair. Given his difficulty in inventing a plausible or engrossing plot, and given his determination at the same time to write a novel a year, he really had no choice but to draw upon his own continuing experience, touching it up here, smoothing it down there—mere grist for the fictionist's mill. But at the rate he was going—Burma done, London and Paris underworld done, schoolteaching done, even the gentilities and gossip of Southwold done—he really had no choice but to start acquiring a new set of experiences. He was sitting at his desk writing a novel: that was virtually the sum of his winter and spring activity in Southwold now. As usable capital, to be drawn upon in the future, it was alarmingly meager: was he next to write a novel about a novelist writing a novel in a seaside town out of season? No wonder he was eager to be finished with Dorothy Hare and the awkwardly connected chapters of sordid experience he had imposed upon her, and to be on his way to London. He had set October as the deadline.

His comments as he was writing A Clergyman's Daughter grow bleaker the further he gets into it: it was dreadful, it was loathsome, it was awful; reading over the manuscript made him want to vomit. Even as one makes allowances for the conventional exaggeration and discontent of an author in midbook, one senses a malaise here that goes deeper. For him there was really nothing and no one of significance (except his mother) in Southwold any longer. There were only the trivialities of everyday life, as enervating to the spirit as the round that Dorothy Hare was being made to experience in Knype Hill: a hedgehog, small as an orange, turns up in the bathroom; the daily stroll with his mother and the poodle down the High Street to the lighthouse, the landmark of the town, with perhaps a pause, on the walk back, at Avril's tea room; he goes to a film, which his father already has seen and spoils for him (as fathers will) by insisting on telling him the plot beforehand. The significant thing was the departure of Eleanor and Dennis Collings for Singapore—a marriage and a departure that had deprived him of "two friends at a single stroke," as he complained to Brenda, and even she, his other close friend in Southwold, had given up her job at St. Felix and gone to teach at another school, not as far away as Singapore, but no longer as readily available as she had been.

His sense of isolation was almost total. Still, with no significant happenings to engage his emotions or distract him from the daily stint at the typewriter, there was nothing to do but write, which he did—his novel, his reviews for the *Adelphi;* and on the third of October, precisely on schedule, he informed Leonard Moore that he was sending him the completed manuscript of *A Clergyman's Daughter.*

PART TWO

EILEEN

TEN

D URING HIS NINE MONTHS (JANUARY TO OCTOBER) OF
convalescence, creativity, and boredom in Southwold, he
had kept in touch with his friends at the *Adelphi*, in particular its editor-proprietor Richard Rees, who came from
London for a weekend visit in the summer and found the
family house in the High Street perfectly comfortable; Avril
and Mrs. Blair, whom he was now meeting for the first time,
excellent company; and the elderly father more benevolent
and less intransigent than the son had allowed him to believe. Throughout these nine months of exile, Eric, while
writing his next novel as George Orwell, had continued to
be a frequent contributor to Rees's magazine, always, it
will be remembered, in his own person—that is, as Eric
Blair. Now that the time was finally at hand—health recovered and novel finished—for his next move, the *Adelphi*
connection led directly to a job and a place to live.

There had never been a question of his remaining in
Southwold. At this period in his life London was where he
wanted to be. "Coming to London" was a strategic move for
a young writer whose career was in its early postapprentice
phase—so, for example, Rayner Heppenstall from Yorkshire
and Dylan Thomas from Wales, both of whom Blair was
soon to meet under Rees's auspices, were arriving in Lon-

don and writing for the *Adelphi* at almost the same time as he. But the fact that he was still making professional use of both his pen name and his own name suggests some uncertainty in his mind as to the nature of the career he meant to pursue: a writer, yes; but beyond that, a realistic novelist? or a poet and man of letters, at ease with French Romanticism and medieval Catholicism (on both of which he wrote for the *Adelphi*) or whatever else an editor, usually Rees, sent his way? (In fact, for George Orwell—if not for Eric Blair, whose signed work terminates at the end of 1934—a literary career could and did include a wide variety of genres, far more than he must have contemplated, starting out. In his own fashion he was to prove almost as versatile a writer, if not as prolific, as his sometime master of French at Eton, Aldous Huxley. And in Orwell's career, as in Huxley's, the poet and realistic novelist ultimately would give way to the fabulist and polemicist.)

In August, still in Southwold, Eric was informing Brenda Salkeld that it would choke him to live in Bayswater, where a friend had offered him a lease of part of a flat, and which must have figured for him as a London version of Knype Hill (or Southwold). His preference, he told her, was for "somewhere in the slums." When she took this to mean a return to the common lodging houses and squalor of three years back, he hastily explained that his intention was nothing so drastic: simply, he wanted to avoid a respectable quarter. At that moment, Islington seemed a likely possibility.

But once he came up to London, he was to live from mid-October 1934 until August 1935 in Hampstead, where respectability and the Bohemian life are blended in an altogether congenial and very English way: he was anywhere but in the slums.

At that time in Hampstead, at No. 1 South End Road, there was a secondhand bookshop with the Knype-Hillish name of Booklovers' Corner. Its owner, Francis G. Westrope, a Welsh pacifist and friend of the *Adelphi* people, mentioned to Rees's co-editor, Max Plowman, that he was looking for an assistant to work in the shop afternoons. For mornings he already had a young man named Jon Kimche. (Kimche would later become well known as a writer on Jewish and Middle Eastern affairs, and editor of the *Jewish Observer and Middle East Review*.) Plowman mentioned the job to Rees, who thought immediately of Blair, just up from Southwold and staying with the Fierzes until he found some way to support himself. Here, surely, was a lucky find for a writer in need of money, whose chief aim was to have as much free time as possible for his writing—which had not been the result when he was a schoolmaster—especially since, in addition to a small salary, Westrope would include, rent-free, a furnished room in the family flat, directly round the corner from the shop. Rees promptly mentioned the job and its attractive perquisite to Blair. It did appear to solve both his working and living problems simultaneously, and he went round to be interviewed by Westrope, who hired him on the spot.

Two days later Eric moved from the Fierzes' house in Golders Green to the small block of flats in Pond Street that bore the rather too grandiose name of Warwick Mansions. Mabel came along with him to help him settle in, and to inspect the dim furnished room with its view of the backs of the row of shops in South End Road. Privately she thought it a bit dingy, which of course would not disqualify it in Eric's eyes, but she kept her counsel; at the least it promised a fair amount of independence and privacy. And the neighborhood itself was agreeably villagey, with large trees

all along the rising slope of Pond Street, an attractive ter-
race of perhaps-Georgian houses adjoining Warwick Mansions, and directly in front of Booklovers' Corner, a small
triangle with benches where passersby might contemplate
the fountain and horse trough a civic-minded Miss Crump
had caused to be erected in 1880.

As for the job itself, it seemed to Mrs. Fierz, as it had to
Rees and even to Blair, pleasant in prospect, making small
demands and ideally suited to someone of bookish temperament. Alas for optimism and fine beginnings! Although he
was at Booklovers' Corner some fifteen months, he grew to
loathe it, and in the novel he would be writing at this time,
Keep the Aspidistra Flying, he described it, or revenged
himself upon it, with acerbity and wit and spleen—also,
according to Kimche, with a good deal of exaggeration.

Since Kimche's hours to clerk were between nine-thirty
and two, and Blair's between two and six-thirty, they were,
in a manner of speaking, ships passing in midocean, with
barely time to semaphore a message of sympathy and good
will before disappearing over the horizon. But Blair had the
key to the shop, and would come down after making his
breakfast to open the door and wait for Kimche's arrival,
and they would talk a bit then before he went back to his
room to begin his morning's writing. When he returned
after lunch, for his own stint in the shop, he and Kimche
would talk a bit again.

Gradually a kind of friendship—the Blairian kind, affable
but reserved—developed between the two young clerks with
literary ambitions, though in this respect Blair was much
ahead, for he had already published two books (the second, admittedly, only in America thus far), he had just
finished a third, and was starting work on his fourth. Sometimes he would invite Kimche to come round to his room in

Warwick Mansions (and to the bed-sitter to which he would presently move), where he held a sort of court. His circle of acquaintances had begun to widen, drawn from Sunday afternoons at the Fierzes', Wednesday evenings at the Sturge Moores', casual visits to Rees's flat in Cheyne Walk (which was now also being used as the *Adelphi* office), and the occasional evening in Soho with Rees—it was in those circumstances, early in 1935, when they were having dinner in Bertorelli's in Charlotte Street, that Rees would introduce him to Heppenstall and Dylan Thomas. Evidently his social life was a good deal less circumscribed and more enjoyable than the life he permitted to Gordon Comstock, the angry young man and anti-hero of *Keep the Aspidistra Flying*, who is sometimes thought, erroneously, to be a portrait from life of the author himself. But whether in a group or with an audience of one, Blair tended to hold forth on subjects on which he held firm views, a favorite in the autumn of 1934 being the baleful influence of the Roman Catholic Church. And for all his affability, he did tend to address one, so Kimche remembers, as if one were a student in a lecture room, or a recruit on the inspection line at a Burma Police parade.

In November 1936, several months after he had given up his job at Booklovers' Corner and only a month before he was to leave for Spain, Orwell published in the *Fortnightly* his brief and generally even-tempered "Bookshop Memories." Here, as in the much more caustic first chapter of *Keep the Aspidistra Flying*, which Gollancz had published in April of that year, he describes the haphazard visitors, intruders, browsers, time-wasters, would-be shoplifters, and occasional customers he had had to put up with in the shop. They ranged along a spectrum from the rare person who knew and cared about books to the "not quite certifiable

lunatics," of whom, as he remarks, there are always "plenty
. . . walking the streets, and they tend to gravitate towards
bookshops." But from this heterogeneous, even lurid, catalogue of bookshop types there is a significant omission in
the light of his own experience: namely, the women a male
clerk such as himself was in a position to become acquainted with, first as a clerk, then as a friend, moving
from the dusty precincts of the shop to the world outside,
and with whom, if circumstances were favorable, he might
eventually embark upon a "relationship" of considerable
intensity. This, for Orwell the author and Blair the man,
was the chief reward of working at Booklovers' Corner.

As we have already suggested, his experience of women
thus far in his life—he had celebrated his thirty-first birthday in June—seems to have been meager and belated, and it
was reflected in those stumbling attempts at female por-
traiture in his first two novels: in *Burmese Days*, the stereotyped Elizabeth Lackersteen (blond, cold, English, and
snobbish) whom Flory loved in vain, and the stereotyped
Ma Hla May (dark, spicy, Burman, and vicious) whom he
took to his bed; and in *A Clergyman's Daughter*, the hapless Dorothy Hare, implausibly pressed into service as the
author's surrogate. Now, thanks to two women he met at
Booklovers' Corner—one succeeding the other as object to
be pursued, though there was some overlap for a time and
he continued seeing them both—his experience was considerably enlarged, broadened, and deepened. (Love itself
he had still to experience, for though they were fond of
him, neither of these two women was in love with him, nor
he with them.) Meanwhile the literary consequence of
these new "relationships" made itself evident in the novel
he was writing precisely while they were in progress. Rosemary, the heroine of *Keep the Aspidistra Flying*, drawn

from his experiences rather than his fantasies of women, is an achievement he had never managed before: a credible female portrait.

The first of the two women—each of whom recognizes aspects of herself in Rosemary, and both of whom were kind enough to see the authors of the present work and share their memories of Eric Blair as they knew him in 1934/1935—was Sally; the second was Kay.

The daughter of an American mother and a South African father of European descent, Sally had been brought up in the south of England in conventional, traditional middle-class circumstances—"boarding school and all that"—and although she felt that she and Eric were, temperamentally, both "odd people out," she was essentially a girl of her class. The point is worth emphasizing, for it holds true of all Orwell's women, then and later: they all came from the middle class—say, from middle-middle to middle-upper-middle, to borrow Orwell's own gradations, with Orwell himself in the lower-upper-middle. Whatever compulsions drove him to explore the lower depths, to go down and out, they stopped short of urging him towards women of the working class or below: there was no hint of *nostalgie de la boue* in that particular, nor of a missionary impulse such as inspired George Gissing, a novelist Orwell especially admired, and made Gissing's life, unlike Orwell's, a misery. Orwell's ladies, one and all, were ladies who might have been introduced without embarrassment to Mrs. Vaughan Wilkes, the headmistress of St. Cyprian's.

A commercial artist and illustrator, Sally was twenty-seven ("But holding on to her girlishness," as she puts it) when she first met Eric. This would have been towards the end of 1934. At the time, she was working for an advertising agency (see Rosemary in *Keep the Aspidistra*), but in retrospect she makes no claim to having supplied Eric with the details about advertising or agency routine that are scattered through the novel—"Hardly necessary, do you think? Anyone who looks at a newspaper or magazine could invent that sort of thing, the slogans and the rest of it." She lived in Hampstead, in the vicinity of Booklovers' Corner, and came into the shop late one afternoon in search of a copy of *The Decameron*—there was a possibility, which never materialized, of her doing an illustrated edition. She returned to the shop for further books, and after the second or third time, she and Eric were on chatting terms, friendly enough for him to ask her name and where she lived.

Discovering that they were neighbors made it easy for him to suggest that they have dinner together, which they did, and soon they were seeing each other quite frequently and continued to do so, in spite of a basic disagreement that was never resolved, for more than a year. He would have her come to his "evenings"; he brought her round to the Fierzes' (as he would presently also do with Kay); they went on an excursion to Brighton; they had dinner fairly often at local restaurants, where he kept up a constant complaint about having no money, but was adamant (as he had been with Ruth Pitter) in not allowing her to share the bill (and as Gordon Comstock would be with Rosemary). At their dinners they drank lots of chianti, which she thought fine and he thought sordid. That they couldn't afford a better wine—having lived in Paris, he was something of a wine snob—was simply one more proof, like his being obliged to work in a bookshop, that the world was awful. In his conversation he was very much the ambitious, nonstop, hardworking professional writer (which indeed he was, unlike Gordon Comstock with his single slender published volume of verse, *Mice,* and the long poem he worked at fitfully but never finished). Politics, after 1936 a ruling passion in his life, figured in his conversation then almost not at all, except for an occasional disparaging reference to William Morris and Socialism—no matter that he was *pro forma* a Socialist himself. But at this time, early in 1935, his view of the world was more solipsistic than Socialistic; his concerns were chiefly with himself and his deprivations: the wine he wanted and couldn't have; the literary success he wanted and didn't have—would it come with his next novel, or with the serial he was thinking of writing?—and, most vexingly, so far as the immediate moment was concerned, the woman he wanted, Sally herself, and was not to have. That, of course, was the basic disagreement between them.

The difficulty was that Sally knew what *she* wanted, not marriage especially, for she thought of herself as a woman of advanced ideas, but a Grand Romantic Passion, and early on she recognized that Eric was not that. She felt that he regarded her, and women in general, as "a plate of greens," which she had no intention of being or of serving up to him. So while she was prepared to go back with him to his room—no ogre barred the door as in the Gordon/ Rosemary story—and was prepared to indulge in playful kisses and caresses, a line was drawn and adhered to, prompting a good deal of quarreling, and from him the ultimate period epithet, that she was a "Victorian." Nevertheless, they continued to see each other for more than a year, even after he had met and was frequently seeing another woman, Kay, who was more amenable than Sally, and even after he'd met a third woman, Eileen, with whom he fell instantly in love, though that epochal encounter did not deter him for some months further from continuing to see both Sally and Kay, all three separate relationships being maintained simultaneously. One does have an impression of Blair on a carousel in this almost Schnitzlerian season of his early thirties, making up enthusiastically and adroitly for time lost in his early twenties.

However pleasurable, vexing, tantalizing, satisfying, and educational the pursuit of women might be, he was concerned even more with the literary pursuit: his determination to become a writer—what Richard Rees described to us in conversation as "Blair's obsession." So it followed naturally that in those first months in London in the autumn of 1934 he would be preoccupied above all with the fate of the novel he had just completed, *A Clergyman's Daughter*, and the future of the as-yet-untitled novel he had just begun. His experiences with *Down and Out* and with *Burmese Days*—the latter still to be taken by a publisher in England—would make him wary of optimism in any case. He knew now, as he had not known two years earlier, that between sending a novel to a publisher and a publisher's accepting the novel, much could intervene, usually of a frustrating nature. But in the case of *A Clergyman's Daughter*, he was especially uneasy because he believed that what he had written fell short of being a truly successful novel: "It was a good idea, but I am afraid I have made a muck of it."

Moore, as an efficient agent with a manuscript to place by an author of proven talent, was not put off by his client's regrets and self-depreciatory judgments—they were as much a part of his "style" as another author's exuberant egotism. After all, only two years before, Blair had made an impressive start as George Orwell with *Down and Out in Paris and London*. That book had sold well enough for him to be remembered by booksellers, and certainly he would not be overlooked by reviewers such as Compton Mackenzie, who had so conspicuously "invested" in him. Although Gollancz, on the advice of lawyers, had rejected *Burmese Days,* and in so doing had forfeited official option rights to the author's future work, it occurred to Moore that he might be strongly attracted to the "down-and-out" aspects of this new, and so far as English readers were concerned, this "first" novel by George Orwell. Accordingly he sent the manuscript to Gollancz, from whom in early November came a qualified acceptance. There were the inevitable complaints that portions of the book were libelous, and there were passages marred by obscenity—all of which would have to be attended to. But other, more serious objections were raised, chief among them that Dorothy's grim-to-grotesque experiences as a teacher at Mrs. Creevey's School were thought to be incredible. However—and this was the crucial point— Gollancz wanted to publish the novel, and would do so if the author was amenable to making changes.

From Warwick Mansions, having received the essentially good but peripherally irritating news, Blair wrote to Moore in mid-November. His mood was at once despondent and docile. He had feared all along that there might be difficulties with the publication of the book, which he himself seemed to value for a few of its parts rather than as a whole. But it was precisely for those few parts that he was anxious that it be published, and therefore he was prepared to revise. The libel and the obscenity (swear-words) presented no problems at all. Still, he did need to know specifically what was wanted done before setting to work, and with that in mind he asked that Moore arrange an interview for him with Gollancz—an hour, he thought, should be sufficient to decide upon the revisions.

About the adverse reactions to the school scenes he was both amused and bruised. When first sending the manuscript to Moore, he had emphasized that the school was imaginary, and this was not merely a precautionary declaration. Indeed, he admitted that a fault in the novel was that it was "rather unreal." Much of what is described as happening at Mrs. Creevey's School belongs to the world of caricature and nightmare, though when Dorothy makes suits of armor for the school play, struggling with wrapping paper and glue, she suffers precisely the same agonies that Blair had suffered in precisely the same situation at Evelyn's. But whether or not the particular school in the novel was invented or faithfully described, he was sure that there were still beastly abuses in the private schools in general—he had suffered them himself only twenty years before at his own school, St. Cyprian's, even though it was so much grander and more respectable than Mrs. Creevey's, at the very top of that particular heap—and to say, as Gollancz's incredulous readers had done, that such abuses had been ended thirty or forty years ago, was simply an easy way of dismissing them from one's mind and conscience. Still, though he claimed to be willing to tone down the details a little, and presumably did so, the picture of Mrs. Creevey's School as it appears in the published novel is, at the least, "rather unreal," and it is hard to think what it must have been like before revisions. One has only to compare the fictional Mrs. Creevey's with the actual Frays College to realize how ill-judged it is to read this portion of the novel as though it were a factual account.

Which is not to claim that Blair did not hate teaching, which so interfered with his writing; hated it at the deeper levels of his being, while outwardly he appeared to be enjoying himself at Frays, just as he was soon to hate being a clerk in a bookshop. If, as we have seen, he drew upon details of his own experience as a schoolmaster to produce an air of verisimilitude, it was hatred, festering within and bubbling to the surface, that compelled him to exaggerate and undermined his credibility. Hatred, rancor, and unforgiving responsiveness to pain in whatever form (the social wound and the battlefield wound)—all these can be animating forces for the writer, and were to be so for Orwell throughout his career. In the novels before 1936, especially in *A Clergyman's Daughter* and *Keep the Aspidistra Flying*, such forces tend to turn inward. The result is a subjective response to private experience: the nightmare that mistakes itself for a true account of life as it is. But once these forces that were so much a part of his nature could be turned outward, and he could concern himself with the plight of *others*, identify with the existence of others, objectify the angers that stirred him and transmute them into a concern for others, which he began to do in 1936 in *The Road to Wigan Pier* and in "Shooting an Elephant," his identity as a writer would come into sharp focus: he would be truly Orwell.

But on the fourteenth of November 1934, writing to Leonard Moore, he was still "yours sincerely, Eric A. Blair," and what concerned him was a flaw in the structure of *A Clergyman's Daughter* that he did not think could be corrected. In his letter to Moore, he fails to identify the flaw; but whatever it might be, it had not bothered him until now because he hadn't meant the novel to be read as a realistic account (as the people at Gollancz were reading it), nor to be judged on that basis. This would seem to contradict his position of a month before when he acknowledged as a fault of the book its being "rather unreal"; yet he could hardly pretend to himself that much of his subject matter was not drawn from his own experience, faithfully recorded, in the hop-picking episode literally so. True, the novel does contain a slightly *expressionist* interlude, the night scene in Trafalgar Square, told entirely in dialogue, which most critics have accepted as written under the influence of *Ulysses,* as it strives for the intensity one associates with poetry rather than prose—and with Joyce rather than Orwell. But most of *A Clergyman's Daughter* has the specificness of detail that is characteristic of the English novel even when it is crossing the border of nightmare and fantasy. If his novel was being read as a kind of document of experience—as his generally straightforward style invites one to do—Blair may have decided that the flaw was his failure to provide any details of the missing five days in Dorothy's life, not even a shadowy explanation of how she got from Knype Hill to London and what happened to her on the way. This is a conspicuous omission, certainly; and assuming that it is the "flaw," one wonders why he should have thought it could not be corrected—unless his imagination simply did not take in and respond to the intimate details of female existence, of female degradation.

He met with Gollancz later that week. Everything went smoothly enough between them so that he could tell Moore that a month's time would be sufficient for the revisions and changes wanted. A month later, on Christmas eve, he sent off to Gollancz the novel in its final form, and was through with it. Once again he began to suffer something like the despondency he felt after he had given the twice-rejected manuscript of *Down and Out* to Mabel Fierz and told her to "Read it, burn it, and keep the clips." For he announced to Moore that if Gollancz decided not to publish this revised version, he would extract from the manuscript the one chapter that he liked—presumably the night scene in Trafalgar Square—and try to have it published separately in a magazine. As for the rest of it, the implication was clear: he would simply throw it away. But such drastic action was not necessary. Less than a month later Gollancz had decided that he would definitely publish *A Clergyman's Daughter,* and his terms were so good as to elicit from Blair the rueful comment, "I am afraid he is going to lose money this time, all right."

That was in mid-January. Immediately the wheels began to turn, at a rate that reminds us again how much simpler and more efficient publishing was in the old-fashioned 1930's than at present, after four decades of technological advance. Proof copies existed and were sent out for comments to the famous before the end of February;* bound copies of the finished book were in hand the first week in March; and the official publication day was March 11, 1935.

Pleased Orwell undoubtedly was to have the book published, and pleased at the terms Moore had secured for it. He was also pleased when Gollancz in mid-February reopened the question of publishing *Burmese Days* and soon had agreed to do so. But he could not persuade or deceive

* Sending advance copies of a book for flattering comment is a tradition of the trade that continues unabated in the 1970's, even though the proportion of replies is discouragingly low. One famous writer to whom the publicity people at Gollancz sent *A Clergyman's Daughter,* along with the traditional polite letter hoping for a laudatory sentence or two, was Sean O'Casey. He declined to comment at the time, but the request seems to have lingered in his mind, and he finally did make a comment in 1954, in his autobiography, *Sunset and Evening Star.* "They were sure the scene in Trafalgar Square was one of the most imaginative pieces of writing they had ever read—equal to Joyce at his best," he recalls. Then, with evident relish: "Orwell had as much chance of reaching the stature of Joyce as a tit has of reaching an eagle." O'Casey was convinced that his refusal to comment favorably on *A Clergyman's Daughter* was the reason for Orwell's unfavorable review of his own book, *Drums under the Window,* in the *Observer* many years later—a fine example of authorial paranoia, a state of mind from which Orwell himself was known occasionally to suffer.

himself, then or later, that he was pleased with *A Clergy-man's Daughter*. Sending a copy to Brenda Salkeld four days before publication, he assured her, "It is tripe, except for chap. 3, part 1 [the night scene in Trafalgar Square], which I am pleased with, but don't know whether you will like it." Did she like it? Years later she spoke of *A Clergyman's Daughter* without enthusiasm—it had never been one of her favorites among his works, she said.

Gollancz published the novel in an edition of 2000 copies, and it was widely noticed in a gamut extending from the *Sunday Times* to the nonconformist *British Weekly*. Compton Mackenzie predictably led the van in the *Daily Mail*. As enthusiastic as when he had reviewed *Down and Out* just two years before, he had recourse yet again to the Dantean allusion, warning that "the book should be avoided by all readers who lack the courage to descend to the innermost circle of the social inferno. . . . [It] chastens without revolting, horrifies without disgust. . . . By telling the story through the medium of a woman Mr. Orwell has secured a perfect objectivity, and thereby avoiding conveying an impression that he is once more exploiting his own experiences in the guise of fiction . . . definitely a novel, and a very fine novel at that."

Other reviewers were more restrained. Bonamy Dobrée, in the *Morning Post*, while he thought "The description of a night in Trafalgar Square . . . unforgettable," extracted a social moral from the text that one suspects was not present in the author's mind when he wrote it: "A patchy book, at times brilliant, which raises the question of the position of the clergy in outlying districts."

The young V. S. Pritchett, in what must be the first of many perceptive attentions he was to pay Orwell over the years, gave the book second place in the fiction column in the *Spectator*. He was rather taken with Dorothy, enough to think her quite badly treated by her creator. The satire, Pritchett felt, was essentially "a whip for the vicarages," and in the circumstances it was not surprising that the "plain, obstinate, stoical and delightful Dorothy at last breaks down," though he was constrained to add that "one does not believe that she would not have put up a more intelligent fight." About the episode in Trafalgar Square, unlike Dobrée, he had his reservations: "This scene shows an immense knowledge of low life, its miseries, humours and talk, but unfortunately has been written in 'stunt' Joyce fashion that utterly ruins the effect."

In the *New Statesman and Nation,* the novel was one of eight reviewed together by Peter Quennell, who found it ambitious and unsuccessful. He, too, raised objections to the Trafalgar Square episode ("would be more impressive if it were less reminiscent of the celebrated Nighttown scenes at the end of *Ulysses*") and his final judgment was that "We have no feeling that [Dorothy's] flight from her home and her return to the rectory have any valid connection with the young woman herself."

There was a rather patronizing review from L. P. Hartley in the *Sketch,* who complained that the book was "hardly constructed at all," and then paid Orwell a double-edged compliment: "It is not a work of art, but it is worth reading for its vivid, if overcolored pictures of certain unfamiliar aspects of social life."

So it went: a characteristic English reception for a not especially notable novel, with here and there the usable quotation—"A brilliantly clever, brilliantly disagreeable book" (Sylvia Lynd, *Harper's Bazaar*); "Interesting and exciting reading" (*Times Literary Supplement*)—along with a fair amount of caviling.

Reviewers, especially of fiction, have only so much space and time at their disposal: novels arrive in alarming quantities from publishers each week. Even writers as gifted as Pritchett and Quennell, faced with the impossible problem of the omnibus review, must be done before they have hardly begun, to make room for the next novel awaiting its turn. It could be argued that Orwell was fortunate to be paid as much attention as he was, the more so as it became apparent that he was going over ground that in many respects he had already covered in his first book. (From this point of view it is regrettable that *Burmese Days* hadn't followed directly upon *Down and Out* in England, showing a broader range for Orwell as a writer and defusing the argument that he could only do "down and out.") But having made all allowances for the difficulties imposed upon the London book reviewer practicing his trade, it must also be added that the most pertinent and valuable review would not appear until the novel was published in America more than a year later, with a slight change of title as *The Clergyman's Daughter*.

Only the streak of quixotry that makes publishing so odd a business can explain the American publication at all. Harpers', in spite of having failed twice with Orwell, decided to try once more, though there was nothing in the English reviews to suggest they would fare any better this time than before—unless, perhaps, the notion of a novel of a *woman* going down and out might titillate readers who had hitherto been obstinately indifferent. But having been twice burnt, Harpers' in the matter of *A Clergyman's Daughter* behaved cautiously as well as quixotically, and at a very stately pace. It was not until December 1935 that they decided they would import 500 sewn sets of sheets (that is, unbound books) from Gollancz—rather than go through the more expensive process of printing it in America—for which they would pay a royalty of 1/10½d a copy, and Gollancz accepted the offer. Publication was scheduled for August 1936. In July, when there appeared to be a shade more interest in the bookshops than Harpers' had anticipated, they asked for another 500 copies from Gollancz, but it was too late. By then, some fifteen months after the novel had been published, the first printing of 2000 copies had been sold; no second printing had been called for; and the type had been distributed. Harpers' solved the problem by acquiring a further 500 copies by photographic process, and for these they agreed to pay a royalty of fifteen cents a copy, terms Moore readily accepted. This meant 1000 copies were available in America; more than were needed, as it turned out, for 256 copies ultimately were remaindered. *A Clergyman's Daughter* was the last book by George Orwell to be published in an American edition until *Animal Farm* in 1946.

Such facts and figures, while dismal to contemplate, have little relation either to the quality of the book itself, or to its critical reception, which, generally speaking, was enthusiastic or reserved in a way comparable to its reception the preceding year in England. But the review by the young poet and novelist Vincent McHugh, which appeared in the *New York Herald Tribune Books*, deserves to be singled out, for it must be the first in which Orwell's affinities with George Gissing, the late-nineteenth-century writer he so greatly admired, are recognized and declared.

"The motto for this novel," McHugh began, "might have been taken from George Gissing's reflection on 'the life which is not lived for living's sake as all life should be, but under the goad of fear.' " Poor Dorothy Hare, with "her faith and her almost gallant drudgery," living a life that in all its turnings has fear as its base, is the heroine of "a minor novel in Gissing's tradition, a shade more lively as to tone, rendered in a quiet, fluent texture which has a way of making detail count, and garnished with modest incidental ironies."

McHugh had a fine awareness of Orwell's difficulties with characterization and structure—"Dorothy's peregrinations have been arranged more to bring the author's various materials into play than to set up an internal pattern for her life. Perhaps for this reason she remains a little indistinct. . . ."—and an equally fine awareness of the skill with which he evokes the village of Knype Hill, "so minutely and with such honest grimy detail that it becomes almost a new picture. . . ." No small feat, since McHugh felt constrained to add that by this time "The English village has been chronicled almost to extinction."

But his aim was not simply to award a reviewer's pluses and minuses, but to place the novel in a particular tradition, that of Dickens and Gissing:

Mr. Orwell too writes of a world crawling with poverty, a horrible dun flat terrain in which the abuses marked out by those earlier writers have been for the most part only deepened and consolidated. In all his characters . . . there is the present equivalent of that sense we have been accustomed to think of as Victorian: the subjectively unquestionable, even remotely comforting conviction of the eternity of English social forms. It was this belief which lay at the root of what has been called Gissing's "pessimism"—the rigid round of custom, the loneliness, the causeless ennui. And it is precisely this almost unrecognized social compulsion by instilled pattern which determines Dorothy Hare's final decision that it would be best to take up once more the service of a church she no longer believes in.

McHugh was at his most prescient in his final paragraph, especially if one remembers that the year was 1936—decades before Orwell was to become a subject for critical explication—and that he knew nothing of the author beyond the two books of his that he had read (the other was *Down and Out*) and what he inferred from them:

It may be that the theme of *The Clergyman's Daughter* has the extra value of an ironic symbol unnoted by its author. The stages of Dorothy's plight—the coming to herself in the London street, the sense of being cut off from friends and the familiar, the destitution and the cold—enact an almost perfect dream-logic for the secret nightmare of that lower middle-class she had come from: the nightmare in which one may be dropped out of respectable life, no matter how debt-laden or forlorn, into the unthinkable pit of the beggar's hunger and the hopelessly declassed.

Whether or not Orwell noted the ironic symbolism of which McHugh speaks one can't answer with certainty—there are no contemporary diaries or journals to call upon, and his comments on the novel are brief, disparaging, and uncommunicative—but there is no doubt that the nightmare itself was one with which he had been made familiar from the time that he was a schoolboy at reduced fees at St. Cyprian's, threatened with the consequence of failure on the scholarship exam for Eton: "to go down to the depths of degradation, to be cast out from the charmed circle." That was the logic not only of a dream, but also of life itself, as it had been set forth for him in his childhood.

ELEVEN

CONSIDERING THAT ORWELL WAS A MAN WHO YEARNED
to put down roots, there is a special poignancy in the way
he was virtually always on the move, never quite coming
to rest or at home anywhere for an extended, uninterrupted
period, at any time throughout his life. Of all the many
addresses that were to be his in his forty-seven years, beginning with Motihari in Bengal, where he was born, and
ending with University College Hospital, London, where
he died, it seems fair to say that none was to lead to greater
happiness for him than 77 Parliament Hill Road in Hampstead, where he lived from March to August in 1935.

On the sixteenth of February, in the course of a letter to
Brenda Salkeld, he remarked that he would have to give
up his room in Warwick Mansions within a few weeks.
"Isn't it sickening," he began, but that was merely a way
of speaking, and it would seem that Eric might have given
a more circumstantial account had he been so minded.
There was no suggestion that he might have some alternative available; when he next wrote, on the seventh of
March, replying to a letter of hers, he was already at his
new address, 77 Parliament Hill Road, NW 3, with no hint
as to how he had happened upon it.

There had been a growing strain with Westrope, not in

the shop, where his work was entirely satisfactory, but in
the flat in Warwick Mansions, where his life was not. The
proprietor, anticipating a solitary lodger of whose existence
one would hardly be aware, was irritated by the considerable and no doubt audible social life being lived in the
back bedroom, and the situation was not improved when
Mrs. Westrope fell ill. Presently it was agreed that Blair
would move elsewhere, though continuing to work in the
shop, and his wages would be adjusted upward to take this
into account. He was relieved, actually. Except for its
proximity to Booklovers' Corner, he hadn't been especially
happy with the room, and Mabel, who had disliked it from
the first, had a solution to the problem of his finding another place to live as soon as he came to discuss it with her.

Her friend, Rosalind Henschel Obermeyer, whom he
would have met at the Fierzes'—a pleasant woman in her
early forties, a niece of Sir George Henschel, the conductor
and composer, and herself pursuing an advanced course in
psychology at University College, London—lived at the top
of Parliament Hill, on the very edge of Hampstead Heath.
There, Mabel felt, was where Eric should live too: so much
healthier, especially considering his weak chest, the next
best thing to living in the country itself, and so much nicer
than the small back room in Warwick Mansions. Rosalind
and her husband were separated; he was traveling in
America for an indefinite period, lecturing on philosophy;
her flat, very comfortable, light, and airy, was too large for
her alone. She might be willing to let out a spare room. Mrs.
Fierz remembers saying that she would ring up Rosalind
there and then to make sure it was all right, and she did,
and it was—in fact, Rosalind had already let a room to a female medical student. But there was one further room that
should do nicely, nor would the rent for it be beyond his

means, for what Rosalind wanted primarily was to have someone there, someone of the right sort, and Eric, as a rising young author and friend of the Fierzes', obviously qualified.

By the end of February he was comfortably installed in his bed-sitter in Mrs. Obermeyer's first-floor flat. It was a ten-minute walk uphill from Booklovers' Corner, and he had indeed moved upward in every sense, from Warwick Mansions. No. 77, the last house of all in Parliament Hill Road, is a smallish but solid brick structure—it then contained only three flats, one to a floor—built in the later years of the nineteenth century, and overlooking at the back a small garden of its own. It was the sort of house, typical of its style and period, that was meant to suggest a certain degree of affluence and stability, and continues to do so to this day. What made it remarkable was that one stepped from the front door and almost immediately was on the Heath, had only to ascend a knoll and there before one were great grassy stretches of field; clumps of woodland; birds and insects and plants to observe, the life of nature that Orwell would always value; and far in the hazy distance, the panorama of London, unfolding as far as the eye could see. It was a very different country from the land of the aspidistra to which he consigned poor Gordon Comstock.

The flat, arranged in a square around the central staircase, three bedrooms, living room, kitchen, and bath, was large enough and so arranged as to offer privacy as well as comfort. Mrs. Obermeyer, Blair, and Janet Gimson, who was studying medicine at University College, were all occupied with their respective careers—the two women were away weekdays from morning to evening—and there was no attempt to create a bogus family of three. Nor, contrariwise, was there that anonymous, dispiriting atmosphere of the usual respectable furnished flat segmented into rooms to let. Mrs. Obermeyer was anything but the nosy, emotionally impoverished landlady for whom a place has been made in so many realistic novels since Balzac—a monstrous specimen of the stereotype, Mrs. Wisbeach, is exhibited in *Keep the Aspidistra Flying*. From the start she and Blair got on well together: within the month they had progressed from Mrs. Obermeyer and Mr. Blair to a more cordial, even amiable, Rosalind and Eric. But she never failed to recognize that his room was his domain, and the sound of the typewriter behind his closed door meant that he was not to be interrupted.

Similarly, Janet Gimson, living in the room adjoining his and so particularly aware of him at work—out of sight but within earshot—respected his privacy. Indeed it might be more accurate to say (as she herself has said, some forty years on) that this straightforward young woman—who had been Head Girl at Bedales, one of the most progressive Public Schools of the period, and who had just turned twenty-one—was perhaps more indifferent than respectful in her attitude towards Blair. To her he seemed so old— he was past thirty—and looked ill and cadaverous besides, and so (as she thought) almost as much out of things as "Obie"—her nickname for Mrs. Obermeyer—who was over forty! Older than that she couldn't imagine, then. Now, older than that herself by some twenty years and a distinguished physician, she recalls having seen Eric continually, a part of everyday life in the flat, as they would pass through the doors of kitchen and bathroom, and to that degree she was "conscious" of him. But she had no "feeling" about him, one way or another. As she remembers, she was neither in a state nor had the time to pay much attention to Eric, except in a perfunctory way. She had failed her medical exam, the consequence of a romantic attachment that distracted her from her studies and now was ending badly, and she had to work particularly hard to catch up. Even so, there was some social life of a pleasant, low-pressure sort among Eric, herself, and "Obie." They led their separate lives, and the motto of the flat might have been "Do What You Will," but on those occasions when one or another of them would have people in for wine or coffee parties, the others were frequently asked to join in. Characteristically, Mrs. Obermeyer would change for these parties into a flowered tea gown, while Eric came as he was, looking weathered and a bit scruffy, like a perpetual research student who would never take his degree.

As a former Head Girl, Janet tended to be censorious where cleanliness and neatness were concerned: in those respects Eric's room simply would not pass. She thought it then and remembers it still as "filthy." He seems to have been a firm believer in the principle of "sweep it under the carpet" or "move it out of sight." The result of the latter was that forgotten, half-finished boxes of biscuits grew old at the back of his cupboard and were taken over by mice —at night Janet could hear them rustling about; and after Eric moved from Parliament Hill the next summer, she and Obie discovered a family of mice nesting in an extra blanket he had tossed out of sight on the floor of the closet.

The difference between their rooms must have been remarkable to anyone who would notice such things, and not merely because she was neat and he was not. Janet had agreed to take her room unfurnished—an advantage from her point of view—and proceeded over the three and a half years that she lived in "Obie's" flat to fill it sparely but beautifully with furniture of remarkable quality, much of it the work of her great-uncle, Ernest Gimson, perhaps the most famous and gifted maker of furniture in England in this century. Eric's room, by contrast, had been furnished rather higgledy-piggledy with Rosalind's "discards," serviceable still but hardly beautiful—not that it would have mattered to him if they were, for he tended to be loftily or gloomily indifferent to such details in his surroundings. The important thing was that the room was large, and filled with light from the window that looked down on the shrubs in the back garden. Unlike Janet and Rosalind, he had no "view" from his room, though if he opened the window and crawled out on the roof of the adjoining garden shed, he could catch a glimpse of the Heath. The absence of a "Heath view" was not a disadvantage; indeed, if it had been there to look at, gaze at, daydream over, it might have distracted him from the manuscript on his table and the blank sheet of paper in the typewriter. The flat was quiet, and his room excellent to work in. Religiously he did three hours of writing each morning, determined, as he wrote Brenda Salkeld, that this new novel, unlike *A Clergyman's Daughter,* was to be truly a work of art. And in the evenings, when he was not otherwise occupied, he would write again.

Rosalind had arranged the room as a bed-sitter, so that he could and soon would entertain there: no restrictions were placed upon him, he was free (as he hadn't felt himself to be in Warwick Mansions) to do as he pleased, which meant that many evenings were occupied otherwise than with writing. In an alcove curtained off with India-print fabric, he had a gas cooker, the "Bachelor Griller," upon which he cooked deftly, for himself and sometimes for others. Rayner Heppenstall and his friend Michael Sayers, also an aspiring young writer, who shared "two rooms on a top floor in Kilburn at a combined rent of ten shillings a week," were asked to dinner in Parliament Hill. Heppenstall, describing the occasion in his memoir *Four Absentees*, recalls that "Blair cooked for us himself. He gave us a very good steak, and we drank beer out of tree-pattern mugs, which he was collecting."

Evidently these aesthetic appurtenances made a greater impression upon Heppenstall than upon Janet Gimson, who would have been less likely than he to be impressed by a collection of tree-pattern mugs and has no memory of them; indeed, there were many other niceties of Blair's style of living that struck Heppenstall as unusual, not to say unforgettable, yet that to another eye might have seemed commonplace. He remembers (again in *Four Absentees*) that when they would meet in restaurants, Eric "would order red wine, feeling the bottle and then sending it away to have the chill taken off, a proceeding by which I was greatly impressed. I had never seen it done in France, but then," Heppenstall adds, "my French experience, like most of my English experience, had been provincial, while Eric had worked as a *plongeur*, long after he had learned how to order up a bottle of *vin ordinaire*." But, as we shall presently see, there were between Blair and Heppenstall significant little failures to connect, such as Eric's believing that red wine was better drunk "unchilled," the differences of age, of background, of experience, and of attitudes towards life, art, drink, and each other, which would affect the course of their friendship as it moved through 1935 and into the future.

A more frequent guest in the bed-sitter than Heppenstall or Sayers was Eric's new girl, Kay, who had not so

much replaced as been given a place alongside or perhaps
to the front of Sally on the carousel. Typically, and in this
instance quite sensibly, he was at pains not to introduce
the one to the other. As Kay wrote to the present authors,
"he compartmentalized his women friends so much that
one only met one's predecessors or successors by accident,
mostly elsewhere than with him."

Like Sally, Kay had wandered into Booklovers' Corner
—she too lived nearby—and there the friendship had its
beginning, progressing fairly rapidly from bookshop to tea
room to restaurant to theater to Parliament Hill. Unlike
Sally, she had no fantasy to come between them of a
"Grand Romantic Passion," certainly not with Eric, about
whom she entertained no illusions or expectations. She
was another who felt he did not understand women very
well and was afraid of being committed to anyone. Since
her own wish was to be independent, this posed no problem, and a fondness developed between them, a kind of
intimacy without depth. They agreed, however, that if
either of them found "someone else," they would not hesitate to say so; and in the summer of 1935 he did tell her of
his feelings for Eileen. Thereafter she saw him less and
less frequently, like Sally gradually fading out of the picture, and they met for a last time several months before
he and Eileen were married. It was an amicable but complete severance, although she wrote to him after the publication of *The Road to Wigan Pier* to object to the more
extravagant generalizations and assertions of its second
part, wherein he set forth his own idiosyncratic views of
Socialism, past, present, and future—a not uncommon reaction among readers, beginning with Victor Gollancz, who
published the book.

This is virtually to end the story before it got under way.

They happened to meet in Booklovers' Corner, but they might as easily have met first in Richard Rees's flat in Cheyne Walk, for Kay, who had literary aspirations, in the fashion of the time had struck out on her own, and supported herself by running a small typing and secretarial service which did a good deal of work for the *Adelphi*. Hence her acquaintance with Rees, whom she saw quite often (sometimes in company with Eric) and whom she thought exceptionally nice.

"Nice," let it be said, was not the first word that would have come to Kay's mind to describe Eric when she knew him, nor did it occur to her, first or last, when she sat down to talk about him some forty years later. He was too prickly to be nice, too cynical, too perverse, too contradictory, too paradoxical, a strange mix of shyness and assertiveness, endowed with a fundamental honesty and common sense that she never questioned, along with small-minded envies and prejudices that she did not hesitate to call into question. (With no noticeable effect, it must be added; perhaps she took him too seriously, or allowed herself to be baited by his rather malicious sense of humor. Eileen's was evidently the more effective technique: not to rise to the bait and argue, but to smile and ever so gently to lead him on, question by question, until he would have to acknowledge the silliness of his more extreme impromptu pontifications.) What was one to say, for example, to a man who declared that the best proof of Conrad's genius was that women disliked him? Or who saw "conspiracies" everywhere? In the Roman Catholic Church; in the highbrow literary world, where, as he put it in *Wigan Pier*, you succeeded only by "kissing the bums of verminous little lions." Even PEN—that rather innocuous and well-intentioned international organization of writers, of which Kay

was a member, and which, at her mild suggestion that he
do so, he indignantly refused to join—was not an organization to be trusted. Then there was his dislike of the Scottish—his hatred of them, really—which he justified to her
by his aversion to the whisky-drinking Scottish planters he
had met in Burma. (Cyril Connolly thought this particular
prejudice could be traced back to St. Cyprian's, where the
pretty little Scottish boys of good family wore kilts on Sundays and were much in favor with Mrs. Vaughan Wilkes.)
So that when Kay proposed taking him to meet her friends
Edwin Muir, the distinguished poet, and his wife Willa
(together they were the translators of Kafka) at one of
their informal "literary evenings," he refused outright, because Muir was Scottish and hence beyond the pale. No
matter that, as she reasonably pointed out, Muir was the
gentlest of men, no one less like a whisky-spewing planter
was to be imagined, and a native of Orkney besides, with
a dislike of his own of mainland Scotland. That argument
got her nowhere: Eric went on to proclaim a detestation
of literary salons, which might have carried more weight
had he not been himself a frequenter of Sturge Moore's
evenings in Well Walk, an "aesthetical salon" if ever there
was one—on two occasions he asked Kay to come with him
there, forgetting his earlier declaration. For that matter, his
own little evenings of seven or eight people in Parliament
Hill were, whatever he might choose to call them, salons
of a sort, where the discussion was predominantly literary,
with only the briefest of excursions into politics.

In short, he was too inconsistent to be nice. But niceness is not all. Niceness is not necessarily stimulating or
exciting, and what drew her to him was his powerful intelligence, his articulateness, his integrity, his sense of
literary vocation from which he would not be swerved.

He was at this time, she felt, heart and soul a writer, and his writing took precedence over everything else in his life, including, of course, their own quasi-romantic attachment. What puzzled her then was the envy and resentment that seemed inseparable from the vocation, the more puzzling because in her eyes, as an aspiring writer herself, he was so clearly on the way to being recognized: his poems, essays, and reviews were regularly in print in the best magazines; his books were not merely being published but were conspicuously and favorably noticed. True, he was not yet making much money from them; but did he not claim to despise money? And the writers for whom he had an abiding contempt were the Priestleys and the Walpoles in all their lordly affluence. So that as a grievance it hardly held up. Yet the grievance was there. It was as though he enjoyed thinking himself ignored and a failure—unloved, so to speak.

About his writing itself he was, as one would expect, close-mouthed: intimacy did not bring about a rush of disclosure. He did tell her that, after finishing *A Clergyman's Daughter,* he had begun work on what he intended as a kind of contemporary version of *The Canterbury Tales,* in which the characters would embody the various political views of the day; but he had had to abandon the project because, as he candidly admitted, he did not know enough about politics to write it. Instead, he was now writing a new novel, which he slaved at each morning before starting down the hill to Booklovers' Corner. What he did not tell her was that he was using her, along with Sally, as a model for the character of Rosemary in the novel, and that certain of their experiences were being virtually transcribed in its pages: a painfully embarrassing lunch at a Thames-side restaurant in Maidenhead, when for all his Etonian assurance he was intimidated by the waiter into ordering a much grander meal than either of them wanted or he could afford; a dinner with Richard Rees at the Café Royal, which Eric had insisted upon paying for, during the course of which he got blind drunk, though not, as in the novel, arrested.

Between fiction and reportage the line was becoming increasingly blurred as he had to draw upon more and more recent experience; this at a time when he was determined to write "a work of art." Even so, his powers of imagination are more in evidence in *Keep the Aspidistra Flying* than might have been expected, particularly in the creation of Gordon Comstock, the failed, nonwriting poet who is best understood as the anti-self of George Orwell, the failure he feared he might be but gave no evidence of becoming. Not surprisingly, it was at this time that Rees said of him that he was "doomed to success"—the conjunction of doom and success having their special Orwellian irony.

One does have the sense of his beginning to emerge at this period, if not into the limelight, then out of total obscurity. Before, when he had lived in London or its fringes, and despite a few early literary friendships—with Ruth Pitter reading his first faltering attempts; with Richard Rees opening the doors and pages of the *Adelphi;* with Mabel Fierz introducing him to a variety of types in and around the arts—he had led a sort of isolated, subfusc existence. Certainly he had not figured in the literary life of the capital: from that point of view he had been nobody. Now—let us arbitrarily choose as a date the end of March 1935, a few weeks after the publication in London of *A Clergyman's Daughter,* a few months before the publication there of *Burmese Days*—even though he himself might not think so, he was becoming a small somebody; his pen name, which he was affixing by this time to his articles, poems, and reviews, as well as to his novels, would not be unfamiliar in the literary world. He began to meet more people, began to contribute to more journals, began to enjoy himself more. By the end of the year he would be in a position to live entirely, if frugally, by what he earned as a writer. It was not an altogether unpleasant existence—writing in the morning, clerking in a bookshop in the afternoon, going out in the evening to a cinema or pub or music hall or theater or dinner party or giving an occasional small dinner party of his own—though no trace of its pleasant aspect found its way into the novel he was busily, angrily writing then as a work of art.

One of the very first of his dinner parties in 77 Parliament Hill—and it suggests the widening spectrum of his acquaintance—was for the elderly, white-bearded, skull-capped poet T. Sturge Moore and his daughter Risette, to whose house in Hampstead, 40 Well Walk, he had been introduced some time previously by Mabel Fierz. Mabel herself completed the party that evening. Though the same tree-pattern mugs might make their appearance, and the menu be modest (for there are limits to what one can do on the "Bachelor Griller"), the tone of this dinner would have been a good deal more "serious" than that with Heppenstall and Sayers. To judge from his own account, Heppenstall was then living the life of a rowdy young writer in and out of Bohemian Soho, often in the company of a writer even younger and rowdier than himself, the cherubic-looking Dylan Thomas, recently arrived in London from Wales. T. Sturge Moore was a very different case, a survivor from the aesthetic eighteen-nineties of irreproachable character who still kept in the nineteen-thirties, at least in certain quarters, a most impressive reputation. The

American critic Yvor Winters, for example, writing in *Hound and Horn,* declared: "In my opinion, Mr. Moore is a greater poet than Mr. Yeats." It would be rather like having an Institution to dine.

Frederick L. Gwynn in his study of the poet, significantly titled *Sturge Moore and the Life of Art,* tells us that "in the mid-1930's, 40 Well Walk became a kind of minor Garsington Manor."

> Moore and his wife [Gwynn continues] instituted the custom of Friday Evenings at Home, to which writers and artists like George Rostrever Hamilton, John Gawsworth, Christopher Hassall, Owen Lewis, Ruth Pitter, Edward Garrick (Gordon Craig Jr.), and nearer contemporaries like Mona Wilson and John Copely came to read and discuss traditional and experimental art. The house was also a haven for literary men of other lands, and one might meet the Indian Ranjee Shahani or the Chinese Seyuan Shu appreciatively absorbing the host's discourse and hospitality. . . .

> Wilfred Gibson's recollection of this period vividly describes the poet

> with snowy beard
> And dreaming eyes declaiming a new work
> To a hushed circle in his house at Hampstead,
> A visionary mosaic of coloured words
> That, with a craft, half poet's and half painter's,
> Aural and visual, to the inner eye
> Revealed in rhythm the old heroic world. . . .

It may be difficult to credit the presence of the author of *The Road to Wigan Pier* at this aesthetical salon in Hampstead. (Even Gwynn's qualifying "minor" hardly seems to cover the realities of Well Walk: there was no pride of lions there comparable to Lady Ottoline Morrell's at Garsington, no D. H. Lawrences, no Virginia Woolfs, no Aldous Huxleys or Lytton Stracheys.) Perhaps Blair was present chiefly as an onlooker and listener to the discussions of "traditional and experimental art," but Adrian Fierz, the son of Mabel and Francis Fierz, recalls attending one such evening in Well Walk with his mother and Eric, where Eric read aloud a sonnet to the company, either Keats's "When I Have Fears That I May Cease to Be" or Milton's "On His Blindness." The important fact is that Eric was there, in Well Walk, fairly frequently—once he even brought his mother, visiting from Southwold, but the event bored her and she slept through most of it—and on sufficiently close terms with the aging poet to lure him out of those aesthetical precincts to come to dinner in Parliament Hill. But that was in the years *before 1936*, when Blair's ambition was still to write a novel that would be a work of art, a decade before Orwell's declaration that nothing he had written since 1936 hadn't been at least implicitly political—in opposition to totalitarianism of the Left or the Right; when he had not yet turned in revulsion against the Life of Art, that is, against his own life as a novelist before 1936, in which politics had played so negligible a part. Orwell as a writer would always need something to stir up his anger, something to be in revolt against: it was the spur that drove him, paradoxically, to his most enduring achievements. If we are to understand the emotional and intellectual impact upon him of the events of 1936 and 1937 in which he participated, we must accept him also as he was in the years preceding them—poetical salon, tree-pattern mugs, and all—however disharmonious with the realities and legends of the later Orwell.

TWELVE

SOMETIME THAT SPRING ERIC SUGGESTED TO ROSALIND Obermeyer that they give a party together. An evening was decided upon, each was to invite a group of friends—but when it came to the point, it turned out that Eric had only one friend whom he wished to ask, and that was Richard Rees. Jointly he and Rosalind invited Janet Gimson. The rest of the guests were friends and acquaintances of Rosalind's, the greater number being fellow students of psychology at University College, London. One of these was Elizaveta Fen, a Russian emigrée in her early thirties, who had been living in England for more than ten years, had been married to a scientist at Cambridge, and was later to have a distinguished career as a psychiatrist, translator, and author of memoirs. Another was an attractive young woman whom Rosalind did not know especially well although they often sat next to each other at lectures: her name was Eileen O'Shaughnessy.

Of the party itself, a major event (as it seems to us now) in the life of George Orwell, only a few recollected details survive. This is hardly surprising, for with only one exception those who were present would have had no reason to think it unusual, and Orwell, who knew from the moment of Eileen O'Shaughnessy's arrival that it was, never wrote a word about the occasion, which again is hardly surprising, given his instinctive reticence in personal matters and the highly selective and polemical character of his auto-biographical writing.

Mrs. Obermeyer, years after this first meeting of Eric Blair and his future wife, could recall with preciseness a particular detail from the party itself: Eric and Richard Rees standing in front of the fireplace, both of them tall, thin, and ungainly, talking together, glancing at guests as they entered the room and going on with their conversa-tion. Elizaveta Fen, who came to the party with Eileen—they had first met in 1933 and were very close friends—also remembered the two men "draped" at the fireplace, look-ing, she thought, "moth-eaten and prematurely aged."

Nevertheless, at the first glimpse of Eileen's face across the room, Blair was sufficiently stirred to detach himself from the fireplace to go to be introduced to her. Once, years afterward, attempting to describe the effect upon him of certain phrases in Yeats's poetry—inside the political Or-well there was an aesthete always struggling to get free—he remarked that they "suddenly overwhelm one," and then, as the most powerful comparison he could find, added, "like a woman's face seen across a room." Accept-ing the remark as one of those "impressions" that have more to tell us about Orwell than Yeats, it would seem to provide a clue to his feelings that spring evening in 1935 at the party in 77 Parliament Hill. Especially in the light of the immediate sequel, it is a reasonable conjecture that Blair was himself overwhelmed then, for when the last guests had departed and he and Rosalind were cleaning and straightening things in the living room, he turned to her —it is the only other detail of that far-off occasion that Mrs. Obermeyer still vividly, exactly remembers—and said, "Eileen O'Shaughnessy is the girl I want to marry."

The next day at University College Eileen sought out
Rosalind to thank her for the party: she had enjoyed herself very much.

And what, Mrs. Obermeyer recalls asking her, had she
thought of Eric Blair?

Oh, a very interesting man, full of the most curious and
decided opinions, Eileen replied, one of the most interesting men she had met in a long time, and it would be nice
to see him again; but whether she did or not, she intended
to read his books. This was hardly comparable to Eric's flat-
out declaration, but there was a warmth in her tone that
was sufficient to kindle Rosalind's matchmaking proclivi-
ties. She suggested that Eileen might come to the flat for
dinner one evening soon, all very informal: it was understood that Eric would be there too. That dinner, when it
took place, was a success. It reinforced him in his conviction that she was the woman he wanted to marry, and her
in her conviction of his oddness, his remarkableness—and
also his fascination. Walking her to the Hampstead tube
station for her long journey home to Greenwich, he suggested they meet again, and she readily agreed. He also,
she afterward reported in an offhand way to Elizaveta Fen,
"as good as proposed to her."

"What! already?" [Miss Fen] exclaimed. "What *did*
he say?"

"He said he wasn't really eligible but . . ."

"And what did you reply?"

"Nothing . . . I just let him talk on."

"What are you going to do about it?"

"I don't know . . . You see, I told myself that when
I was thirty, I would accept the first man who asked me
to marry him. Well . . . I shall be thirty next year . . ."

"That remark," Miss Fen tells us, "was typical of Eileen. One could never be certain whether she was being serious or facetious." But perhaps in this instance facetiousness was a way of concealing from herself, as well as from her closest friend, the seriousness of what she was already beginning to feel for this very interesting man.

ONE CANNOT EMPHASIZE TOO STRONGLY THE IMPORTANCE OF Eileen O'Shaughnessy in the life of Eric Blair, and hence of George Orwell—indeed, her entrance into his life would hasten the transformation. It was as though, in choosing her that night at Rosalind Obermeyer's, though they did not actually marry until June 1936, he was obeying an injunction of Rilke's that became famous in the 1930's: "You must change your life."

Eileen did not actually *change* him—at thirty-three he was much too set in his manners and habits for her to do anything but accommodate herself to them, which she did quite willingly and with a certain affectionate asperity—but her *influence* upon him was profound, in his life and his work. That being so, it seems both ironic and sad that in the years since her death in 1945 so little attention has been paid her. An unexpected consequence of Orwell's request in his will that no biography of him be written is that his wife should have gradually faded, been obscured, in the perspective of time. Humbling though it may be for a biographer to admit it, a writer will live in his work whether or not a biography of him ever be written, and no matter how much at variance his work may be from the facts of his life. A writer's wife, however—unless by chance she is a writer herself, as capable as he of sustaining her "image"—grows dim and shadowy when there is no biography, inevitably so; she becomes no more in the end than that useful, enigmatic, unilluminating phrase "his wife."

Fortunately we have had the opportunity to talk with a number of Eileen's friends and acquaintances, some of whom knew her as Eileen O'Shaughnessy, others, in the early years of her marriage as Eileen Blair, still others, coming later upon the scene (the wartime years) as Eileen Orwell. From their testimony, generously given, some of it surprisingly vivid—considering how long ago they last saw her—we have materials for at least a partial portrait, and taken together, they are persuasive enough to justify the claim for her importance we are making in these pages.

ORWELL, WHO WAS ENDOWED WITH A SENSE OF SOCIAL PLACE-ment worthy of Proust or Henry James, a quivering enraged responsiveness to who and what and where one was in the English class system, from which he could never quite get free, described himself as coming from the lower-upper-middle class. On a calibrated scale of such distinctions, upper-middle is conspicuously further up, and even lower-upper-middle ranks higher, than mere middle. In lower-upper-middle, who-you-are counted for more than what-you-had, which counted for a great deal in middle—hence the seeming paradox of a prosperous burgher locked firmly into the socially inferior middle class, while an impoverished civil servant or clergyman, making do on an inadequate pension, could cling, however precariously, to his superior social position, in the lower-upper-middle. Within that subtle subclassification, Orwell explained, a fairly wide spread of income was permitted: from two thousand down to three hundred pounds a year. But what happened to the luckless born gentleman who fell below the three-hundred-pound mark? Or the rare eccentric who chose to opt out of his class, and fell down, down to the nether regions below? Where did one land, then, in that decisive tumble? Obviously not in the middle class, for he didn't begin to have enough money to qualify. But not, dropping a notch lower, in the working class either, from which he was debarred by certain ineradicable indicators of class that betrayed him: his accent, for one; a certain authority of manner, for another. It seemed that one was doomed to one's class, as Orwell discovered in his down-and-out explorations: disguised in rags and tatters, he opened his mouth and was recognized at once as a gentleman down on his luck. And, as we shall see, when he journeyed among the coal miners in the North, he had only to speak in that Etonian way of his for them to know him for what he was: not one of them.

The upper-middle class—without lingering any further here over Orwellian subdivisions—included civil and colonial servants, members of the professions and clergy, officers of the army and navy—the respectable center of the nation, above whom (as by right) were the upper class, above whom were the aristocracy. So much for social calibrations! Their usefulness, simply, is that they locate the class background out of which Eric Blair had come, and out of which came Eileen Maud O'Shaughnessy, born in 1905, the daughter of a civil servant (Eric's father had been a colonial servant). Adjusting the calibrator more precisely, one could say that the O'Shaughnessys (Anglo-Irish) were a shade more securely placed than the Blairs (Anglo-Indian) because they were a shade better off.

All this might seem like worrying a trivial matter more than it deserves, were it not for the legends that accrete to Orwell like barnacles to a boat and are as difficult to dislodge. Elizaveta Fen, in the vivid memoir of Eileen she published in the *Twentieth Century* in 1960, begins on a note of understandable indignation:

> Years ago I happened to overhear a youthful admirer of George Orwell telling another young enthusiast with a splutter of excitement: "Here's a man for you—he practices what he preaches: He's married to a woman of the people, and leads the life of a labourer."
>
> A woman of the people [Miss Fen bursts out]: No two words could be less appropriate in describing Eileen O'Shaughnessy. . . .

Born in South Shields and raised in the North—ultimately the family would settle in London—she was educated at the excellent Sunderland High School. In the autumn of 1924, she entered St. Hugh's College, one of the women's colleges at Oxford. Like most undergraduates—and unlike her adored older brother, Laurence junior, who was a dedicated medical scientist from the beginning—she seems to have been somewhat uncertain as to her particular aim. Perhaps she would teach, and being of a literary bent, possessing a marked gift for storytelling (her friends confirm this) and a lively prose style (her letters reveal this), she decided to read English. In 1927 she received a very good Second, and in the Michaelmas term she took her B.A. Missing her First, however, she gave up all thought of an academic career: either the standards she set herself were unyieldingly high, or, as is probably more likely, the notion of teaching was no more than that—certainly not a dedication comparable to Laurence's—and so could be put aside without regret.

Still, it left a question: what was she to do with herself? In prewar days the question would hardly have arisen. Pretty, and pert, and intelligent, and charming, she would simply have stayed at home and chosen among the suitors who would in due course present themselves. But that was not at all the kind of action, or inaction, that appealed to Eileen—any more than it had to Sally or Kay, the girls she was to supplant in Eric's life—and there was no reason why a bright young woman, just down from Oxford in 1927, shouldn't think of having a career (1927 was also the year when Eric Blair returned from Burma and resigned his commission in the Indian Imperial Police, determined to have a career as a writer). The difficulty—not only for Eileen but for so many young women, and for that matter, for so many young men, down from the ancient universities —was to find a career that would engage her deeply, in which she could put her undoubted gifts to their best use. And that did not happen all at once. Indeed, one has the sense of her floundering in search of a solution for some years.

By choice she was in and out of a succession of jobs, of no special consequence and with no connection from one to the next, which she held briefly (though sometimes as long as a year), which amused her and provided her with a fund of entertaining, sometimes fantastic, stories to draw upon afterwards, and, in much less impressive quantity, with funds to live on—fortunately, like so many young women of her class, she was never wholly dependent on her earnings. (Like so many young men of her class, too— it will be remembered that Eric, during the most arduous years of his long apprenticeship, when his savings from

GEORGE ORWELL

ERIC BLAIR, MABEL FIERZ, AND THE DAUGHTER OF A NEIGHBOR
PICTURE TAKEN BY ELEVEN-YEAR-OLD ADRIAN FIERZ

FRAYS COLLEGE, UXBRIDGE

BLAIR IN THE FIERZES' GARDEN, NURSING A PET RABBIT

AT THE ARAGON FRONT. BLAIR IS STANDING, EILEEN IS
SITTING AT HIS LEFT

EILEEN

SALLY

KAY

Burma were used up, received just enough financial help from his mother and his aunt so as not to have to take a job.)

Eileen began as an assistant mistress at Silchester House in Taplow, in the Thames valley, a girls' boarding school, comfortably housed and set in pleasant grounds that included a playing field and a large swimming pool: evidently a very different sort of establishment from the nightmarish Mrs. Creevey's School that Orwell invented for *A Clergyman's Daughter*. She seems to have enjoyed herself there, "making a humorous study of the species of female who own and staff such schools," but not to the point of staying beyond one term. Her next job, we learn from Elizaveta Fen, was "secretary to a formidable business woman who revelled in reducing all her female staff to tears. Eileen led a successful 'revolt of the oppressed' against her before she walked out in triumph." After this industrial imbroglio, a period of quiet: she became a reader for the elderly Dame Elizabeth Cadbury, a member of the well-known Quaker and chocolate-manufacturing family. Her next job was with the Archbishop's Advisory Board of Prevention and Rescue work—which has a fine Gladstonian ring—presumably, social work among prostitutes. That didn't suit, however, and in 1931 she became the proprietor of an office in Victoria Street, London, for typing and secretarial work, experience that would prove useful to her later when she was helping her brother, and later still her husband, with their manuscripts. But the early years of the Depression were not an ideal time for such a venture (as Kay also discovered), and after a year she closed it down, in favor of free-lance journalism, selling an occasional feature piece to the *Evening News*. However, the work she most enjoyed was helping her brother Laurence, "a brilliant chest and heart surgeon, by typing, proof-reading and editing his scientific papers and books."

At that time Eileen and her mother were sharing a flat and having their differences in Greenwich, while Laurence and his wife, Gwen, also a doctor, were living in Black-heath. But early in 1935 the Laurence O'Shaughnessys moved to Greenwich, to 24 Crooms Hill. It was a large, handsome house, directly across from the park, with more than ample room for Laurence's mother and sister, and thereafter that was where they all harmoniously lived—a tribute to Gwen O'Shaughnessy in particular; from all one can learn, a most intelligent, warmhearted, and under-standing lady. Laurence senior had died sometime earlier, with no discernible major effect—with the O'Shaughnessys, as with the Blairs, the father was a subordinate figure. Laurence continued to be his mother's favorite child; and for Eileen, certainly, he was the dominant figure: someone to worship. Perhaps it was merely the example he set of a dedicated, unselfish life, or perhaps he may even have con-fronted her with the purposelessness of her existence, but by 1934 she could no longer avoid the palpable truth—that her years since leaving Oxford had been largely wasted: the time had come for something better than another in-consequential job.

So it came about that in the autumn of 1934 she enrolled at University College, London, in a two-year graduate pro-gram in Educational Psychology that would have led, in the ordinary run of events—preliminary course, thesis, advanced course—to her M.A. degree. It was an atmosphere in which she thrived; her fellow students were anything but dilet-tantes. Dedicated to their work, they were aiming for ca-reers of one sort or another in psychology. From the first Eileen threw herself into her studies with interest and enthusiasm, urged on by Professor Cyril Burt, who recognized in her a more than ordinary aptitude. She was particularly attracted to intelligence testing in children, and quite early decided upon that as the subject for the thesis she would presently be writing.

Elizaveta Fen—a fellow student who went on, as Eileen did not, to become a professional psychiatrist—met her then for the first time, and has recorded a vivid impression of her:

> She was then 28 years old and looked several years younger. She was tall and slender, her shoulders rather broad and high, giving an impression of a slight stoop. She had blue eyes and dark brown, naturally wavy hair. George once said that she had "a cat's face"—and one could see that this was true in a most attractive sense— it was rather short, soft in outline, the nose slightly up-tilted, the eyes large and round with a look of disarming innocence. Those eyes could dance with amusement, like a kitten's watching a dangling object. Her skin had a milky whiteness, and without makeup her pallor could look unhealthy. She was, in fact, far from strong, but she somehow succeeded in doing more work than many strong women I know.

Elizaveta Fen became one of Eileen's closest friends and continued so until her death. By contrast, John Cohen, now the professor of psychology at the University of Manchester, knew her only as a fellow student. He and Eileen acted as partners in psychological experiments, which are usually conducted by pairs of students, and although he was to lose touch with her after the University College years, he still keeps a vivid recollection of how she looked, and a diagnostic impression of her as "bright, rather tough, could be argumentative and 'provocative.'" Rosalind Obermeyer was yet another fellow student and friend of Eileen's who made a postgraduate career in psychology. It was Rosalind who was responsible, as we have seen, for Eileen's meeting with Eric Blair, and so, albeit unwittingly, for her abandoning the career as a child psychologist in which Elizaveta Fen continues to believe she would have had a notable success. Perhaps so. Certainly there was reason to assume in the early part of her time at University College that Eileen, at last and however belatedly, had found in her study of psychology something to which she could dedicate herself. It is an irony of some importance to literary history, that, having done so, only a few months later she would meet the man to whom she dedicated her life.

Eric's dedication, his obsession, had been declared long before his meeting Eileen: to be a writer, first, always, and last. And so he was: only in *kind* was there a progression—from an "art" writer to a political writer. Falling in love with Eileen, wanting her for his wife—this for him was an additional dedication, not, as in her case where Eric was concerned, an alternative.

The year of their meeting, 1935, the year also of the publication in London of *A Clergyman's Daughter* (March) and *Burmese Days* (June), was the beginning of the most important period in Blair's life, continuing through his return from Spain in 1937. During that time he transformed himself from a self-absorbed, minor novelist with little or no interest in politics to an important writer of fiction and essays who had a view and a vision and a mission. *Keep the Aspidistra Flying*, the novel he was writing in the mornings in 1935—in the afternoons he was still a clerk at Booklovers' Corner—would be the last of the "art" novels. In-

tending it to be "a work of art," Orwell himself judged it
a failure. He may have been too harsh in his judgment: the
novel, restored to the canon after his death, has won its
admirers, notably Lionel Trilling, who found it "a *summa*
of all the criticisms of a commercial civilization that have
ever been made." But whether accepted at Trilling's or
Orwell's evaluation, *Keep the Aspidistra Flying* has too
often come to be read as autobiography in the form of a
novel, with wee Gordon a calculatedly shrunken version of
the very tall Orwell (Gordon is a mere five feet seven
inches) and Rosemary, his girl friend, so a recent reference
book would have us believe, "a portrait of Orwell's wife,
Eileen." Part of the misapprehension must be blamed on
Orwell himself: his habit of drawing upon experiences of
his own, while they were still fresh in mind, and reproduc-
ing them in the novels virtually unchanged. And often
Orwell's later nonfiction seems to corroborate what he has
written earlier as fiction. His *Fortnightly* essay "Bookshop
Memories" runs over the same ground, rather more amiably,
that he covers with such ferocity in the first chapter of
Keep the Aspidistra Flying. In the nonfiction version, the
account of working in a bookstore is told in the first person;
in the fictional version in the third—but the *voice* in both is
unmistakably Orwell's. *Ergo*, the innocent reader of the
two accounts will conclude, same setting, same voice,
change the names and it's the same life: the novel is *really*
autobiography.

In general, it seems fair to say that the further Orwell
was away from an experience, the more likely he was to
write of it objectively and without exaggeration. He had
three goes at Booklovers' Corner, and the third time, in an
autobiographical note in 1940 for an American reference
work, he wrote that working in the shop had been interest-

ing, and that his chief resentment was that it forced him to live in London, which he hated. Yet in spite of its disagreeable aspects—chiefly the people who came in to browse, and the dust-laden air of the underheated shop—the work cannot have been excessively demanding; in October 1935 he contemplated taking three weeks off in the country and coming up once a week to tend the shop, and although the plan didn't materialize, the idea of it raised no objections from Mr. Westrope.

But if the picture of life at Booklovers' Corner, as drawn in *Keep the Aspidistra Flying*, is grimmer than the reality warranted, it points to a curious paradox, involving the novel itself and the circumstances of its composition.

Nineteen thirty-five was by any standard a happy year for Eric. He was living comfortably in Parliament Hill; his career as a writer was perceptibly advancing; his social life was richer and more varied; he had girls aplenty, and one girl in particular with whom he had fallen in love—something altogether new to him. As the months passed, his love for Eileen deepened; and she, having first found him "very interesting," gradually responded to him, grew to love him, fell in love with him, and by the autumn of that year agreed to marry him the following June when she had completed her courses. It was now customary for him to have dinner in Crooms Hill, usually on Sunday evenings, after an afternoon in the country with Eileen, or sometimes at the Westminster Skating Club, with Elizaveta, Eileen, and Laurence and Gwen O'Shaughnessy—no matter that he was the clumsiest of them on skates, the sheer pleasure of being together with people who were fond of him was invigorating. Toward Laurence O'Shaughnessy—who was known in the family by his second name of "Eric," which made for a certain amount of amusing confusion—he enter-

tained a slightly cautious attitude at first; perhaps at first
there was the slightest tinge of jealousy, knowing as he did
how Eileen worshipped her brother. (And here it seems
reasonable to interject that if Eileen had not met and fallen
in love with Eric Blair, she might well have ended as Dr.
E. O'Shaughnessy, and the beloved Aunt Eileen of Laurence and Gwen O'Shaughnessy's children.) But once Eric
felt assured of Eileen's love, he was able to recognize his
prospective brother-in-law's remarkable qualities. He listened carefully when Laurence talked of politics—which
were less doctrinaire Socialist than those adhered to by
Rees and other Adelphians—and especially to his account
of the rise of Hitler, which Laurence had seen at first hand,
during a period of research in Germany. It was he who introduced Eric to the idea, which seems not to have occurred to him until then, that Hitler intended to carry out
the program of *Mein Kampf*, and if allowed to go on un-
checked, would bring down catastrophe upon the world.
However foreboding these conversations might be in themselves, the occasions on which they occurred were conviv-
ial and affectionate, creating an atmosphere of civilized
discourse and good feelings—within a family—such as Eric
had seldom experienced before. As against his inveterate
pessimism, here was the possibility that one could, after all,
be happy.

And then, after those pleasant Sundays in Greenwich,
he would go back to Parliament Hill, or, later in the year,
to the flat in Lawford Road he shared with Rayner Heppenstall and Michael Sayers, and continue writing what
proved to be the grimmest, bleakest, and most obsessive of
any novel he was to write until *1984* thirteen years later.
The mood of splenetic despair that hangs like a pall over
most of *Keep the Aspidistra Flying* owes nothing to Or-

well's situation in 1935 and everything to those months in
the winter and spring of 1932, when Jonathan Cape and
Faber & Faber rejected his first book, and Blair had given
up on it and left the manuscript with Mabel Fierz to do
with as she pleased. As we know she turned it over to
Leonard Moore, who sent it to Victor Gollancz, who decided to publish it. But the depression he had felt during
those intervening months, the conviction of failure, had
been almost overwhelming, and the memory of it stayed
with him vividly, oppressively, like a nightmare that had
to be exorcised. It would be written out in *Keep the Aspidistra Flying,* and to that extent the novel is undeniably
autobiographical, but to that extent only. No matter that
Orwell drew upon his later experiences to fill out the narrative, or that his *obiter dicta* and extravagant generalizations are strewn through its pages, or that the poem Gordon Comstock is writing during much of the novel appeared, virtually unchanged, in the *Adelphi* that November as "St. Andrew's Day, 1935" under the name of George
Orwell—no matter how many such resemblances, coinci-
dences, and parallels turn up (and they are inherent in Orwell's method of writing naturalistic fiction), Gordon Comstock is *not* a disguised self-portrait of the author, nor even
a consistent spokesman for him. He has his own fictional
reality.

Keep the Aspidistra Flying is a very peculiar book: there
are many passages and episodes of great power and interest, but they tend to be vitiated by the incessant harping on
money, money, money that goes on and on and on through
the novel—as though it were not only the root, but also the
trunk, the branches, and the fruit of all evil. Surely the
view presented here is too constricted to sustain the weight
of generalizations about life and the contemporary world

that are drawn from them. When we first meet Gordon he is a clerk in the bookshop, loathing it and the people who frequent it, earning just enough for a miserable existence, barely above the poverty level, returning at night to his bleak bed-sitter, and there, as Gordon Comstock, author of a promising first book of poems, writing fitfully and despondently at what is meant to be its successor. And all the while he rages against the injustice of life—for he has no money, and without money, how can he write, how can he be accepted in the literary world, how can he have friends, how can he have women, how can he be loved, how can he have cigarettes enough to last him through the week until the next installment of his meager earnings? It is only toward the end of the third chapter that we discover that Gordon's grim situation has been self-imposed: that he has quit his job as a copywriter for an advertising firm and chosen near-poverty as a gesture to himself—his private war against the money-god who rules over modern life. As Orwell puts it in a sentence whose echo of D. H. Lawrence is too clear to have been unintentional: "One's got to get right out of it, out of the money-stink."

It is one thing to choose poverty, as a Franciscan does, to live among the poor and alleviate their suffering; it is another to do so for one's own salvation, to cleanse one's nostrils of the money-stink. There is nothing selfless in Gordon's defiance of the money-god. It is one of the peculiarities of this novel set in 1935 that its rebellious poet hero should be only fitfully aware of the hundreds of thousands of unemployed in England, living through no fault of their own below the poverty level, looking for work and unable to find it. And he is equally indifferent to any sort of political solution to the evils of the money world from which he is in flight. The Socialism espoused by his friend Ravelston, the editor of *Antichrist* (a character based in outline, but not in detail, on Orwell's friend Richard Rees, and a magazine suggested by the *Adelphi*), elicits from Gordon a profound boredom, a cynical No to everything Socialism claims to stand for: indeed, for Gordon there are no political solutions; the world must fend for itself. Cleansed of the money-stink, he will have his integrity, be free to bring his promise to fulfillment. The view is resolutely blinkered and solipsistic, as befits a poet to whom poetry is the beginning and end of existence. But does Gordon answer to this description? Orwell's attitude toward the question is ambiguous, perhaps because he recognized only when he was fairly deep into the novel that the struggle to be a poet and the struggle against the money-god are not synonymous. In any event he was committed to a poet hero, and he gives us as the one example of Gordon's poetry, line by by line as it is being written, a poem of his own, which he must have thought well of, for, as we have noted, he offered it to Rees for the *Adelphi*.*

It seems fair to conclude, then, that Gordon's flaw, in Orwell's view, is not in the quality of his verse but in his dedication to writing. Orwell himself had never wavered in this respect: he had continued to write under the most adverse conditions and in circumstances that would have discouraged anyone less determined than he. Life was difficult, yes; but if one wanted to be a writer, one wrote—otherwise one was not a writer. This was a basic conviction of Orwell's. His work came before anything and anyone else—it was as simple and ruthless as that, and he knew it, and so did Eileen. But Gordon was irresolute; he did not

---

* In all he would publish seven poems there; three—not, however, "St. Andrew's Day, 1935"—have been included in *The Collected Essays, Journalism and Letters.*

seriously write—oh, there were reasons enough to explain (to himself) why he did not; and many of the reasons were valid—up to a point—but the dedicated writer got past that point, and wrote, as Orwell had done and would continue to do until his final illness, no matter what.

Better than Orwell may have suspected, he had learned the lesson Mrs. Vaughan Wilkes had taught the boys of St. Cyprian's—character, character, character—and it is a defect of character in Gordon, his failure to work, which his creator held against him, and for which he is "punished." He will lose his war against the money-god; he will drop the manuscript of his unfinished book-length poem *London Pleasures* down the drain and never be a poet again; he will marry Rosemary, whom he has accidentally impregnated; he will return to the New Albion advertising agency and spend his life writing slogans; he will even have an aspidistra, that symbol of lower-middle-class respectability, in the front window of their flat—and that is the ending that Orwell devised for Gordon Comstock, failed poet and failed rebel.

However one chooses to interpret its ending—as the justified defeat of an unjustified ideal (immature, unworthy Gordon); or the victory of the age-old life force over the modern death-wish (symbolized for Orwell in the use of contraceptives, the French Letter being for him truly a *bête noire*); or a simple coming to terms with reality (mature, sensible Gordon)—the novel as a whole reeks of bitterness, grievance, and festering discontent. From its pages can be garnered a wealth of evidence to support the generalization Isaac Rosenfeld was later to make about Orwell in an article in *Commentary:* "Under the bland, fair, mild, empirical and fair-minded manner which he perfected in the essays, I feel he was full of self-hatred, rage, spite and contempt.

. . . He condoned his own failure to be a gentleman or—
it came to the same thing—managed to forgive himself for
being one." Any fair-minded admirer of Orwell will recognize a degree of truth in this; but it is our contention that
in the writing of *Keep the Aspidistra Flying,* he was exor-
cising a ghostly, malignant companion, the man he feared
he might have become—Mrs. Vaughan Wilkes's "failure"
—and in doing so, liberated himself as a man and a writer.
That he should have done so at a time of great personal
happiness is a paradox, but not, as any student of psychology will verify, an impossibility.

THIRTEEN

JUNE 1935: A MONTH OF LANDMARKS IN THE LIVES OF Eileen O'Shaughnessy and George Orwell.

Eileen, at University College, successfully passed her qualifying examination for the M.A. In one more year she would have the degree, she and Eric would marry, and then . . . But "and then" brought them into a region of potential disagreement that neither of them—in June 1935 —was willing to explore. Eric had his old-fashioned lower-upper-middle-class notions and was no more likely to approve a wife pursuing her career than he would allow a woman he'd invited to dinner to pay the bill or even her share of it. And Eileen, as an independent-minded woman whose sister-in-law was a successful M.D. in her own right, was not likely to believe that a wife must subordinate her life to her husband's. But "and then" remained a region neither need explore for a while longer. Sensibly, they chose to see the landmark as a midpoint; they were halfway on the way to being permanently together.

For Orwell, June was the month of the belated English publication of *Burmese Days*, bringing his work into the bookshops for the second time in four months. Familiarity was not a deterrent: *Burmese Days* sold better than either of his previous books. A first printing of 2500 copies was soon exhausted, and Gollancz ordered a second impression of 500—this proved sufficient for the demand. So far as sales were concerned, Orwell was still a decade away from the success to which he was doomed. Nor were the reviews much consolation. *Burmese Days* was less extensively noticed than its predecessors—very likely it suffered in this regard from having come so soon after *A Clergyman's Daughter*—and most of the reviews it did receive were tepid and condescending. The anonymous reviewer in the *Times Literary Supplement* was prepared to admit that "The book has traces of power and it is written with a pen steeped in gall. That gall is merited for these people exist, but a little less would have carried more conviction." What especially bothered the reviewer, and others of similar mind, was the sweeping character of Orwell's attack on the British establishment in Burma. He (or she) pointed out, snobbishly but perhaps with some justification, that when Orwell says that few of the Burmese magistrates' English superiors "work as hard or as intelligently as the postmaster in a provincial town, he shows he can hardly have mixed with the men who really run the country." In the *Spectator*, Sean O'Faolain, not likely to be troubled by an anti-imperialist point of view, nonetheless found the novel rather heavy-handed. "Poor Flory," he lamented, "hasn't a dog's chance against his author"—a remark that might equally be applied to poor Dorothy in *A Clergyman's Daughter*, and to poor Gordon in *Keep the Aspidistra Flying*. All was not disapproval, however; from Compton Mackenzie came the by now customary, but even more fervent, tribute in the *Daily Mail*,* and in the *New Statesman and*

---

* "It can hardly be much more than a year ago that there apppeared a remarkable volume of personal experience called *Down and Out in Paris*

Nation there was a highly favorable brief notice by Cyril Connolly, which, in a biographical study of Orwell, deserves to be treated separately.

Although Connolly and Blair had been close friends at St. Cyprian's and quite close friends at Eton, there was no communication between them thereafter, through the five years that Blair was in Burma, and even after his return to England. This was not unusual: virtually none of Blair's Etonian friends were allowed to keep in touch with him, and those who persisted and made the effort found themselves politely but firmly discouraged. As Connolly recalled the sequence of events for us, he knew that Blair had returned from Burma and had been in touch with Maurice Whittome, who arranged a reunion dinner with several other Old Etonians that Connolly had been unable to attend. Then Blair dropped from sight again. He chose to go underground, and evidently did not intend to surface until he had firmly established himself as a writer. But the Etonian network is pervasive and enduring and more powerful than the whim of a sometime member to drop out. Early in 1935 Connolly heard from a mutual Etonian friend that Blair had become the writer George Orwell. So when *Burmese Days* appeared he asked for an advance copy, read it, admired it, and determined to review it for the *New Statesman and Nation.*

---

and London. It is not six months ago that there appeared an even more remarkable novel called *A Clergyman's Daughter.* Last week there was published by the same author a more remarkable book than either of its predecessors, and after reading *Burmese Days* by George Orwell I have no hesitation in asserting that 'no realistic writer' during the last five years has produced three volumes which can compare in directness, vigour, courage and vitality with these three volumes from the pen of Mr. George Orwell."

The difficulty was that Connolly's column there, "New Novels," was expected to cover the week's crop of fiction, and in the week of July 6, 1935, he had eight novels to deal with. The luck of the game depended on the company you kept; even so, it is rather disconcerting, forty-odd years later, to discover one of the enduring novels of the century in the company of seven others that must be gathering dust on the top shelf of a Booklovers' Corner somewhere, earning the contempt of some latter-day version of Gordon Comstock. But Connolly was not the man to be daunted by a situation with which he was all too familiar— viz., his vastly entertaining "Ninety Years of Book Reviewing"—and he very deftly sandwiched *Burmese Days* between *She Fell Among Thieves*, an adventure story, and *Star Against Star*, a novel of "a normal young girl toppling into the well of loneliness." He begins briskly and quotably, in a way that must have gladdened the heart of Gollancz: "*Burmese Days* is an admirable novel. It is a crisp, fierce, and almost boisterous attack on the Anglo Indian." And he has a very winning way of balancing criticism with praise: "His novel might have been better if he had toned down the ferocious partiality of the Lawrence-Aldington school, but personally I liked it and recommend it to anyone who enjoys a spate of efficient indignation, graphic description, excellent narrative, excitement, and irony tempered with vitriol."

Conceivably this burst of enthusiasm played a part in furthering Orwell's career; what is not in doubt is that it revived the friendship between Blair and Connolly. Blair wrote to thank Connolly for the review; Connolly replied; soon they were meeting frequently, the old bond was restored, and the friendship continued without interruption until Orwell's death in 1950, and thereafter, in an impres-

sively loyal and generous fashion, until Connolly's death
in 1974.*

He was not the only friend of Orwell's to write admir-
ingly of his work at this time. Michael Sayers reviewed *A
Clergyman's Daughter* and *Burmese Days* together in the
Adelphi for August 1936, more than a year after their publication. He managed the difficult feat of being both prais-
ing and perceptive. "George Orwell is a popular novelist
sensitive to values that most other novelists are popular for
ignoring," he began. "At present Mr. Orwell appears to be
most concerned with presenting his material in the clearest
and honestest way. . . . The lucidity—so to speak, the
transparence—of his prose is a necessary quality of the
realistic novel, which aims at exhibiting action rather than
significant language. . . . Neither pity, nor bitterness, nor
cynicism, nor contempt, is permitted to obscure the insidi-
ous degradations of Imperialism acting on white and col-

* The conversation with Connolly referred to above, the last we were
privileged to have with him, occurred on July 29, 1973. In the course of
it he corrected an error, concerning himself and Blair, in our *The Unknown
Orwell*. The portion of the sentence there that begins "It is suggestive, too,
that the friendship with Connolly should have been kept in abeyance until
the *early* 1930's, by which time Blair was already a published author with
two books to his credit," should be revised to read, "It is suggestive, too,
that the friendship with Connolly should have been kept in abeyance until
the mid-1930's, by which time Blair was already a published author with
three books to his credit," and continue unchanged, "while Connolly,
though a well-known critic, would not publish his first book (the novel
The Rock Pool) until 1936."

In this same conversation, Connolly said he was puzzled by the remark
of Orwell's quoted by Denys King-Farlow and repeated in *The Collected
Essays, Journalism and Letters*: "Without Connolly's help I don't think I
would have got started as a writer when I got back from Burma." Connolly felt Orwell may have made some oblique reference to the review of
Burmese Days as having helped him in his career, which King-Farlow
must have misheard or misinterpreted.

oured alike . . . the consciousness of being an interloper
and a despoiler, or a victim. . . . All this is shown rather
than stated by Mr. Orwell." And he concluded propheti-
cally, accurately, "Mr. Orwell's career has only begun."
Granted that there was some ambiguousness in his use of
"popular novelist," which Orwell all too evidently was not,
and granted that the word "popular" itself was not a word
of high praise in the vocabulary of Sayers and Rayner Heppenstall, who fancied themselves as unpopular highbrows,
the review paid Orwell the compliment of treating him
with the utmost seriousness, as though his as yet entirely
theoretical popularity needn't debar him from serious con-
sideration. Sayers's review would contribute to Orwell's
growing reputation in literary circles, but it had no practical effect. Even if the *Adelphi* had had a considerably
larger readership than it did, and even if all its readers had
rushed off to the bookshops in search of the novels, it would
have made no difference, for by that time (a year and a
few months after publication) both *A Clergyman's Daughter* and *Burmese Days* were out of print, and their type had
been distributed.

WITH EILEEN HALFWAY TO HER DEGREE AND HALFWAY TO
marrying him, and with *Burmese Days* at last published
in England and selling sufficiently to ensure him at least a
little more money than he usually had, Eric allowed his
dissatisfaction with his living arrangements, which he had
hitherto felt but not expressed, to come to the surface.
There was much to be said for Parliament Hill, but as his
social life broadened in general, and his relationship with
Eileen deepened in particular, the disadvantages of Rosa-

lind's flat began to outweigh whatever might be said for it;
it remained *her* flat that he had a room in. The theoretical
"room of one's own" that Virginia Woolf had written of
with such fervor as all a writer needed no longer would
satisfy him: however tactful Rosalind might be, she was
there, on the other side of the door, and he was never more
conscious of this than when Eileen was with him—her being
Rosalind's friend and fellow student added to the vexing
aspect of the situation, for one couldn't pretend Rosalind
didn't exist and simply close the door in her face. "Liberty
Hall, Liberty Hall" was the cry, but he felt himself increasingly imprisoned. Still, he had no wish to hurt Rosalind's feelings, there was a certain delicacy in his situation,
and he turned for advice, as he so often did in the years
before he married Eileen, to Mabel Fierz.

Eric's position in the Fierz household, which he fre-
quented from 1932 on whenever he lived in London, is
difficult to sum up precisely—"visitor" is too distant, "guest"
too formal—perhaps one does better merely to approximate
the reality and say that he was welcomed as a friend, a
quasi-son-and-older-brother, and as a sage. "Eric says . . . ,"
"Eric says . . ." was a phrase much heard in the household,
Adrian Fierz recalls, and what Eric said, as readers familiar
with his work might expect, was often a wildly exaggerated
generalization—"Eric says all scoutmasters are homosex-
uals," for example—and while Eileen, at such a pronounce-
ment, might have smiled and said quietly, "*All*, Eric?"
Mabel was quite prepared to accept it as true because Eric
said it, although part of her knew very well that he was
going too far. Exaggeration never bothered Mabel: she
liked enthusiasm, living boldly, being in touch with what
was new, what was going on, what was exciting, in the arts,
in politics, in philosophy, in psychology. If she had been

a painter—rather surprisingly, she was not, for she was ready to try anything—she would have painted in vivid colors, in a free self-expressionist manner. Eric was her candidate in the literary sweepstakes, which was astute of her, before anyone else had heard of him, even, one is tempted to say, before he had heard of himself. Francis, her husband, a businessman associated with the Baldwin Steel firm, took a skeptical view of most of her protégés, who were forever overrunning the house and often, it must be said, taking advantage of Mabel's generous nature—there is a fictionalized, not especially accurate sketch of her in Rayner Heppenstall's memoirs that bears this out—and of them all, Francis really liked and approved of only three: Eric was one; another was the arts-and-craftsman Richard Middleton Murry, a brother of John Middleton Murry; and the third was the composer Ralph Vaughn Williams. As for the Fierz children, Adrian and Fay, they were always pleased to see Eric, for they knew he would always have time for them. Adrian's recollections of him are preeminently happy: Eric coming out in the garden to play cricket; Eric talking about books—Sherlock Holmes, P. G. Wodehouse— and giving him a copy of Marlowe's *Doctor Faustus;* taking him to the British Museum, and a few years later to see Maurice Evans in *Hamlet* at the Old Vic. His last memory is of Eric and Eileen coming to his, Adrian's, wedding in 1941—a very simple occasion in wartime, with no more than ten people present, but it was understood that the Blairs would be there, though it must have been difficult for them to arrange. (About Eileen, Adrian is equally enthusiastic: "She couldn't have been nicer and sweeter, and much better looking than the run of his girls—he was very lucky to get her.")

Mabel was always good at giving advice, and one of the

reasons she was good at it was that she never nagged at one with objections that put one off from what one had already decided. She recognized over the first cup of tea that Eric was determined to move from Parliament Hill into a flat of his own. Therefore she agreed that he should. The only questions were How was it to be managed? and How was Rosalind to be tactfully told? This was the sort of situation on which Mabel thrived. Before Eric had downed his second cup, she had the answers to both questions. By a lucky coincidence, Rayner Heppenstall and Michael Sayers, whom he already knew and liked, of course—that was Mabel's "Of course," though Eric did know them, and did rather like them—were just at the point of being evicted from their grimy little rooms in Kilburn. Why, she proposed, shouldn't the three of them share a flat? It would be much more sensible, *financially*, for Eric, since Michael, the drama critic of the *New English Weekly* and a promising short-story writer, would be able to contribute at least a third of the rent. True, Rayner was having a hard time of it at the moment—with a little here from the occasional poem sold, and a little there from the occasional review, and a small advance (already mostly spent) from a publisher for a book about the dance. But he would contribute what he could when he could. Three congenial chaps, she reasoned, wouldn't get in each other's way; essentially it would be Eric's flat, only he wouldn't be paying as much for it as he would if he were trying to swing it alone. Furthermore, this particular solution would please Rosalind: when she heard that Eric was leaving for the sake of Michael and Rayner, as an act of kindness and charity to them, she would not be offended by his departure. Even Eric, for all his eagerness to leave Parliament Hill, must have realized that Mabel's logic was highly questionable, but at such moments she was rather like a force of nature, and he fell in with her plan. So too, when she consulted them, did Heppenstall and Sayers, who had a great deal less to lose by it than Blair. Sayers was interested in a flat, any flat, only as a kind of *maison de passe*, a place to bring his girls, of whom he had a number; at other times he intended to go on living at his parents' very comfortable house in Golders Green. As for Heppenstall, he was in no position to quibble—he wanted a roof over his head—and though it did occur to him to wonder why Blair would want to share with him, Mabel (he tells us), in an enthusiastic flurry of invention revealed a surprising secret; that Eric had a suppressed homosexual passion for him, or so she deduced from his having mentioned that he admired Rayner's hair. Whatever the particulars, and it is not unlikely that time has distorted them, in August of 1935 Blair left his pleasant room on Parliament Hill to share a flat with Heppenstall, and at times Sayers, at 50 Lawford Road in Kentish Town.

The area was rather slummish and grubby, which would not distress him, and a relatively short distance from the pleasant airs and graces of Hampstead—one of those contrasts in which London abounds—which meant that he was still able to walk in the afternoon to his job at Booklovers' Corner. The flat itself was in a small house in a row of semi-detached villas, but with some land between each pair of houses. It contained three rooms, the largest going to Blair, and the smallest, hardly more than a cell, to Heppenstall, with the middling room serving Sayers as his occasional love nest. In this characterless flat Blair would live until the end of January 1936, when he set out on the road to Wigan Pier, and for the greater part of the time he was there it was his exclusively: the ménage of Blair, Heppenstall, and Sayers was doomed, one is tempted to say, virtually from the moment it came into being in the mind of Mabel Fierz.

It was not one of her happiest inspirations, for she had failed to take into account differences in age, temperament, education, experience, and class, all of which (to judge from Heppenstall's memoir, *Four Absentees,* the only document of the ménage) were brought into sharp relief as soon as the three men began to share the flat. Until then, after all, their relationship had involved little more than occasional meetings in a pub or a restaurant. They had been friends of a pleasant, uninvolved sort—"intimacy" is not the word that springs to mind—and once they were free of the flat, they would be friends of that sort again, Heppenstall and Blair particularly: one has only to read Blair's letters to him over the years to recognize it. But in the confinement of the flat, Michael and Rayner, though ten years younger than Eric and far less established as writers than he, tended to patronize him. Heppenstall—and it cannot be emphasized too strongly that this account is based entirely on his —found him in many ways naïve and foolish. In his attachment to little bits of Old England, "country parsonages, comic postcards, *The Magnet* and *The Gem,* anecdotes about Queen Victoria and bishops," he was "quite inaccessible" to them. As young *littérateurs* only recently in London from their provincial universities, and keenly responsive to "the New" in literary fashion, they could not share his admiration for Samuel Butler (old hat) or Henry Miller (not yet really being worn, although stocked by Eliot & Co.). They also rather patronized Eric's writing, finding it too "commercial" for their taste: good enough novels in their way, but very traditional, and with no attempt to absorb the crucial modernist influences. As for the poems he was writing and that Richard Rees, the mutual friend of all three, was publishing, they were no further along, with their carefully metered, neatly rhymed quatrains, than the late Georgians, whereas Rayner's experiments in verse that appeared in the *Adelphi* had the look and feel of the 1935 avant-garde—not likely to appeal to an anthologist such as Thomas Moult, who had chosen one of Eric's for *The Best Poems of 1934*.

But in spite of literary differences, Rayner and Eric would have quite a jolly time together, chatting away about this and that, when Rayner would emerge late in the morning from his room after a rowdy night in Soho and Eric was finishing his three-hour stint at the novel. Some subjects, books apart, were less satisfactory than others. Rayner felt he was not providing the sort of information about the working class (from which he was rising) that Eric expected of him. As he puts it in *Four Absentees*, "Orwell was already contemplating a guide to working-class life. With my information on this subject he was dissatisfied. He wanted leaky ceilings and ten in a room, with scrabblings on slag-heaps if possible. Himself he hankered after the simple life. He compared the process of writing, unfavourably, with that of making something *real* like a chair, on which you could then sit down. I thought him a wonderfully nice man, but confused."

Eric ran the household, the flat was rented in his name, and he did most of the cooking. Meals were served in his room, at the large plain table that at other times he used as a desk. He was also the one who tried to keep the place straight; he felt about Rayner much as Janet Gimson had felt about Eric himself in Parliament Hill, that he was very messy. (And very likely he was—a young man attuned to the ways of Soho would not worry if his few possessions were scattered about his tiny room, or the mattress that served him as a bed was in perpetual disarray.)

In due course the inevitable occurred: there was a parting of the ways, over the now notorious shooting-stick incident. It was first brought to light by Heppenstall in the
reminiscences of Orwell that he published in the *Twentieth
Century* in 1955 and went on to incorporate (with some
revisions) in *Four Absentees*. His motive in writing of the
man he knew as Eric Blair, he explained in a second volume of memoirs, *The Intellectual Part,* was that "There
was growing up a whole Orwell mythology, which seemed
to me to bear no relation to the man I had known." Heppenstall's less than reverential tone, as evidenced in the
mildly ironic passage quoted above, "nice, but confused,"
was not likely to please the uncritical admirers of Orwell,
and it drove his hagiographers up the wall. The man in
the shooting-stick episode was impossible to reconcile with
the secular saint they were then in the process of canoniz-
ing. Perhaps Heppenstall would have been on safer ground
if he had limited himself to a bald recital of facts, but he
drew upon a wide range of literary devices—as Orwell himself was wont to do—to enrich his account: heightening for
effect, introducing offhanded generalizations that don't
bear too close inspection, a tone of ironic condescension
that at times is indistinguishable from malice. In short, as
one might say of Orwell writing of St. Cyprian's, Heppenstall was carried away by the occasion, and he too had some
old scores to settle. Orwell had drawn an unflattering vi-
gnette of him, which he recognized, in *The Road to Wigan
Pier,* and it is not inconceivable that he caught more than
a glimpse of himself in Gordon Comstock. The ironic result,
however, so clear after the passage of two decades, is that
the official portrait hasn't been redrawn; the saint remains,
but poor Heppenstall has been incorporated into the mythology as a kind of devil figure. Scandal gave to the shoot-

ing-stick episode an importance that, as we shall now see, it scarcely deserved.

A shooting stick is a cane-shaped, cane-sized object that has the virtue of opening at the top to form a small seat or perch: one goes out into a field, opens one's shooting stick, perches upon it, and looks in an approving, upper-class way at the surrounding landscape. Yes, class has to be brought in, even here, for as Heppenstall makes clear, a shooting stick is not a traditional appurtenance of the well-equipped working-class home. Eric, however, owned a shooting stick. So, too, we learn from Heppenstall, did Eileen, in spite of which he liked her very much, thinking her much the nicest, prettiest, and most intelligent of Eric's girls. Eric and Eileen would take their shooting sticks with them on their Sunday excursions into the country, and when they had walked to a picturesque point, they would open them, and perch, side by side, admiring the view in the best upper-class manner, which was theirs by right.

Most of this, it has to be said, is pure supposition by Heppenstall: he did not accompany Eric and Eileen on their Sunday excursions, and hence did not see them perched; he did not know for certain that Eileen even *had* a shooting stick, and it is highly improbable that if she had, she would have brought it round with her when she visited the flat in Lawford Road. Conceivably Eric told him that she had one, though it seems an odd bit of information to impart. Out of all this prefatory business, the one sure fact that emerges, and all, really, that matters to the episode, is that Eric had a shooting stick.

One evening Rayner had come home to the flat very drunk, and according to his account, Eric had made very upper-class noises at him; it wouldn't do, it was not the sort of thing one did, and so forth and so forth. Rayner, a good deal shorter than Eric, drew himself up and said he would hit him if he didn't go away, and when he tried, Eric punched him on the nose, knocking him down and briefly out. Rayner than dragged himself as far as Michael Sayers's unoccupied room, where a bed was more or less made up, and lay down, bloodied nose and all, to try to sleep. A moment later he heard the key turning in the door: Eric, he realized, had locked him in. This had the effect of waking him entirely. In a fury he began shouting and tried to crash through the door. At which point Eric opened it and stood there, holding aloft his shooting stick, and when Rayner lunged forward, he struck him with it, his face alight "with a curious blend of fear and sadistic exaltation." By this time the people downstairs, aroused by the noise, came up and separated them. The next morning, in his best district commissioner's way, Eric told Rayner he would have to go.

This is the story as Heppenstall told it, and no doubt it has the elements of exaggeration: after all, it is the work of a gifted novelist. There would be no reason to take the episode seriously—or any more seriously than Orwell and Heppenstall themselves did, for it did not, as one might expect, put an end to their friendship; apart, they were on better terms than ever before—except that, in certain quarters, it has been taken too seriously. Heppenstall's lurid phrase "a curious blend of fear and sadistic exaltation" has had the unfortunate effect of calling into being a stereotype of "Orwell the sadist" that is as exaggerated as that counter-stereotype, "Orwell the virtuous man." Undoubtedly there were elements of sadism—more properly, brutality—in Orwell; he has emphasized them in his exemplary accounts of his experience as an Imperialist, and there are pages in 1984 that are shocking in their cruelty. Certainly from the time of his return from Burma, and through the remainder of his life, his "sadism" was principally turned against himself. Perhaps in making this statement, we seem to be falling back upon the third stereotype, "Orwell the masochist." But it is our belief, reinforced by what we have learned of him from admirers and detractors alike, that he had to suffer himself, to experience suffering in his own person, before he could understand the suffering of others and so re-create it on the page for his readers.

THE IMMEDIATE EFFECT OF RAYNER'S DEPARTURE—HE went off to stay with the Middleton Murrys in Essex—was that Eric at last had a flat of his own, as he had wanted from the beginning. (Sayers, who had never been deeply involved in the Lawford Road scheme, withdrew from it even before the shooting-stick debacle, having made other arrangements.) The advantage of Eric's being in sole possession was that now he and Eileen could be together as often and as long as they pleased, and without having to converse in whispers behind the closed door of his room. The disadvantage was that a flat of his own, no matter how thriftily and frugally he lived, used up his money at an alarming rate. At this time, autumn 1935, he was living on his small wages from Booklovers' Corner, the remains of his small advance from Gollancz for *Keep the Aspidistra Flying,* and the small trickle of royalties from *A Clergyman's Daughter* and *Burmese Days.* In all it came to just barely enough, and he cast about for ways to augment his income. For a brief time he put aside the novel, deluding himself that he could turn out commercial formula fiction to order—a serial story for a newspaper—and like many another gifted writer who turns to hackwork of the sort that makes hacks rich, he found it more difficult than he'd anticipated. After four tormented days he'd written just two pages of manuscript, and although, ultimately, he was able to produce a synopsis and a first chapter, it was a hopeless enterprise. To discover that he was not born to be a serial writer, he had wasted three weeks of time that might have been spent on the novel, and it was with a sense of relief that he got back to it.

In the light of Orwell's full-blown emergence as a Socialist in 1936, it may be hard to credit that he should have been so unremittingly nonpolitical as late as 1935. And yet only by a feat of verbal acrobatics can *Keep the Aspidistra Flying*, his principal literary preoccupation in that year, be made to seem a *political* novel, and then only by implication. Gordon's hatred and all-out condemnation of the money-world are too infuriated and subjective to permit a calm "analysis of the situation," but indirectly he might be thought to be arguing that the evils of the money-world must be wiped out—not however, by a political solution, but in an apocalyptic catastrophe. Hence those fleets of bombers, pouring down death on London, that recur so excitingly in his fantasies. (Of course, by a still more agile feat of acrobatics one can read those fantasies as no more than a realistic political prophecy—a prefiguring of the Luftwaffe in action during the Second World War.) But if Orwell held any firm political ideas in 1935, one might logically expect a more straightforward, less symbolic expression of them to find its way into his journalistic writing. Not so, however. That year, as it happened, most of his time was devoted to the novel, except for a handful of reviews in the *Adelphi* and the *New English Weekly*, the two journals with which he was most closely associated at this period. Neither was free of a certain crankiness in the principles and the politics it espoused: the *Adelphi*, under Middleton Murry and Rees, a mix of Marxian Socialism, Tolstoyan Christianity, and Pacifism; the *New English Weekly*, under A. R. Orage and Philip Mairet, a mix of Major Douglas's Social Credit as elucidated by Ezra Pound, Christianity as practiced by T. S. Eliot, and Tolstoyan Agrarianism. For all their differences, the two journals were alike in being firmly political in their point of view, and each had its literary side. Orwell, with his sweeping generalizations, his sometimes odd but always strong opinions on so many subjects, was not without his own elements of crankiness, and he found the atmosphere of the two magazines congenial. Richard Rees, who had succeeded Middleton Murry as the editor of the *Adelphi*, was perhaps his closest friend; and he got on very well with Philip Mairet, who had succeeded to the editorship of the *New English Weekly* upon the death of Orage. Still nonpolitical in 1935, Orwell made his contributions only to the literary side of each magazine, and Rees and Mairet were resigned that it should be so.

For the *Adelphi* that year he wrote a very favorable review of the autobiography of a working man, *Caliban Shrieks*, by Jack Hilton, which had, he felt, the rare and invaluable quality of giving one, "instead of a catalogue of facts about poverty, a vivid notion of what it *feels* like to be poor"; an unfavorable review of a biography of Henry Crabb Robinson; and a scathing review of Amy Cruse's *The Victorians and Their Books*, in which he "dipped his pen in gall" and held forth on the difficulty of dislodging the Victorians from their pedestals. (This was in 1935, seventeen years since Lytton Strachey had done that particular job so efficiently that it would take another two generations before the despised Victorians would be restored to something like their original eminence.) In a fit of bad temper he excoriated Mrs. Cruse for her affection for those "slimy Low Church scoutmasters," Charles Kingsley and Thomas Hughes. But not even the fact that Kingsley and Hughes had been Christian Socialists imparts a political color to his anger; one comes away from this forgotten review—it has never been resurrected—with an impression of Gordon Comstock in possession of George Orwell: an angry young man still uncertain of what to be angry about.

The two pieces that he wrote for the *New English Weekly* are as untouched by politics as the three for the *Adelphi*, but one of them is of enduring interest: his early, appreciative review of Henry Miller's *Tropic of Cancer*, where anger gives way to discernment and a generosity of spirit that are wonderfully invigorating. It is something of those qualities that would illuminate the best of his political writing. But politics were still for the future: the surprising thing is that they proved to be much closer than Eric must have anticipated late in the autumn of 1935 in Lawford Road, finishing *Keep the Aspidistra Flying*, adding to the manuscript twiddly bits of verbal decoration, and contemplating an Epilogue he never bothered to write. As Richard Rees wryly observed, long after Orwell's death, "I spent more than three years trying to convert him to Socialism, and he remained unconvinced, and not really interested. Then he went North. When he came back in the Spring of 1936, the conversion had already taken place."

PART THREE

THE END OF ERIC BLAIR

FOURTEEN

EARLY IN DECEMBER THE LAST OF THE TWIDDLY BITS HAD been applied to *Keep the Aspidistra Flying* and Blair delivered the manuscript to Leonard Moore, who sent it on to Gollancz, who accepted it as a matter of course. By now Orwell was an established author on his list, perhaps so well established that it was thought unnecessary to read him with very close attention; he was in danger of becoming predictable: ". . . another scathing . . . poverty . . . depression England . . . worthy to stand beside the same author's . . ." Hence everything got under way with the usual startling speed. The novel was scheduled for publication at the beginning of March 1936. Proofs were in hand in January. And then, belatedly, someone at Gollancz seems to have subjected the text to the closest scrutiny, for all at once a crisis over the possibility of libel erupted: the name of the advertising firm where Gordon and Rosemary worked bore some faint resemblance to an actual firm. Once again Orwell found himself in conference with Norman Collins, to whom he had taken a firm dislike—the aftermath, no doubt, of that earlier, similar conference over *Burmese Days* —discussing the potentially actionable points that would have to be altered. As before, Orwell yielded to reason— what could one do? But the anger he had suppressed in the Gollancz offices he vented in letters: to Richard Rees, on

February 29, he reported that the required alterations had spoiled an entire chapter; by the time he wrote to Jack Common a fortnight later he felt that they had utterly ruined his novel. (Remembering his despair over the changes he had had to make in *Burmese Days*—a matter of a few names—one is prepared to recognize here some slight Orwellian exaggeration.) There is no record of his having prepared an unamended, pristine text for American publication, perhaps because it was not needed. Harpers' decided against *Keep the Aspidistra Flying* as "too English."

With the novel written and in the hands of his publisher, a crisis of a different but equally familiar sort confronted him, which he had had to face with each book since *Burmese Days*: what was he to write next? He was a dedicated professional writer, whose life, as we have said earlier, was his literary capital. He had drawn upon it continually for the events and substance of the four books he had written during the past four years. Even in his novels, where he was free to invent, the reality of his own experience sustained what he invented, imparting to it a convincingness and a conviction it would not otherwise have had. What would he write next? The question had a particular urgency now, for it seemed he had used up his capital: he had come to a point where he would have to live more before he could write more.

Here, providentially, Victor Gollancz enters the picture.

Gollancz was not only a successful publisher but also a dedicated social reformer. Sometimes he confused his two roles: but for a brief period, from 1936 to 1939, as founder, owner, and chief spirit of the Left Book Club, he united them with historic consequences.* In 1935 he had already

* These years were the heyday of the Club; it would continue until 1948.

published within a space of months two novels by Orwell; the arrival of a third in December, which he admired and marked for publication in early spring, provoked a belated act of recognition: that here was an author who responded as deeply as Gollancz himself to the "abomination" of poverty and who was able, indeed was compelled, to describe it in all its cruel, degrading, and abominable reality. As a social reformer, a Socialist, and an idealist, Gollancz had an unquestioning, perhaps overly optimistic faith in education: if only people could be made to know the nature of poverty, he thought, if they could be educated as to what it was, then, surely, they would want to eradicate it, remove from power the government that tolerated it, and transform the economic system that brought it into being. As a successful publisher, however, he was realistic enough to know that if a book about poverty in England in 1936 (not, on the face of it, a subject of broad appeal) was to reach the large audience he wanted for it, it must be something more than a well-intentioned, carefully researched collection of facts, statistics, graphs, and hortatory conclusions. It must, instead, be a sympathetic report from outside—the account of an eyewitness rather than a victim (so that the middle-class readers whom Gollancz intended to be moved could identify with the reporter as one of themselves), written by someone with experience enough to know what to look for, and with the ability to describe what he saw so vividly as to make it unforgettable. Who better to undertake the task than George Orwell?

The proposal—that Orwell should travel through the depressed areas of the North, observing the effects of unemployment among the coal miners, and write about what he had seen—was made by Gollancz through Moore. He offered a larger advance for whatever book might result from the journey than he had ever paid Orwell before; and, as a further inducement, the likelihood that the book would be made a selection of the Left Book Club, which was already germinating in Gollancz's mind, would be announced at the end of February, and come into existence in May, with himself, John Strachey, and Harold Laski as selectors, choosing from amongst books to be published and often commissioned by Victor Gollancz Ltd.

When Moore put the proposal to Orwell, he accepted it immediately. It resolved in a challenging and very stimulating way the crisis of what he was to write next. And the prospect of earning more money as the time approached when he and Eileen would marry was agreeable to contemplate, though in no sense crucial. The sheer elation that went with being in love with her persuaded him that they would somehow manage: things would arrange themselves, as he told Rayner Heppenstall. (Besides, neither of them cared that much about money.) Perhaps inspired by just having married off Gordon to Rosemary, Eric did suggest to Eileen that they might marry earlier than June. But he deferred to her sensible objection: immersed as she was in her course, she hadn't time to earn anything herself and so would be a drag on him; whereas after she had finished and taken her degree, almost certainly she would have a job and would be able to make her contribution. Things would arrange themselves.

The chief attraction of Gollancz's proposal was that it offered Orwell a way out of the enclosed world of the realistic novel, where the characters a novelist invents are in a leech-like relation to him, preempting his experiences or fantasies of life. Even the notion of the journey exerted a powerful attraction: he would be going towards new experience. Secure at last in his own life, thanks to Eileen, he could allow himself to be responsive to the lives of others, become absorbed in a world outside himself—and in so doing, replenish his literary capital. He started without pre-conceptions, literary or political. He had no idea, beginning the journey, of what the book he would ultimately write about it would be, and when the journey was over and he was settling down to write, he was only certain that it would not be a novel. He had no clearly defined politics to preju-dice him or to assist him in evaluating what he saw. Gol-lancz, noting the affinity between his own response to the "abomination" of poverty and Orwell's, may have assumed that, like himself, Orwell was a dedicated Socialist. He would not have been the first to make that sort of assump-tion, depending upon instinct rather than concrete evi-dence. The present authors were told by Philip Mairet, of the *New English Weekly*, that when he first met Blair in the early 1930's, he took it for granted from his manner and general style of conversation that he was a man of the Left —though they never actually talked much about politics— and so, in 1936, when Orwell publicly declared himself a Socialist, Mairet wasn't surprised, but felt—again depend-ing on instinct—that he would not make a very good "party man." On the whole, Mairet seems to have been sounder in his instincts than Gollancz, who got in *The Road to Wigan Pier* a very different book from the one he'd anticipated. In 1945, in the introduction to the Ukrainian edition of *Animal Farm*, Orwell would make the rather surprising claim that he had been a Socialist since 1930; still more surprisingly, he would state that for many years he had made a sys-tematic study of the life and labor of the miners of the North. Perhaps he felt that for Ukrainian readers he needed to give his credentials a more impressive sound. But what is truly impressive is how fast and perceptively he traveled

—in a more than literal sense—along the road to Wigan, even though he never succeeded in finding the pier. (He thought, mistakenly, that it had been destroyed.)

A WRITER MUST WRITE, AND IN JANUARY HE DASHED OFF BOTH a memorial tribute to Kipling and an omnibus review of ten novels for the same issue of the *New English Weekly*. Then he gave up his detested job at Booklovers' Corner and the flat in Lawford Road—he would not live in London again until 1940—and on the last day of the month set out on his journey. It was winter, cold and rainy, and in the North there would be snow. Rather unusually for him, he was prepared to concede something to the hostile weather: he wore a raincoat and scarf. In his haversack he carried a minimum of personal belongings, and the proofs of *Keep the Aspidistra Flying*, which he intended to read, correct, and alter (as agreed with Norman Collins) while he traveled.

There was a loosely improvised quality about the expedition that was very much in accord with Gollancz's proposal, which left him on his own, free to write as he pleased within the expandable/contractable boundaries of the subject. He made no plans in advance, beyond consulting with Rees, who promised to send him the names of people in the North connected, one way or another, with the *Adelphi* or the Adelphi summer school, who might be helpful to him. And they were—it is difficult to imagine how the first part of *The Road to Wigan Pier* could have been written without their interventions. At the least, it would have been a more impressionistic, less documented and explicit account than it turned out to be.

But if he had chosen to travel without plans—simply to go and see, letting each day lead to the next—he had one principle to which he held firmly during the next two months, following a jagged crescent route from Birmingham to Manchester to Leeds, and when he sat down in April to write about what he had seen. Orwell would not be writing "from the inside" as Jack Hilton had done in his autobiography, but he was determined to get as close to the inside of working-class poverty as he could, and to convey the *feeling* of it—precisely the sort of thing that tended to be lost in an objective book by an author who had not known, or was not prepared to know, the experience of living on two pounds a week. He had abandoned the elements of masquerade and disguise of his earlier adventures, on the bum among down-and-outers. He was content to be what he was, but he knew that if he was to write honestly and sympathetically of the lives of working-class men and women, he must live as they did. Hence the stringencies he imposed on himself.

The first days and nights of the journey are illuminating in this respect: they set a pattern of extreme thrift and a willingness to endure discomfort and hardship, not out of guilt and a need for expiation, but simply to make the experience as near to unexceptional as possible, and hence, closer to the inside. Arriving in Coventry late in the afternoon of the thirty-first, he has one pound in his pocket: in theory, enough for the first half of the week. That night he stays in a "bed-and-breakfast" rooming house; the next day he walks in the occasional rain twelve miles towards Birmingham, then takes a bus into the city, where he has lunch. Afterwards, a bus again, this time to Stourbridge, then another four- or five-mile walk to a Youth Hostel for the night. The next day, returning on foot to Stourbridge, he takes a bus to Wolverhampton. Lunch there; afterwards a ten-mile walk to Penkridge in the rain, a warm cup of tea, and a further two miles on foot, at which point he manages to catch the bus to Stafford. That night he stays in a Temperance Hotel that hasn't even the virtue of being cheap. The next day he travels by bus from Stafford to Hanley; thence on foot to Eldon, where he has lunch in a pub; continuing on foot to Rudyard Lake, and another mile to a Youth Hostel for the night. End of four nights and three days: he had walked forty-four miles, and spent some two shillings less than the pound he had started out with; another pound would see him through the week.

Most of the details in the paragraph above are culled from the diary Orwell kept from the thirty-first of January through the twenty-fifth of March, which records, virtually day by day, the unretouched material that he would in due course develop into the first part of *The Road to Wigan Pier*. The diary, a work of unusual interest, was found among Orwell's papers after his death, and published for the first time in 1968 in the *Collected Essays, Journalism and Letters*. One hopes that it may eventually be published together with the book it inspired in a single volume, as has been done with *The Counterfeiters* of André Gide and his *Journal of the Counterfeiters*. The relation between Orwell's unretouched diary and the artfully rearranged and highlighted final version of the material it contains is a fascinating example of what a creative writer brings to nonfiction, as a reading of the two together in sequence will immediately make apparent.

The self-portrait of Orwell that emerges un-self-consciously from the diary is, we would argue, far more sympathetic and credible than the highly stylized, self-conscious *portrait moralisé* he painted of himself in the

second part of *The Road to Wigan Pier*. It is not difficult
to account for the difference: in the diary (and in the first
part of the book) he is *learning;* in the second part of the
book he is *lecturing,* never Orwell's most impressive or convincing literary posture. (Compare, for a definitive example, the indictment of Imperialism made by implication in
"Shooting An Elephant" with the attack on it by direct
statement and overstatement in the second part of *The
Road,* the two works written within a few months of each
other after his return from the North.)

The Orwell of the diary is earnest, serious, a little naïve—
that is, uncynical about, and given at moments to senti-
mentalizing, what he sees—but also eager to learn, un-
pretentious, making no claims to expertise, grateful for
kindnesses shown to him, which he is quick to notice though
sometimes too shy to acknowledge, liking many of the people whom he meets and hopeful that they will like him in
return, above all admiring the virtues of the working class,
as he learns to recognize them, even under conditions of
extreme adversity. And following as it does immediately
upon the all-inclusive angers and phobias of Gordon Comstock in *Keep the Aspidistra Flying,* the diary is even more
impressive for its freedom from "self-hatred, rage, spite and
contempt." In its unretouched pages, perhaps more clearly
here than in any other single work, we have the sense of
Orwell *changing:* of his accessibility to new experience.

At first, new experience was not forthcoming. There was
a possibility that he might penetrate no further than the
bleak edge of poverty, sampling the marginal existence,
nasty enough in itself, of a solitary man on the move from
the slummy areas of one town to the next, a dismal roster
of "bed-and-breakfasts," of quirky encounters and conversations with commercial travelers, lodging-house keepers,

and odd types in buses, pubs, and teashops, along with some townscapes and landscapes meticulously observed. Then, on the fifth day of the journey, he arrived in Manchester, and found a letter waiting for him there from Rees, with a list of people in the North whom he should see. One of them, Frank Meade, lived in Manchester—a Trade Union official and the business manager of *Labour's Northern Voice*, who also had in charge the printing of the *Adelphi*. Orwell went to see him two days later, having spent the day before in a common lodging house (shades of *Down and Out*), and Meade couldn't have been more welcoming. He insisted that Comrade Orwell must stay with the Meades in their house at 49 Brynton Road until he got launched in his investigations, and he was with them there from the sixth to the tenth of February. Brynton Road turned out to be in one of the new building estates, and the house itself, with bathroom and electricity, set a standard for comfort that Orwell would only rarely encounter during the rest of the journey, most notably when he spent a few days with his sister Marjorie and her husband, Humphrey Dakin, in their house outside Leeds, and with John and Mary Deiner —she had been Middleton Murry's secretary at the Adelphi summer school—at their house in a suburb of Liverpool. But Meade, Orwell decided, had suffered the inevitable, ironic fate of the working man who becomes a Trade Union official (or a Labour party politician). Earning perhaps four pounds a week, he adopts the ideology appropriate to his class—despite which, both Meade and his wife persisted in the habit of calling Orwell "Comrade," discomfiting him. Still, he was careful to note that they had been very decent to him; and Meade, bourgeoisified or not, would direct him towards the new experience he must have if he were to write a book of the sort Gollancz had proposed, rather than

—the risk inherent in the proposal—"Down and Out Revisited." For once Orwell had made it clear what it was that he wanted—to be among working men, and to live as they did—Meade sent him on to Wigan to meet his friend Joe Kennan. Kennan, an electrician and a militant Socialist, like Meade had a "decent Corporation house" but he struck Orwell as "more definitely a working man." He was "very anxious to help" and gave him a letter to Paddy Grady, an unemployed miner and secretary of the local branch of the National Unemployed Workers Movement. He, too, was "very anxious to help." Indeed, all the men at the NUWM shelter were friendly and helpful: when they heard that Orwell was a writer gathering material about working-class conditions, they were anxious to supply him with information. At this point in the diary he notes with a quite winning naïveté, "I cannot get them to treat me precisely as an equal, however. They call me either 'Sir' or 'Comrade.' "

To live in a decent Corporation house was an impossible ideal for the majority of working-class men and their families in 1936, and Orwell, reasonably enough, chose to do without the comforts of Parliament Hill or even the basic amenities of Lawford Road in favor of getting closer to the "inside." Guided by Paddy Grady, he found lodgings in Warrington Lane, in the house of the H.'s—five rooms, outside lavatory, for Mr. H., unemployed miner, Mrs. H., their fifteen-year-old son, working night shift in the pit, a cousin also on the night shift, and two lodgers, both unemployed. Orwell would share a room with one of the lodgers, be supplied all meals (in the kitchen) and would wash (no hot water) in the scullery sink—for twenty-five shillings a week.

He began in Warrington Lane, planning to fan out through Lancashire and Yorkshire, and almost immediately he realized that the two months he had allowed himself for the task wouldn't be sufficient; he liked the miners, they were nice and warmhearted and took him for granted, he would have liked to spend a year among them. But that was impossible: first, and crucially, it would have kept him away from Eileen far too long; besides, in a couple of months he would have to get back to work, by which he meant his writing. (Oddly, he seems never to have thought of his day-to-day life among workingmen in the North as "work.") Considering that he was in Wigan for only three weeks (the longest single stop he would make), and that he was not a professional journalist dropping in for a "crash course" in poverty before hurrying off to another, different assignment, it was no small feat that he should have gathered enough material, and responded to it deeply enough, to present a vivid picture of life in a mining town where a large proportion of the miners were unemployed, and where employment itself was no guarantee of living above the poverty level.

Wigan, of course, was not the only stop on his itinerary, but as it was the longest, it seems worthwhile to let his time there represent the scope and method of his activities in Lancashire, and the next month in Yorkshire. In Warrington Lane, he took carefully detailed notes, on the conditions of the house itself and on the existence of the H.'s, what they ate, and earned, and how their meager earnings were spent. He walked up and down the streets of Wigan, bleak vistas of the terrible houses of the poor, and along the industrial canal—"one-time site of Wigan Pier," he notes in the diary—towards the mountainous slagheaps in the distance. He attended a political talk in the Co-op Hall by a Communist speaker, Wal Hannington, head of the NUWM, that in spite of being padded with Socialist clichés ("Socialist" and "Communist" seem to be used interchangeably) excited the audience. And he notes in the diary: "surprised by the amount of Communist feeling here." But perhaps he ought not to have been, for, as he also noted, the members of the audience were "all obviously unemployed."

He went out with the NUWM collectors on their rounds, wanting to see for himself the terrible housing conditions Mrs. H. had already described to him (by comparison, the H.'s were well housed)—a harrowing visit among the crowded, primitive caravans. From that day he took away an impression that, as he recorded it in the diary, is one of the most moving passages he would ever write. Coming up an alley, he saw a woman "kneeling by the gutter outside a house and poking a stick up the leaden waste-pipe, which was blocked. I thought how dreadful a destiny it was to be kneeling in a gutter in a back alley in Wigan, in the bitter cold, prodding a stick up a clogged drain. At that moment she looked up and caught my eye, and her expression was as desolate as I have ever seen; it struck me that she was thinking the same thing as I was." He would reproduce this in *The Road*, as a glimpse caught from a train, and while more details are added—for a sense of exactness—and it is skilfully finished, it is no more *moving* than in the hastily noted first state.

He moved to squalid lodgings over a tripe shop in Darlington Road, the setting he would choose for the opening chapter of the book. He attended an NUWM "social" to raise money for the defense fund for Ernst Thaelmann, the German Communist leader, imprisoned and awaiting trial by the Nazis since 1933—some two hundred people were present, the greater number women, dispirited and sheep-like *en masse*, but he supposed them to be the more revolutionary Wiganers. Which prompted him to add in the diary a significant "If so, God help us."

He witnessed one of the most exotic but characteristic

experiences available to a "foreigner" visiting Wigan in the 1930's and eager to describe its life as it was. With Paddy Grady he went out to watch the unemployed miners at their dangerous and illegal "coal-picking." Waiting by the railroad tracks, they would leap onto the fast-moving train bringing carloads of dirt and shale from the mine to be dumped on an ever-growing heap at Fir Tree Siding. As the loaded cars were uncoupled, and before they could be dumped, the men began shoveling the stuff to their women and children below, who would scrabble through it for pieces of coal to put in sacks, boxes, carts, anything that could be used to carry away the "loot," useless to the companies but precious to the scrabblers as fuel.

And he witnessed, too, the most central experience in Wigan life, upon which all else—even, as he would presently argue, life in England—virtually depended. He made his first descent into a coal mine ("Crippen's"). He went down with Joe Kennan and a number of other men, in the charge of an engineer who worked in the pit, crowded into a cage that very swiftly went down nine hundred feet. From there, he proceeded painfully, torturously—such it was for Orwell anyway; for he was in a bent-over position throughout, too tall ever to stand upright—almost a mile to the coal face.

All these "events," summarized here, are described in sharp, flashing notes in the diary: the immediate impressions he intended to draw upon and develop for the book. But there was a significant portion of his time in Wigan that is not accounted for in the diary: certain tasks that went with his being a writer that couldn't be put aside entirely while he was on the journey, and that couldn't be done in his crowded lodgings in Warrington Lane and Darlington Road. He had the proofs of *Keep the Aspidistra Fly-*

ing to correct and send back to Gollancz, and he had research to do. Although he had no intention of writing a dry-as-dust handbook, he knew that he wanted his book, however amorphous it still might be in his mind, to carry more weight than a mere collection of impressions—he would need facts and figures to reinforce them (on unemployment, and housing, and conditions in the mines, the sort of thing one got from *The Colliery Year Book* and the *Coal Trades Directory,* from government documents and from a close reading of the local newspapers). Correcting proofs; looking things up—these were the nonwriting parts of his work as a writer; they couldn't be postponed, and he found time to do them, day after day, in the library at Wigan, among all the unemployed who drowsed and browsed and used the library as a place to keep warm.

Carlton Melling, who was then in charge of the reference library in Wigan, still remembers Orwell. In 1974 he offered an entertaining glimpse of him in the library to the novelist John Farrimond, which Farrimond has generously shared with the present authors: "Very soft-spoken, with a handsome, intelligent face. He never spoke except on the subject in hand. I spent two weeks 'looking after him' at the library. He signed the visitors' book as Eric Blair, and an excited assistant came upstairs to tell me, 'Do you know who that is, Carlton? *George Orwell!'* "

He went down Crippen's mine on Monday the twenty-fourth of February, and the next day was too done in by the experience to move from his bed. But time was running short, March was already allotted to Yorkshire: on Wednesday he persuaded himself that he was well enough to spend the day in Liverpool, where he still had to look up the Deiners and George Garrett, who were all on Rees's list. But by the time he arrived there he was feeling "unwell." When he

presented himself at the Deiners' door, Mary Deiner realized he was in no state to collect facts about housing or
anything else, nor was he up to even the restorative cup of
tea and biscuit. Almost at once, he was "ignominiously sick,"
and Mrs. Deiner put him to bed in the spare room. There
was no question of his going back to Wigan that night: indeed, she thought he ought to stay two or three days more at
least. But that was not Orwell's way. The next morning he
insisted he felt appreciably better and must get on with his
work. From Mary Deiner he now learned—with some surprise, for Rees had neglected to mention it—that George
Garrett, under the pseudonym of Matt Low, was a writer
of stories for the *Adelphi*. Orwell knew the stories, thought
them impressive, and the man himself, when they met late
that morning, equally so. A Communist absorbed in party
politics, a seaman, a docker, as well as an occasional writer,
Garrett was more often than not unemployed: he had had
about nine months' work in the past six years, being "blacklisted everywhere as a Communist." His checkered history,
which included a period of bootlegging in the U.S.A. in the
prohibition era, was fascinating to listen to. Orwell, already
impressed by his literary gift, suggested that Garrett should
write an autobiography. But the plain facts of his situation
—on the dole, married and with kids, the family crowded
into two rooms—made it impossible for him to attempt any
extended piece of writing. They also made a striking contrast to the situation of poor Gordon Comstock, dreadful no
doubt when seen from a middle-middle- or upper-middle-
class vantage point, but how would his situation look from
a working-class point of view—quite so dreadful, or perhaps
a little self-indulgent? Indeed, the more Orwell would see
of the working class on this journey—their poverty and, so
often, their courage, their endurance—the more he must

have begun to have qualms about *Keep the Aspidistra Flying*. Obviously he couldn't deny having written it, but it becomes understandable that he should claim in his letter to Jack Common—himself a writer from the working class —that the alterations he had been forced to make in the text had ruined it. As the years went on, he wouldn't seek even this sort of excuse: poor Gordon's keening displeased him to the point of disavowing the novel entirely.

Garrett—evidently *not* the sort ever to be thought of as "poor George"—proved to be yet one more of the working-class men Orwell met in these two months who were eager to be helpful. He took him around to the docks, and to see the new housing estates and the great slum-clearance projects. It was a full afternoon of learning; even so, between lessons, he'd found time to indulge himself by browsing in an antique shop near the docks. When he got back to the Deiners', he showed Mary Deiner a pair of brass candlesticks and a ship in a bottle he'd bought there, and told her that he was thinking of opening an antique shop of his own. That evening, the Deiners drove him back to Wigan, and he took the candlesticks away with him, but the ship in the bottle was too fragile to be carried around Yorkshire in his haversack. He left it temporarily with the Deiners. He would write, he said, as soon as he was settled, telling them where to send it on. But he never did. Very likely he had intended from the first that they should have it: this was his diffident, Orwell-like way of thanking them for their kindness to him. And the ship in the bottle remains with them to this day.

March was for Yorkshire, and he began in Sheffield. By this time he had established a network of contacts through the NUWM, and it led him, in Sheffield, to the Searles' house—two up, two down, outside WC—in Wallace Road.

They were a very likable couple, with a five-year-old child, living on the dole—Mr. Searle unemployed, Mrs. Searle working as a char at sixpence an hour. Orwell noted in the diary: "I have seldom met people with more natural decency." They were kind and helpful, and so too was William Brown (on Rees's list), unemployed, a sometime contributor to the *Adelphi*, who played a Garrett-like role and took him at a nonstop pace all over Sheffield, showing him slums, housing estates, and factories—supplying him with facts and more facts, grim and unavoidable, to add to those he had already collected in Lancashire. Once more the familiar note—of kindness that asks nothing in return, as he encountered from first to last in his travels—was made: "very anxious to help." But in the privacy of the diary Orwell felt constrained to add that B. was "tiresome . . . to be with," being "too conscious of his Communist convictions." Immediately he had pigeonholed Orwell as a bourgeois, remarking on his "public school twang." But in spite of this initial difficulty, they got on well together, inspiring a famous phrase in the diary—that Brown (Orwell felt) was disposed to treat him as "a sort of honorary proletarian." Too much has been made of the phrase by later admirers of Orwell, who fail to recognize that he himself was not deceived by it (as he might have been four years before, as a part-time down-and-outer), however much it may have pleased him. One of the lessons he was already learning from his two months of collecting facts was that between the working class and the middle class was a gulf that could not be bridged. He could admire, sympathize, support, fight for, and some would say sentimentalize the working class; he could and henceforth always would be *with* them; he could never be *of* them.

After Sheffield, he spent a week with the Dakins outside

Leeds, a reminder, if one were needed, of the gulf—not that Marjorie and Humphrey lived grandly. In fact, they lived very simply, in their house in Headingley, and in their cottage on the edge of the moors. But oh, the differences: theirs was another world. And he left to return to the working-class world, across the gulf, to a house in Barnsley—lodgings with a miner and his family—arranged by Wilde, the "kind and helpful" secretary of the South Yorkshire Branch, Working Men's Club and Institute Union. Again, there was the collecting of facts: by now he knew what his principal themes would be: the appalling housing to which the working class, employed and unemployed, were fated; the appalling conditions under which they worked, when they were lucky enough to have work; and the appalling poverty that befell them—the humiliations of the Means Test and the inadequacies of the dole—when there was no work for them and they became that abstraction, "the unemployed." But Barnsley, from which he doubted he would learn much that would be of interest, nonetheless was close to the mines: and he arranged to go down a "day hole" pit on Thursday, and on the Saturday down the Grimethorpe pit, which was very up-to-date, and promised to be less physically taxing. These two further "descents" would give him an authority, when he came to write about the mines, that he would not otherwise have had. But the impact of the first time, the descent in Wigan, was "devastating"—physically, and (more important) psychologically and intellectually. From the physical aftermath of those three hours underground in Crippen's, he would recover (as Joe Kennan remembered) after a couple of days in bed. But the psychological and intellectual consequence—the chief legacy of the journey North—stayed with him through his life, shaping his politics and his vision: here was a world underground, which he had not been aware of before, a world in the dark where men—not in the abstract, but men whom he'd met and liked and admired and who had been decent and kind to him—were spending the greater part of their lives. Theirs was an existence—and thousands of men like them shared it—that would have been unimaginable to him if he had not seen it, if he had not experienced it himself, however briefly and incompletely. He came away from the mines and the North in a state of guilt, anger, and compassion, and with a new, untested belief in the necessity of a political resolution.

FIFTEEN

WHEN ORWELL GAVE UP THE FLAT IN LAWFORD ROAD at the end of January and started on his journey to the industrial North, he had no intention of returning to London to live. He wanted, in a modest sort of way, to be a countryman, with a bit of land, enough for a vegetable garden and flowers, some animals to tend, with great trees, birds to observe and recognize, and a nearby stream to fish. As though to make certain that he would not backslide from his intention, he went ahead in February, while he was still in Lancashire, to rent sight unseen (through friends) a very small house at a very small rent (7/6 weekly) in the very small rural village of Wallington in Hertfordshire, midway between London and Cambridge. The nearest town was Baldock, three miles distant along the narrow, winding road that twice each week was the route for the bus between Baldock and Wallington. There was, along with other amenities in Baldock, a railroad station, and it was there, after more or less an hour train ride from London, that Orwell alighted on the second of April. As it was not a bus day, he walked across the fields to his new home, The Stores, Wallington—his sixth address since the publication of *Down and Out in Paris and London*. Although he would be away from it for considerable periods—most dramatically when he went off to fight in Spain—it would be his for a longer time than any other house (or flat) in his adult life; and when Eileen came to live with him he would be happier there than anywhere else.

The village was small, unspoiled, dull, remote in feeling if not in actual distance from London, and free of the dangerous quaintness that might attract tourists or stockbrokers. It had a population of less than a hundred, mostly aging—the school had been closed and converted into a lending library, and the dozen or so children were taken by bus to school in Baldock. The landmark was predictable: the twelfth-century parish church of St. Mary's. At the point where Kit's Lane and The Street came together, stood the village pub, The Plough (the other landmark), and next to it a low, two-storied, very small, very narrow—it was only eleven feet wide—three-hundred-year-old house of lath and plaster: this was The Stores. There was what passed for a little garden in front, and a somewhat larger one in the back, both, when Orwell took possession, in a state of ruination. Entering the house, you came directly into the main room—also very small—with low ceiling and heavy oak beams, which the previous tenant had fitted out with counter and shelves to serve as the village store, and which Orwell intended to revive. Adjoining it was a slightly smaller room, a sitting-dining room, whose connecting door had a row of peepholes cut out along the top so that one could look through to see if there were customers in the shop, and a minute kitchen with a sink and little oil stove. Upstairs were two small bedrooms and a bathroom (there was only a cold-water tap, and in the winter the toilet frequently froze over). Of course there was no electricity; heat was provided by Calor gas, and a fireplace that smoked and was unmanageable. But these defects, such as they were,

hardly were defects in Orwell's eyes; the house answered
to his practical and imaginative needs—his own place, in
the country, with a little shop that would bring in (perhaps) money enough to cover the cost of the rent, and a
garden that would in time produce a harvest of vegetables
for the table, etc., etc., a good and quiet place to write, a
spare room to put up friends who might come for a weekend; and if living was admittedly a bit primitive, he would
eventually (say in a year or two) put in the conveniences.
Fortunately, Eileen, when he brought her to see it the next
week, shared his enthusiasm for it as well as his indifference
to its defects: they were neither of them "mod-con" addicts.
She was as drawn as he to the notion of reviving the store,
undaunted at the prospect of reclaiming the garden, and
delighted at the idea of their keeping animals—hens, of
course, in a yard of their own, which would supply eggs;
and goats, which would supply milk and be stabled in the
shed behind the house, but put to graze in the common
land, a fairly large area of rough grass and bushes and bram-
bles, some distance from the cottage. Very likely the tini-
ness of The Stores, its being little more than an oversized
"playhouse," appealed to her fantasy side. For if Eileen was
ironic, witty, practical, and immensely rational—always
ready to bring Eric down to earth from one of his wilder
flights—she was also deeply imaginative, and enjoyed "inventing" another world, populated with farmyard animals,
whose traits of personality she developed with the skill of a
psychologist or a novelist, bestowing names upon them—
Kate and Mabel were the goats at The Stores—and creating
for them an ever more complex, interminable series of adventures. For a time she thought of incorporating them into
a children's story that would be set in a farmyard, whose
animal characters, in that ancient tradition going back to

Aesop, would reproduce the traits of their human proto-
types. But when the war came the project was gradually
abandoned (like The Stores itself), and it survived only in
the conversations she and Eric would have in bed at night,
amusing themselves as the bombs fell over London, and
they invented new adventures: foibles and follies for the
animals of their imaginary farm.

But there was one significant flaw in The Stores—evident
immediately to Eileen's closest friends and to her brother
Laurence—that she either did not or chose not to recognize.
It was an ideal place for a dedicated writer eager to get on
with his writing, and to be at a safe distance from the en-
croachments of the London literary and political world. But
for a child psychologist about to embark on a career, living
there would have insuperable disadvantages. The awkwardness of reaching London from Wallington virtually ruled it
out; and Cambridge, the other logical alternative for a starting point, was equally difficult to reach. But when Eric
brought her to the village and showed her the house with
such unbounded enthusiasm, it did not occur to her to raise
objections. She seemed to fall into wholehearted agreement
with his plans, quite as though she had no plans of her own.

THAT SPRING WAS DEDICATED TO SETTLING IN, WITH MRS.
Anderson, a neighbor, coming in to "do" for him—rarely was
an English gentleman so poverty-stricken that he could not
afford a char—and the shop gradually being stocked with a
heterogeneity of things—penny candy, biscuits, tea, string,
rice, flour—that the villagers might possibly want, and the
struggle with the garden under way (he told Rees that he
expected within a year to make it "really nice") and a cer-

tain amount of planting around the house: rambler roses (from Woolworth's), three polyantha roses, two bush roses, six fruit trees, two gooseberry bushes, and he had hopes of planting walnut, quince, and mulberry trees. (According to a later occupant of the house, which is now known as Monk's Fitchett, the survival rate was not high, and there is nothing left to show of Orwell's tenancy but a few of the roses in front of the house.)

But he enjoyed it all—it was the country life that he had not so much idealized as yearned for—and he enjoyed playing the role of a storekeeper, though in the end, as a venture, it had far less staying power than the rambler roses from Woolworth's. Cyril Connolly, when he saw the shop, was immediately reminded, in a rather haunting, Proustian way, of Blair and himself at St. Cyprian's, and the long, long walks they had taken over the Downs, stopping at the little shops of Eastdean, Westdean, and Jevington for penny sweets. It was that sort of long-ago shop Blair had opened in Wallington, and Connolly had the impression that he saw himself as a kind of Edwardian shopkeeper out of a novel by H. G. Wells. Such a shop might have just done in 1910, but it was 1936, and what Eric and Eileen had failed to take properly into account was that the people of the village enjoyed their twice-weekly shopping expeditions into Baldock, which they combined with a visit to the cinema there. So that the most assiduous customers of The Stores were the village children, coming in to buy sweets. Eileen, either to amuse herself or to teach the children arithmetic, had priced the sweets thus: four for a ha'penny, seven for a penny. Obviously one did better coming by the shop twice and buying a ha'penny's worth each time, so that there was rather more bustle in the shop than the day's receipts reflected.

A COUNTRYMAN'S LIFE IS NOT IDYLLIC, AND CERTAINLY NOT the idyll a city man daydreaming of living in the country imagines it to be. Even at best it is demanding. Eric soon realized that if he were to take care of the animals, and the garden, and the shop, and the absolutely essential things that would restore the house to a modestly livable condition, he would have no time at all for what still came first: the work he had neglected while on the journey North, his writing. Accordingly, much of what had to be done was left undone, or postponed until after his marriage to Eileen, when she could share those time-consuming daily chores that are an unavoidable part of living in the country.

He set up his typewriter on the table in the sitting-dining room, and began to write. For the *New English Weekly,* a review of Cyril Connolly's novel, *The Rock Pool.* To friends, letters acquainting them with his changed circumstances. Most importantly there was the new book, on which, as he told Geoffrey Gorer, he'd made "a fairly good start."

Meanwhile, on April 20, Gollancz had published *Keep the Aspidistra Flying.* Its reception suggested that Orwell had arrived at a paradoxical point in his career. This was his fourth book, and by now he had his ready-made reputation, his niche where harried reviewers (and booksellers) could conveniently place him: "The more depressing his theme, the more effectively is his skill displayed" (*Times Literary Supplement*). There is a point at which praise becomes praise-by-rote. He had gone in four books from being unknown to being predictable: something new would have to be said of him to make him an interesting as well as a respected writer; or perhaps he had to write something new, not simply another version of what he had made familiar, to become interesting.

The man in the *Daily Mail*—this time, unluckily, not the faithfully enthusiastic Compton Mackenzie but one Douglas West—having paid the predictable tribute, "No realistic writer of today has produced books of greater vigour and reality," went on to add the ominous *but*. "But among the aspidistra Mr. Orwell seems to lose touch with reality. He gives us, it is true, a measured portrait of an ineffectual young man, and drives home the moral that all he needs to restore his self-respect is the sort of job he could have had for the asking. There is some searching talk, and one or two ideas are given an airing which, though not strictly fresh, will pass as original. A novel, however, needs something more than this."

On the other hand—and once an author has his reputation, there is always a reviewer to play "the other hand"— the poet Richard Church, in *John o' London's Weekly*, rose to the lyrical in his praise: "Mr. Orwell writes (and I hope he will pardon my trite phrase) in his heart's blood. The result is painful, but it is also convincing, human, and beautiful."

Keep the Aspidistra Flying was the third novel by George Orwell to be published in thirteen months, and Gollancz, trusting that by now there was an audience who would recognize his name and be eager to read whatever he wrote, ordered the largest first printing he had yet had: 3000 copies. But the reviewers were not sufficiently enthusiastic, or when enthusiastic were not sufficiently enticing to arouse anyone but a dedicated Orwellian. Three thousand copies turned out to be far more than were wanted; no American publisher had been found to take the place of the disillusioned Harpers' and import sheets; within a month the type was being distributed.

PARADOXICALLY, THE GRAY FATE OF THE NOVEL, HASTENING into semi-oblivion, hastened him towards the happiest period of his life. There was nothing to be gained by postponing any longer his marriage to Eileen, hoping for some dramatic improvement in his financial position that would make things easier for them. Once again the rewards of fiction had been meager. He had given up his earlier notion —never very seriously adhered to—of someday writing a best seller. His experience told him there was little likelihood that he would grow rich from the novels he intended to write in the future—and at this time, it should be emphasized, he still thought of himself primarily as a novelist, the sort who would write thirty novels by the time he was sixty. He appears to have been relieved that this was his situation —to be liberated even from the fantasy of a worldly success so at odds with the kind of life that both he and Eileen valued most. Indeed, his existence exactly as it was then, in the late-arriving spring of 1936, simple, austere, rural, seemingly timeless—living at The Stores, at work already on another book—only needed Eileen as his wife to fulfill an ideal of settled happiness he had never before allowed himself. (And it was an ideal that would be borne out by the reality. As his friend Geoffrey Gorer was later to say, "I think the only year that I ever knew him really happy was that first year with Eileen.")

It had been understood between them for some time that eventually they would be married. The sensible September argument had been that they should wait until Eileen had finished her course and found a job. It was doubtful whether on his own earnings he could afford to support them both. But in the spring, when he returned from the North and moved into The Stores, these scruples evaporated on both sides. They agreed they might be able to eke out an existence with the vegetables, livestock, sale of eggs from the hens, the shillings and pence the shop might bring them, and Eric's chancy literary income. (In fact it was rather larger than usual at the moment, thanks to the advance for the book on the North, of which he'd used up very little.)

For Eric the decision to marry Eileen was so logical and inevitable that it was more in the nature of a culmination than a decision. For Eileen, however, the decision involved a very conscious choice: either to marry Eric or to go on with her course, take her degree, and embark upon a career as a clinical psychologist. The two alternatives were irreconcilable, no doubt had been so from the beginning, and became so unquestionably from the time he settled on The Stores as the place where they would live. But as against the possibility of a career in which she might have done as well as her friends expected (or might not), there was the reality of marriage, and that is what she chose. To be Eric's wife was what she wanted. As for the course, she never bothered to finish it. Ahead of her was a marriage that would occupy her life fully, excitingly, necessitously, and in the years of the Second World War exhaustingly, until her death in 1945.

They decided to marry in the traditional month of June, but with a minimum of traditional fuss. Orwell, though a nonpracticing member of the Church of England, was sufficiently a traditionalist to wish to be married in it—besides, St. Mary's in Wallington was more convenient than the

registry office in Baldock. On the morning of the appointed
day, June 9, he found time to dash off a letter to Denys
King-Farlow, his old friend from Eton, whom he had not
seen since then, and who had written out of the blue to re-
establish the friendship and to invite him to a birthday
party. He had to decline the invitation, but he proposed
that King-Farlow should drop in whenever he was anywhere near, and added the news that he was getting married that very day, and reading the Prayer Book to brace
himself against what he considered the "obscenities" of the
wedding service. Geoffrey Gorer, a more recent friend, also
was told the news in a letter, and to him Orwell confided
the melodramatic prospect that the Blairs and the
O'Shaughnessys might join forces to prevent the wedding,
though there is no evidence on either side to support the
notion.

Mr. and Mrs. Blair and Avril, bearing some of the family
silver as a wedding gift for the young Blairs, drove over
from Southwold, and Laurence and Gwen and Mrs.
O'Shaughnessy came up from London to attend the service
in the church, which was performed by the vicar of nearby
Galston, with Eric's father and Eileen's mother acting as
witnesses. They had a little party in The Stores afterwards
—more than enough with the eight of them to crowd the
tiny house—and at some point Avril and her mother took
Eileen upstairs, as she later told her friend the novelist
Lettice Cooper, to warn her of the burden she was taking
on. (What must Eric have thought? But perhaps the private
little chat occurred when he, his father, and the O'Shaughnessys had already stepped next door to The Plough for a
celebratory drink.)

Actually, what Eileen was taking on was not so much a
burden as a burdensome role: the writer's wife. She proved

to be very good at it, because she was intelligent, sympathetic, humorous, and appreciative of what Eric wrote; and because she recognized and did not struggle against the quite special way his being a writer would shape the course of their lives together.

SIXTEEN

ORWELL BELONGED TO THE CATEGORY OF WRITERS who write. For him a day without writing was not a good one. There were, effectively, no pauses in the process: if not a novel, then a review, or an essay, a letter, a diary, a shopping list. For such a writer, as Eileen once said, not reprovingly, "his work comes before anybody"—even his wife!—and alas for the wife who cannot accept this. Indeed, Orwell's relation to writing was oddly like a marriage: in sickness and in health, for richer or for poorer, till death do them part, it would go on.

In May he was writing the first chapter of *The Road to Wigan Pier*.

On the afternoon of June 9, he was married. That morning, as we have seen, he found time at least to write a letter.

On the morning of June 10 he was back at the typewriter as usual. Work on *The Road* had to wait while he put the finishing touches to "Shooting an Elephant," which proved to be one of his best, and subsequently one of his most famous, essays.

THE CIRCUMSTANCES OF HIS WRITING "SHOOTING AN ELEphant" cast an interesting light on Orwell's tangential relation to the dominant literary movement of the 1930's in England, that group of gifted young poets and novelists who became celebrated during the decade and would enter literary history as "Auden & Co.": W. H. Auden, Stephen Spender, C. Day Lewis, Louis MacNeice, Christopher Isherwood, John Lehmann, Rex Warner, and Edward Upward. Orwell's name would properly be omitted from such a list, no doubt to his satisfaction, by anyone familiar with the politics and *placement* of literary London in the 1930's: he was not in the "movement." But in 1939, in the autobiographical portion of his *Enemies of Promise*, Cyril Connolly had written of Orwell as Eric Blair, his friend at St. Cyprian's and Eton, and in the critical-historical portion he had written of him as the novelist George Orwell, bracketing him with a leading member of Auden & Co.: "In England the ablest exponents of the colloquial style among the younger writers are Christopher Isherwood and George Orwell, both leftwing and both, at the present level of current English, superlatively readable." This would lead to misconceptions. To a critic such as Q. D. Leavis, writing in *Scrutiny* in 1940, it was sufficient evidence to place Orwell in the suspect, charmed circle. In her review of *Inside the Whale*, a collection of three of his essays brought out by Gollancz in 1939, she writes: "Mr. Orwell . . . belongs by birth and education to 'the right Left people', the nucleus of the literary world who christian-name each other and are honour bound to advance each other's literary career; he figures indeed in Connolly's autobiography as a schoolfellow. This is probably why he has received indulgent treatment in the literary press. He differs from them in having grown up . . . by the force of a remarkable character."

But not only did he differ from them, he was not *of* them. In the title essay of the book under review, he had written scathingly of the Auden group, in its literary, social, and political aspects. And this was only the most recent of his attacks upon what he was fond of describing as "the pansy left." In particular he was offended by their politics, which did not seem to him justly earned—"a kind of playing with fire by people who do not even know that the fire is hot." He himself came to politics much later than they—not until 1936—but he stayed longer. From the time of his experience in Spain until his death in 1950, politics would be a center for his life in a way that it never was for the writers we more readily associate with the political 1930's.

Principle prompted his attacks, but especially in the early years of the decade, when he was so obsessively concerned with a literary career of his own, elements of spite and animosity played a part too, as he later acknowledged. Whether they intended to or not, Auden & Co. did rather hog the limelight, and there would have been a sense of revenge on Orwell's part in sneering at Auden as "a gutless Kipling." But from 1936 on, really from the time of his marriage to Eileen, as he became more at ease with himself, more confident and more recognized, he began gradually to renew old acquaintanceships with Etonian contemporaries, and even to allow himself to become acquainted with members of the "movement," some of whom he liked a good deal—notably Stephen Spender, to whom he was introduced by Cyril Connolly.

Nonetheless, old prejudices lingered on, and when, in the spring of 1936, he received a letter from John Lehmann, asking him to contribute to a journal of which he was editor, he was immediately on guard.

Lehmann did have just the sort of credentials that Orwell distrusted. Like Orwell himself he had been in College at Eton. Unlike Orwell he had gone on from there to Trinity College, Cambridge. He was a poet whose books of verse had been published by Leonard and Virginia Woolf at the Hogarth Press. His work had been included in those seminal anthologies, *New Signatures* and *New Country,* at the beginning of the decade that announced the arrival of "the movement," and not only was he one of the right Left people, he also knew and was a friend of the right people who wrote. That spring (1936) he brought out the first number of what was to become one of the most influential and admired publications of the 1930's and 1940's. He called it *New Writing*—evidently everything in the 1930's had to be *new*—and he intended to issue it as a book twice yearly, dedicated to writing of superior quality and to anti-Fascism. These aims were generalized enough to allow him to consider as a prospective contributor virtually anyone who was not an avowed hack or an avowed Fascist. As an editor with a highly developed sense of who was writing what and what was worth publishing, it was highly logical that he should write to Orwell to ask if he had anything he might be willing to send to *New Writing.*

Orwell's reply on the twenty-seventh of May was guarded: he would like to write "a sketch . . . describing the shooting of an elephant. It all came back to me very vividly the other day . . . but it may be that it is quite out of your line. I mean it might be too lowbrow for your paper and I doubt whether there is anything anti-Fascist in the shooting of an elephant." Then, having protected his flank, so to speak—a more diffident reply can hardly be imagined, or a more depreciatory or less enticing "brief description" of what would be one of the great essays of this century—he got to the crucial point: Would, or would not, such a sketch be in Lehmann's line? "If not, then I won't write it; if you think it might interest you I'll do it and send it along for you to consider."

Could Orwell have been serious? Supposing Lehmann

had said "No?" Would we really, then, not have had "Shooting an Elephant"? Such speculations are trivial-sounding,
no doubt, but of such, sometimes, is literary history.

It is literary-historical fact, however, not speculation, that
Lehmann replied promptly to say that he would very much
like to read the piece (knowing that a sketch of shooting an
elephant by the author of *Burmese Days*, which he greatly
admired, would never be confused with the reminiscences
of a big-game hunter), that Orwell sat down promptly to
write it, and sent it off to Lehmann on June 12, three days
after the wedding, that Lehmann read it, admired it,
bought it, and published it in the second number of *New
Writing* in the autumn of 1936. His editorial acumen or
"instinct," for which he would become famous in the next
two decades, had led him straight to a masterpiece.

"Shooting an Elephant" marks the beginning of the major phase of Orwell's career, and it is not just coincidence
that the time of its writing should coincide with the beginning of his marriage. There is an uncramped expression of
feeling, a generosity and humaneness, an acknowledgment
of the complexity of seemingly simple experience that had
been absent from his earlier writing, and that would be
present in his work thereafter, which can be attributed at
least in part to the influence of Eileen. (It is noteworthy
that the vehement bitterness and rancor, so evident in much
of his early work, reassert themselves only after her death,
and reach a kind of culminating, nightmarish intensity in
1984.)

"Shooting an Elephant" is the third of his efforts to draw
upon his Burmese experience. As early as 1931, when he
was still writing as Eric A. Blair, he had made a first attempt with his essay (or "story") "A Hanging"; then in
1934 there had been *Burmese Days;* and now, this sketch of

the shooting of an elephant. It had come back to him vividly, how, as a young police officer in Burma, he had been called upon to shoot a tame elephant that had gone on a rampage. He had no wish to perform what he recognized would be an act of unnecessary murder, for the maddened elephant had subsided and was no longer a danger to anyone; but the Burmese, two thousand of them, gathering to watch their imperialist oppressor in his predestined role, *wanted* him (as he suddenly realized) to play out the role to its bloody end—*to kill*—and in the end he did so, simply not to lose face. But not so simply, of course. In this single episode—exotic to the Western imagination, but a fairly routine part of the life of the police officer in Burma—Orwell found a way, as he had not been able to do before, of suggesting the evil, the dilemma, and the pathos of imperialism: his sympathy for the victims that the system called into being, the ruled and the rulers alike, which made his recognition of its "impossibility" all the more impressive.

THE PROSE IN "SHOOTING AN ELEPHANT" IS SUPPLE AND UNforced, deceptively simple in its intelligent, conversational tone—one hears a voice that is by now recognizably Orwell's. He had arrived at a level of assurance that augured well for the book of the journey North that he had begun a few weeks earlier, and that was to be his principal literary occupation for the next several months. He would have a rough first draft done by October, and he would send off the final version to Moore in December.

A book written in six months suggests a book written easily. In fact, *The Road to Wigan Pier* presented a number of problems that he never solved to his satisfaction, and although it was the book that was to make him famous (and in some quarters, infamous), it is a curiously uneven achievement. He had come back from the North full of impressions and information: it was all vivid and fresh in his mind (and in his diary), and in theory it should have been less difficult to transcribe on the page than an experience in Burma from many years back. But shooting an elephant had been *his* experience, he had been at the center of it. Now he was to write of the experience of *others* as he had observed it—the intent of the Gollancz commission was clear enough—and paradoxically, it made for an odd degree of literary self-consciousness in the early stages of the writing.

He had great difficulty, at first, in finding the right tone. In a book of this kind, art that calls attention to itself is "too much art," and the artist too conspicuous. In retrospect, the answer to the problem seems clear enough: the right note was available all along in the un-self-conscious, unexaggerated, un-"literary" pages of his diary. But he began by thinking of the diary as no more than "raw material" to be reworked, as though he had embarked on a Zolaesque or Dickensian novel of life in the lower depths, rather than what *The Road*, in its first part, became: a sympathetic, honest, and angry report of life in the industrial North, still suffering the effects of a Depression that neither the Tory government nor the capitalist system seemed able to relieve.

Unlike the day-by-day, chronological form of the diary, the book begins—and we are writing here of the book as published; no manuscript either of the "rough draft" or the "revision" is known to have survived—in the middle of the journey. (Indeed, the sense of a journey, of the author being on "assignment," has been artfully suppressed.) In the first chapter we are simply there—in an unnamed industrial town in the North—with "I" the narrator, who is staying in squalid lodgings over a squalid tripe shop owned by a squalid couple, the Brookers. This first chapter is a detailed, leisurely introduction to the elder Brookers, to the other members of the family, to their ill-used lodgers, and the literally disgusting circumstances in which they live. On the first page alone there is such a wealth of unpredictable particulars that one assumes Orwell must have jotted them down on the spot for future reference. But that is not the case. From the diary we learn only that he shared a room with three other lodgers, that one of the other beds jammed across the foot of his, making it impossible for him to stretch out his legs without hitting its occupant in the small of the back. An eloquent detail in itself, but the book adds others even more remarkable. The bedroom, we learn, was formerly a drawing room, into which "four squalid beds" had been crowded alongside a good deal of furniture surviving from drawing-room days: "gilt chairs with burst seats," a horsehair armchair, "something between a sideboard and a hall-stand," and—perhaps most astonishing of all—we are told of "a heavy glass chandelier on which the dust was so thick that it was like fur." It is Orwell in his best "down-and-out" vein, and it goes on for pages, culminating in "a full chamber pot under the breakfast table"—the detail that decides him to leave—but one may wonder if it is the best vein in which to introduce the people of Wigan, most of whom (among those he met) he came to know and admire, with whose lives and struggles he so deeply sympathized, and who would play so significant a role in his conversion to Socialism.

The responses of two very different, differently qualified readers to this first chapter of *The Road to Wigan Pier* are instructive. The poet Edith Sitwell, qualified by breadth of sympathy and highly refined literary sensibility, wrote to the mother of Geoffrey Gorer: "The horror of the beginning . . . is unsurpassable. He seems to be doing for the modern world what Engels did for the world of 1840–50. But with this difference, that Orwell is a born writer, whereas Engels, fiery and splendid spirit though he was, simply wasn't a writer. One had to reconstruct the world from his pages for oneself." John Farrimond, qualified by experience—a Wiganer and a sometime miner, the author of *Dust in My Throat* and *Pick and Run*, who began his career as a novelist at the age of fifty—has written to the present authors: "In all my years around Wigan—I was a lad of eighteen about the time that Orwell was going his rounds researching—I have never met, nor heard of anybody as filthy as the Brookers. Dirt there was in plenty, but *filth* was something different. Unemptied chamber pots? All those I ever saw in those days were spotless. You had only to look over somebody's back yard, and they'd be lying there by the waste grid, emptied and washed."

One might fairly conclude from these so different responses that the poet, unfamiliar with the world Orwell was describing, recognized the truth which transcends particular details, and that the novelist—as a native more familiar with that world than Orwell the short-term visitor—recognized the exaggerations and errors while taking the larger truth for granted. (And viewing the chapters on Wigan altogether, Farrimond felt that they presented "a fairly accurate picture.")

Consulting the diary one discovers that Orwell was in Darlington Road, Wigan, in lodgings over a tripe shop, with people named F—— (who became the Brookers of *The Road*) from the fifteenth till the twenty-fifth of February 1936. Evidently the house, though larger than most in which he stayed, was squalid, smelly, and overcrowded. On the twenty-first of February he noted that it was getting on his nerves. Also that there was an unemptied chamber pot under the breakfast table that particular morning. (Which may, though he doesn't say so, have been emptied and washed out an hour later.) Nowhere else in the diary, except this page at the F——'s, is there a reference to chamber pots, unemptied or otherwise; nor, for that matter, does the diary tell us that at any of the other of the several working-class houses in which he stayed during the journey did he encounter a squalor even remotely comparable to the F——'s. That, clearly, was the appalling exception, and one can only wonder at his willingness to put up with it, as he did, for more than a week—surely his friends in the NUWM could have made a tactful arrangement for him to lodge elsewhere. Comfort apart, to have done so would have served his purposes better: the more he had seen and experienced for himself of housing in Wigan, the more impressive, authoritative (and influential) the total picture might have been. The Brookers, we learn from the diary, were not "so badly off." As a model, then, for the awful housing conditions in Wigan, their lodging house and tripe shop was perhaps too picturesquely awful to be typical. That fur-bearing chandelier, the filthiness of the Brookers themselves, with Mrs. B. wiping her mouth with strips of newspaper and littering the floor with "crumpled-up balls of slimy paper," make the situation seem too special. Or perhaps Orwell, in his eagerness to start out memorably, has worked it up with a shade too much art. There is more than one way to write a purple passage. In June, he would demonstrate in "Shooting an Elephant" the crucial balance between truth unadorned by art and truth heightened by artifice. Getting the new book under way at the end of April, he had yet to strike that balance.

Two further quotations seem in order. On the twenty-fourth of February, after his first descent into a coal mine, Orwell notes in the diary that he "went home [to Darlington Road] and had dinner and soaked myself for a very long time in a hot bath." From which we realize that the F——'s house, squalid though it might be, still had what the houses of most miners didn't have: "A proper bathtub" and "hot water laid on."

Finally, John Farrimond, in the same letter in which he points out exaggerations and omissions in *The Road*, concludes handsomely, "You certainly won't go far wrong in using Orwell as a Guide to Wigan in the thirties."

HE HAD FINISHED "SHOOTING AN ELEPHANT" AND THOUGHT IT good, a rare occurrence with him—for once there seems to have been none of that putting-down of his own work (botched! dreadful! loathe the sight of it!) one comes to expect from him in the thirties. Now he returned to the book for Victor Gollancz. In May he thought he had made a "fairly good start." Then came the Lehmann interruption. The interval away from the Wigan manuscript—so carefully wrought as far as he had gone, so ambitiously more than mere journalism—and the time spent sketching "Shooting an Elephant" had both been salutary. Letting the book simmer allowed him time to reconsider what Gollancz had proposed and what he himself wanted: a report on the North as he had observed it. And the writing of the "sketch" suggested a way to go on more easily and naturally with the book. Writing without exaggeration for literary effect, trusting in the material he had gathered, for its own sake as well as his responses to it, remembering the people he had met, places seen, certain crucial experiences—in *their* coal mines, *their* shelters, *their* houses—allowed him to record the lives and sufferings of others. The tone of the first chapter of *The Road*, those vivid, artfully rendered, and heightened scenes of life in the depths *chez* Brooker—that tone, in itself and certainly by contrast to what comes afterward, seems more appropriate to a novel than to reportage. (It is enlightening to compare the first sentences of Hemingway's novel *To Have and Have Not*—Havana in the early morning—with the first sentences of *The Road*—Wigan in the early morning—and discover their similarities of rhythm and phrasing. In both cases one is aware of the presence of a highly developed and self-conscious literary sensibility.*) This is not to discount the effectiveness of the first chapter—think of its impact upon Edith Sitwell— but simply to agree with Orwell's own decision in mid-June that it was not a productive direction in which to continue. Thereafter, from the second through the seventh chapter, Part I of the book, he was essentially a guide to Wigan, a reporter one comes quickly to trust.

Even so adverse a critic of Orwell as Harry Pollitt, who would trounce the book in the pages of the *Daily Worker*, was forced to concede some merit to its first part, and readers less biased will find in those seven chapters a portrait of poverty and its consequences that catches at the imagination and awakens sympathy and anger even now,

* In *Enemies of Promise* Cyril Connolly called attention to the Hemingway/Orwell stylistic resemblance. In a very ingenious way he fused together sentences from *To Have and Have Not*, *The Road to Wigan Pier*, and Isherwood's "Sally Bowles" into a composite paragraph that illustrated the qualities of "the colloquial style."

some forty years later, when the appalling conditions it describes have long since been ameliorated—perhaps, in some slight degree, a consequence of the book itself. Without consciously aspiring to do so, Orwell had written a work of reportage that endures as a work of art.

SEVENTEEN

P‍ART I, AS WE HAVE SEEN, OPENS WITH A WORKING-CLASS "interior" at its most squalid, and it concludes (in the seventh chapter) with a working-class "interior" at its most idealized, where "you breathe a warm, decent, deeply human atmosphere," not likely to be found elsewhere. The progression from negative to positive in these two dramatically contrasting "interiors" represents the other journey that Orwell made when he went North, the subtext of Part I that becomes explicit in Part II: his own road to Socialism. The journey transformed him, as Rees observed, from a *je m'en foutiste* to a militant Socialist, but he was so much a Socialist of his own sort that perhaps it would have made it easier for those who attempt to write about him if he hadn't bothered to label himself.

The heart of his creed was simplicity itself: a belief that "economic injustice will stop when we want it to stop . . . the method adopted hardly matters." Appalled by the oppressed and neglected lives of the unemployed as he had seen them close up, he felt that something drastic would have to be done to change a social and economic situation that was no longer tolerable—something beyond the makeshifts of private philanthropy or the humiliating, inadequate government dole, something along the lines envisioned by Socialism. What precisely those lines might be, however, he never bothered to say, perhaps because he didn't know, or because, in the first fervor of conversion, he thought it unnecessary to worry over details: it was enough simply to declare oneself a Socialist.

To judge by what he wrote, or what he said to friends such as Rees, it is evident that he did not come to Socialism through ideological commitment. Socialist doctrine, as it argued for state ownership of the means of production and for a planned society, did not excite his imagination or awaken his deepest sympathies. He was much too idiosyncratic to be doctrinaire, and too independent by nature to take happily to the idea of plans (or, to adopt a post-Orwellian version of Newspeak, "social engineering"), even when, as in questions of public housing and slum clearance, the need was inarguable, the advantage undeniable.

What he wanted was a Socialism without planning—surely a contradiction in terms?—founded upon ideals of honor and decency: "Economic injustice will stop when we want it to stop." As he would presently discover, such ideals have only a tenuous connection to the world of practical politics, and honor and decency are not unique to adherents of a given party line, even if the party happened to be his own. The least one can say beginning or concluding a discussion of Orwell's politics in general, and his Socialism in particular, is that a man who believes that "the method . . . hardly matters" will prove to be an unorthodox Socialist.

Unorthodoxy is written all over Part II of *The Road to Wigan Pier*, not simply in its exposition (or invocation) of Socialism as Orwell understood it, but also in the metamorphosis of the book itself. For what had been begun as a work of reportage was transformed at midpoint, and with questionable logic, into a mix of politics, polemics, and selective autobiography. Part I had been, as Gollancz proposed, a report of the working class in the North, *their* lives, their work—and want of it—their struggles, all recorded with candor and sympathy, and as such a prime document of the 1930's. Part II became, as Orwell decided it must, *his* life, his ideas and speculations, his critique of Socialism, drawing upon illustrative moments of theoretical or actual experience, exhilarating in the writing and sometimes infuriating (at least to its early readers), and as such a prime source of confusion in sorting out truth from legend in the story of George Orwell.

The explanation he devises for the shift in the book is simple, and perhaps a shade disingenuous. He had gone—on his own, as it were; there is no mention of the commission—to the North, where unemployment was the worst in Britain, to see it in its true nature, and to be as close as possible to the working class, who were its victims. This self-imposed mission symbolized his two-pronged approach to Socialism. First, you must decide that things are intolerable. Second, you must adopt "a definite attitude on the terribly difficult issue of class," those attitudes, habits, customs, and prejudices that define the classes and come between them. "Terribly difficult"—or, as he put it more pungently in a letter to Jack Common, "Class-breaking is a bugger."

What he had seen in the North, the substance of Part I of *The Road,* proved beyond doubt the intolerability of things. The class question, as exemplified by the history of his own attitudes towards it, and the attitudes of all those others like him who were across the gulf from the working class, is dealt with implacably (and sometimes comically, as in a discussion of table manners and eating

habits that foreshadows Nancy Mitford's U and non-U)
in Part II, though whether the question is satisfactorily
answered therein is hard to say. The facts of unemployment, in all their reams and charts, are something one can
report on objectively. Class "attitudes" and prejudices, and
the hostilities they give rise to—the belief, for example,
that the working class smells, one of Orwell's most notorious animadversions in *The Road*—tend to be subjective and
not susceptible to objective proof. (It was Orwell's bad
luck or peculiarity to be hypersensitive to smells, especially
unpleasant ones, which induced in him both a physical and
a psychological reaction. He tells us that as a young man,
before he had rid himself of the prejudiced class attitudes
he had been taught, he found the smell of sweat exuded
by working-class bodies, even when out of doors in the
sunlight, so offensive that it turned his stomach. Doubtless
his was an extreme reaction, but it does not invalidate his
claim that he was representative or symptomatic of his
class in accepting as true the notion that the working class
did smell.)

At this point a crucial distinction has to be made if one
is to understand Orwell's strategy in *The Road*. Although it
was written primarily *about* the working class, and on their
behalf, the book was not written *for* them. (When the
Wiganers whom he had observed finally got to read what
he had written about them, they were not entirely pleased.)
Evidently the readers whom Orwell envisioned, at whom
the book was aimed like a weapon, were more or less of
his own class—lower-upper-middle—and so he could put
himself forward to them as a "symptomatic figure." His
experience (in his own mind) would stand for theirs—he
thought the working class smelled and so must they; his
progress, beginning in prejudice and ending in enlighten-

ment, might prove exemplary. His tone is that of the man who has been through it all and knows whereof he speaks. Having freed himself from the divisive class attitudes he so deplores (and that make the achievement of a true Socialism impossible), he is determined that they shall do likewise. He brings before them as an object of contempt your typical middle-class Socialist—who would almost certainly turn out to be the typical reader of a book such as *The Road*— and observes disapprovingly that a Socialist of that sort is more likely to associate with someone from the middle rather than the working class. What price Socialism? Such a figure may be Socialist in his politics—meaning that he votes Labour and reads the *New Statesman*—but he is still invincibly bourgeois in his tastes, in food and wine and books and ballet. "Most significant, he invariably marries into his own class."

This damning indictment, drawn up by Orwell within weeks of his making precisely such a marriage himself, sounds odd indeed, the more so as one knows that it was written in a state of unmitigated domestic happiness. But the tone of the sentence on the page carries all before it: it is hard to believe that the man who wrote it would not himself be liberated from so bourgeois a fate. In the circumstances, one can understand why those early readers who knew no more of Orwell than what Orwell chose to tell them in his forthright-sounding prose might leap to the conclusion that had so irritated Elizaveta Fen: "He's married to a woman of the people, and leads the life of a labourer."

Very likely, in the abstract, it would have pleased him to get free of his class altogether—although he seems never even to have entertained the notion of marrying a woman of the working class. His attempts to declass himself were more fantasied than real, and his successes equivocal: at best, as in Sheffield, when he was forgiven his Public School accent and treated for the day as an "honorary proletarian". (Being called "Comrade," a not unusual custom among working-class Socialists and Communists, made him ill at ease then, as we have seen. At the end of the year, however, arriving in Barcelona, he was thrilled to discover that honorary class titles such as "Don" and "Señor" had been abandoned, and everyone was called "Comrade.") He did affect certain habits and attitudes towards food and drink that he considered to be "working class"—especially when with friends and acquaintances who belonged, like himself, to the lower-upper-middle or above—but he was quite aware that they *were* affectations, a form of irony or teasing. (Sometimes, though, it was a case of his left hand not knowing what his right was doing. Life at The Stores was determinedly simple, as both Eric and Eileen preferred it—still, there was the family silver; the portrait of an ancestress, Lady Mary Blair; wine with dinner; vegetables and herbs brought in from the garden; old brass candlesticks; the poodle, Marx. Their life was simple, even austere, in many respects uncomfortable, and they were hard-pressed for money; but by no stretch of the imagination would one say the Blairs were living in a working-class interior.)

No doubt it is unfair to hold a polemicist, whose principal interest is in scoring points, to accuracy in matters of fact, when it's the general impressions, not the minute or exact particulars, that count; nor to expect restraint from him when exaggeration will better serve his purpose. The portrait with which Orwell inaugurates Part II—a portrait of Eric Blair on the way to becoming George Orwell—is as harsh, as biased, and in some respects as misleading, as any that follow of delinquent or deficient fellow Socialists, but it does make up in conviction for what it lacks in precision. We witness the transformation of a snobbish, class-ridden servant of Imperialism (Blair) into a veritable Jeremiah among Socialists (Orwell). With that passion for generalizations so characteristic of him, and with the fervor of a new convert, he launched a splendidly unmoderated attack upon Socialists of the middle class, virtually all of whom are judged and found wanting. There are, in a category of their own, the horror types of the crank fringe—beardless eunuchs and bearded sandal-wearers, fleshy middle-aged scoutmasters in shorts drawn tight across their obscenely bulging buttocks, and vegetarians (a pet hate of Orwell's), immediately recognizable by their peculiar vegetarian smell (whatever that may be). Then, in another category, are those aforementioned bourgeois party members with their gentlemanly waistcoats (bottom button undone) and their insincere table manners (won't drink tea out of saucers). And as a third category, in a chapter or pillory of their own, the latter-day admirers of H. G. Wells (such as Eric Blair had been years before at St. Cyprian's), who share Wells's out-of-date faith in progress and a scientifically perfected future.

If these three categories provide a fair sampling of Socialists—cranks, snobs, and optimistic simpletons—is it any wonder the plain, straightforward, no-nonsense English workingman is put off Socialism? How can he make common cause with these unsavory specimens? Orwell is at pains to insist that he is writing as a convinced Socialist himself, and it is only as a true believer that he takes on the painful role of devil's advocate. Pointing out faults and faults and faults, he does so very much in the spirit of a headmaster (Mr. Vaughan Wilkes, say) administering a caning to an erring schoolboy (Blair, say)—not because he enjoys doing it, but for the good of the boy. What Orwell does, he reminds the reader who may misunderstand, he does for the good of the cause, to bring about the day (still in the future) when Socialism will triumph, as it must, in England's blighted and undernourished land. But as he sweeps along from chapter to chapter, unflagging in his sometimes outrageous, sometimes justified critique, the sheer zest with which he makes the devil's case against Socialism knocks the proportions of the second half of the book askew. The case *for* Socialism is late in coming, and when it does, in the brief final chapter, it proves to be thin and disappointingly generalized. All very well to say Orwell knew he was preaching to the converted—and so needn't resort to argumentation that would already be familiar to them—but here was yet one more paradoxical instance of the devil getting off with the best lines.

Of course there is no reason to believe that he intended this to happen. There is an air of improvisation about Part II that suggests that Orwell started out with a number of notions he meant to pursue, paramount among them the iniquity of class differences, and trusted to luck, instinct, and high spirits to bring him safely to the end. It is indicative that while he had no difficulty in raising the problem of class—he would always be very good at raising a problem—he did not allow himself anything like a rigorous attempt to come up with a solution to it. Apparently, as with economic injustice, he felt that a change of heart was the essential answer; the method adopted hardly matters. Perhaps if he had had more time to reflect before writing, if he had not been writing in so euphoric a state—which makes even his outbursts of extravagant indignation so exhilarating to read—he might have infused his new Orwellian idealism with a saving drop of his old Blairian cynicism. For in the long run, a change of accent might prove more effective as a leveler than a change of heart, though more difficult to achieve.

But he was enjoying himself too much, firing off his salvos in rapid succession—taking aim in every possible direction—to allow himself to be deflected by complicating questions. Never before had he written with such zest and pleasure, no book of his had been turned out in so short a time and with such freedom from self-doubt. If, moving towards the end of the second draft, he felt it perhaps did not quite hang together as neatly as it should, he was not unduly concerned. Certainly he was not troubled by the ever-widening gap between the reality of his own experience and the angry fantasies that enliven his polemic.

ONE EXAMPLE PERHAPS WILL SUFFICE. IN PART II OF *The Road* there is a curious passage on working-class intellectuals, whom he divides into two categories: those who remain working-class (admirable), and those who climb into the middle class (less admirable). The latter have no choice, if they wish to succeed, but to come to terms with the corruption of the London literary world. In that world, Orwell assures us in the accents of bitter experience, you don't get ahead by virtue of ability, but by frequenting literary cocktail.parties and by "kissing the bums of verminous little lions." A vivid summary, worthy of a latter-day Jeremiah (or a Juvenal), but does it square with reality? Well, at the very moment that these scathing observations on how to get published in the most influential places were being written into Chapter 10 of *The Road,* the second number of *New Writing* was being made available in the shops. It confirmed the impression of its predecessor: here was one of the most distinguished and influential literary periodicals that London had to offer (then or later). To appear in its pages was a mark of genuine distinction. Orwell himself led off the list of contributors with "Shooting an Elephant"—and be it remembered that John Lehmann had read and admired his work, especially *Burmese Days,* and it was Lehmann who had written out of the blue to ask for a contribution, not the reverse. There, too, along with Orwell, was V. S. Pritchett, in no sense of the term an "establishment" man, with "Sense of Humour," which has since won an enduring place for itself in the history of the English short story. And in this second number of *New Writing* there was notable work by Ralph Bates, Ignazio Silone, W. H. Auden, André Chamson, Rex Warner, and Ralph Fox. Most remarkably, however, in the light of Orwell's vigorous assertion that bum-kissing and partygoing counted for more than talent in getting on and getting into print, in the same number there was also a story by George Garrett, whom Orwell had met in Liverpool in February. (Garrett seems to have been one of the two working-class writers Orwell actually knew at this time—the other was Jack Common.) His presence in *New Writing,* far more than Orwell's own, would seem to call into question the polemical point being made, for Garrett, as we know, was an unemployed docker, blacklisted as a Communist, living on the dole, an even less likely habitué of cocktail parties than Orwell himself; plainly he had been included in Lehmann's periodical on his merits alone. One would think that this inconvenient fact might possibly have stirred up second thoughts—mightn't the Jeremiad properly be reconsidered, the language moderated? Nothing of the sort happened. The phrase was too memorable to be sacrificed, the point seemed worth the making, and in a polemic it's the most vividly expressed thoughts (however questionable or superficial) that are the best remembered. With what relish, what zest those working-class climbers were fed to those verminous lions!—and so, ultimately, to the folklore of London literary life in the 1930's.

ONE UNDENIABLE ADVANTAGE OF WRITING WITHOUT PAUSING for second thoughts is that a book gets written fast: by the end of September, a mere five months since he'd started, the first draft was finished; he estimated that he would have completed the necessary revision by December. To Jack Common he admitted that he felt he'd made "rather a muck of parts of it," by which, it seems reasonable to assume, he meant parts of Part II. Since no manuscripts of *The Road to Wigan Pier* are known to survive, one can only speculate as to how and what he revised. But the close correspondences between the Diary and Part I constitute evidence of a sort—revision in Part I almost certainly must have been *stylistic*. Whereas a passage in Part II that couldn't have been written at the earliest before the end of October (it refers to the Fascist bombardment of Madrid) is proof of revision by *adding to the text*. But before carrying such speculations further, and saying more about the revised and completed manuscript that would be given to Gollancz in December, we prefer to look back to that marvelous summer during which the first draft was being written.

In any study of Orwell's life, the summer of 1936 must occupy a unique place. His health was good, his spirits high; he was able to work as he wished; he had the pleasure of living in the country, which he had long wanted to do; above all, the pleasure of being married to Eileen, of being

with her, week after week, untroubled by illness or absence, or the strains they were later to experience, working,
surviving, physically worn down, in wartime London. Indeed, only in that summer of 1936 would there be such a
combination of elements and circumstances as to fulfill an
ideal of happiness for him. (Thereafter, one element or another would always be lacking, one or another circumstance would interfere, and after Eileen's death during
minor surgery in 1945, even the ideal itself was abandoned:
the happiness of that long-ago summer would never be
recaptured.)

The friends who visited them at The Stores—Elizaveta
Fen, Geoffrey Gorer, Patricia Donohue, Cyril Connolly,
Denys King-Farlow—testify to the quality of the life there,
the sense of a deep attachment between the Blairs, the mix
of affection and irony (of which Eileen was as capable as
Eric), of mutual appreciation and understanding: they
were, beyond doubt, a couple. (Or, in Elizaveta Fen's
words, "a partnership . . . in which Orwell's needs came
first," an unspoken understanding that Eileen willingly
assented to, even though it had meant, in practical terms,
closing off the possibility of a career of her own.)

Miss Fen, from whose memoir we have quoted earlier, is
the only one of their friends to have written of them at this
period in this setting, and since her 1960 memoir has never
been reprinted, we quote from it again at some length.
(We have also followed her usage in conversation with
us, and substituted Eric for George whenever the name
occurs in the printed text.)

However much I enjoyed Eileen and Eric's company, the
weekends at the cottage were, in a sense, a test of endurance. Like all Russians, I cannot bear being cold

indoors, and the spare bedroom upstairs was as cold as an ice-box, even on June nights. Birds built their nests between the ceiling and the room, and although their singing was delightful in the morning, at night they would sometimes stamp and struggle overhead like an army of demons. "People think they are *rats*," Eric told me with the characteristic smile he had whenever he indulged in being mildly sadistic, and expected you to be frightened and shocked.

Whatever people might think, or Eric might say in that way of his, Eileen knew that in addition to birds in the eaves, the cottage was full of mice—not that this bothered her any more than it did Eric. Patricia Donohue (who had met the Blairs through Elizaveta Fen, and visited them at The Stores from time to time, and continued to see them afterwards in London during the war until Eileen's death) remembers Eileen once telling her that "battalions of mice were standing by at night, shoulder to shoulder on the shelves and pushing the china off."

Visitors unused to that sort of thing might look askance, but birds in the eaves and mice on the shelves were among the amenities, not the vexations, of country life, and Eileen and Eric thrived on it. Eileen, about whose good looks all who knew her are agreed, had never looked fresher or more attractive. "I remember," Patricia Donohue writes (in a letter to the authors), "Eileen as she stood once in the living room of the cottage at Wallington. She was wearing a tweed suit which suited her, and I noted how good-looking she was, with a good figure. At that time she was looking well and cheerful." Later, Miss Donohue goes on to say, "sometimes in London I thought she seemed very tired. [In fact, her physical state was a good deal more precarious than

Eileen or Eric ever realized, or were prepared to admit.]
But of course that was a time of air raids and blackout and
she was doing a good deal—housekeeping and cooking—and
also a fulltime job at the Ministry of Food."

(These latter remarks go a good way to explain Anthony
Powell's impression of Eileen, whom he met for the first
time during the war years and "never knew very well," as
someone "not usually given to making light of things, always appearing a little overwhelmed by the strain of keeping the household going, which could not have been easy."
Here too one should add Elizaveta Fen's observation that
after Eileen's beloved brother Laurence was killed by a
bomb during the evacuation from Dunkirk, "her grip on
life, which had never been very firm, loosened considerably.")

But the grief of 1940, the fatigue and depression that
were to be a kind of background to the Blairs' London life
during the war, while they went on living as though there
weren't time to be upset or unnerved by such minor difficulties as being bombed out of their flat—in short, the future that awaited them—all those complexities of wartime
life were at a still unguessable distance from the rural
simplicities of Wallington in the summer of 1936. Very
early, and without difficulty, they settled into the pattern
of working writer and devoted wife. At 6:30 a.m. the alarm
clock pealed through the house, and George got up to feed
the chickens. By the time he was done, Eileen had come
downstairs to the kitchen and was preparing breakfast:
eggs (from their hens), bread (which she would have
baked the day before), bacon (bought from neighbors who
kept pigs), a pot of steaming coffee with chicory in the
mix—a blend in the French manner Eric had grown fond
of in Paris. Then they went their separate ways: he to the

typewriter or to work in the garden; she, to wash up the dishes, take care of household chores, think about the next meal. (She once told Patricia Donohue, in a half-joking way, that "she reckoned there were only 25 minutes between the clearing up of one meal and the start of preparations for another.") But she enjoyed cooking and was very good at it—her apple meringue pie was delicious and memorable. Inez Holden, the author and journalist who introduced George and Eileen Orwell to Anthony and Lady Violet Powell one evening in the Café Royal in 1941, continued to remember that delicious pie, and evoked it for the present authors years after Eileen and Eric were dead, along with a host of other evocative, affectionate, and poignant details. Her summing-up of Eileen—"so intelligent, so nice"—might stand as a universal verdict. (From the many people to whom we talked about her, we never heard an adverse opinion. The only differences had to do with her complexion. Men tended to speak of her "high Irish coloring"—the phrase comes from Bob Edwards, a member of the House of Commons, who had known her in Spain and liked her immensely; women tended to speak of her very white skin. When we pointed out the contradiction to a woman friend of hers, she explained it thus: Eileen wore rouge, but applied it so lightly men wouldn't recognize it.)

There was, it seems, more than enough for each of them to do to fill their days at The Stores. Eric was racing ahead with *The Road,* or reading books sent to him for review by the *New English Weekly, Time and Tide,* and the *Fortnightly.* Eileen tended the shop, whenever it needed tending, which was not very often. As we have already said, the most assiduous customers were the village children in search of penny candy. (Earnings from the shop generally came to half a crown a week. Balanced against expenses, it was not a munificent return, although there was the advantage, they argued not very convincingly, of getting supplies at wholesale.) Late in the afternoon, smoking furiously, Eileen would walk Mabel and Kate, the goats, along the verges of the common. (One wonders if it was Eileen, with her sense of mischief, who named those goats—Mabel, as in Mabel Fierz, Eric's Egeria; or Mabel, as in Ida Mabel Blair, Eric's mother? One feels certain, in any case, that it must have been Eric who picked out "Marx" for their dirty white poodle, for Eileen's imagination did not tend to run along political lines.) Then there were the hens to be taken care of; she gathered the warm eggs to sell in the shop or for their own use; or to exchange with neighbors for bacon and sausage, or for fruits and vegetables they weren't growing themselves. She was especially fond of hens; for a time, when there were spare hours to fill, she thought that she might even write a children's book with a cast of hens in the leading roles, but, as it turned out, there wasn't time. How much there was to do in a day! Even though, when a friend like Elizaveta Fen, busy with her career, came to visit and one tried to describe to her what one did in Wallington, it seemed that one did nothing—nothing of importance. And yet the day was full. Before one knew where the hours had gone, it was time to prepare dinner. And after dinner, a stroll in the summer night; then homeward across the fields to bed. The logical end of such a life, to which both Eric and Eileen looked forward with a passion, ought to have been children. But Eileen did not become pregnant, and eventually they were to learn—though not for another two years; nothing was to flaw that summer of 1936—that Eric was sterile, as he told Rayner Heppenstall, and as Eileen confided in Elizaveta Fen.

Perhaps the most rewarding visit that summer—from a literary point of view, and at that, inadvertently—was paid to them by Denys King-Farlow, who came out to renew a friendship that had been long in abeyance. We have mentioned how a letter from him, forwarded to Blair by Cyril Connolly, arrived at The Stores on the morning of June 9, an hour or two before Eric and Eileen were to be married. Putting aside the prayer book in which he'd been studying the "obscenities" of the marriage service, he found time to dash off a friendly reply, urging King-Farlow to drop in if he should be passing anywhere near. "I should love to see you again."

They had been in the same Election in College at Eton, and together had been editors, first of the one-copy handwritten paper *Election Times*, and then of the printed "humorous" magazine *College Days*, a considerably more sophisticated and profitable venture—it included a good deal of paid advertising. The two young men had enjoyed a quasi-affectionate, rather peppery relationship; and in an oddly similar style the relationship was picked up in 1936 where it had been left off in Eton in 1922. They had parted then, each to go his own way, Blair to Burma, King-Farlow to Cambridge and then to Princeton and to work for Royal Dutch Shell. They had not been in touch in the intervening fourteen years. As though to emphasize the difference between them now—Eton, their common bond, was something in the distant past!—Blair in his letter of invitation ("I should love to see you") made it a point to say that he'd heard that King-Farlow was "very rich and flourishing," whereas *he* had had "a bloody life . . . but in some ways an interesting one." All in all, a quasi-affectionate but provocative greeting to which King-Farlow responded in kind when he dropped in at The Stores the next month.

Old school friendships only rarely are sustained, and continue to grow, as one grows older oneself. Most such friendships are "living and partly living" in the limbo of a past one has outgrown, however one may choose to remember it—fondly, indifferently, or with active loathing. The meeting of Blair and King-Farlow at The Stores—he dropped in in time for lunch and to be charmed by Eileen and to conclude that in that regard Blair had done very well for himself—did not inaugurate a new, richer, or different friendship on either side. It was all very much as it had been in College.

As King-Farlow has recalled the visit: "He came out and croaked a warm welcome in that curious voice of his . . . rather bored and slightly apologetic. . . . He was burnt a deep brown and looked terribly weedy, with his loose shabby corduroys and a grey shirt. . . . We had some cold lunch and some very good pickles that Blair and his wife were very proud of."

All most amiable; but the reunion had its peppery moments, too. Orwell wrongly presumed that his past experiences and present existence would impress his long-lost friend, offering him glimpses of a world that he, in his rich and flourishing life, would never have known: "He said quite kindly that he supposed a lot of what he was saying must be quite incomprehensible to [King-Farlow] who probably never had to work outside a comfortable office and never had to do a job of any sort with [his] hands."

King-Farlow was not prepared to be patronized: "I asked him whether he'd ever had to do any work with his hands apart from washing a few dishes in French restaurants." And to make the point even sharper, he added that he "didn't regard traipsing about England as a tramp as manual labour."

The game of one-upmanship continued. Blair said, Well, he had done quite a number of odd jobs with his hands from time to time, and he was, of course, now running this store and raising chickens. Unimpressed, King-Farlow said, "I've raised chickens since I was a boy and I never regarded that much as manual labour." Then, as he puts it, "I went on with some pleasure to tell him that when I first went to Texas, I had worked for two years in the oilfields as an oil roustabout, doing every sort of odd job as a tool dresser, then as a driller's help, then as a truck driver."

This was just the sort of give-and-take that Blair had enjoyed at Eton with King-Farlow, and he enjoyed it now; the remainder of the visit went pleasantly, and when it was time for King-Farlow to leave, they agreed that they must keep in touch and see each other often in the future. (In fact, they did not.)

But it would seem that King-Farlow's visit, however fortuitous, couldn't have occurred at a more fortunate moment for Orwell. He had made up his mind by this time that he would write about aspects of his own life—to point a moral —in Part II of *The Road*. In particular he wanted to evoke Eton (though he could not bring himself to name it in the text) as he had known the school in the first years of the postwar period, the time of "anti-*blague*," when he was himself that not-unfamiliar combination of schoolboy snob and revolutionary. Meeting after all these years with King-Farlow almost certainly helped him to recover that mood of mockery and irreverence, and especially the sort of details they had expressed with such youthful glee in *College Days:* "It has been unanimously decided that the Eton War Memorial shall consist of a nunnery. The site for its erection is the School Field."

What had it all come to? Schoolboy revolutionaries they

had been, but what had they ever known of the working class? Nothing—except to rail at their bad manners or to recoil at their smell. And how easily they had shed their revolutionary convictions, leaving Eton! He himself had gone off by choice to Burma to serve in the Imperial Police; and King-Farlow, though he had worked with his hands in the Texas oilfields, had done so, not as a member of the working class, but as someone from the upper-middle having his adventure, and as a first step toward his goal (which he seemed to have achieved) of making a lot of money.

Hardly had this long-lost, newly found friend driven off into the blue whence he came than Eric was back at the typewriter putting the two of them (and all the others like them) in their inglorious place. Eileen, downstairs, cleared away the luncheon plates and began to think about dinner. The even tenor of their ways resumed. Goats to be walked; chickens to be fed; vegetables to be picked; children turning up in the shop for penny candy; the tap tap tap of the typewriter.

It was very quiet in the late afternoons in Wallington: one heard the buzzing of the bees, the sound of the cuckoo. On such a day it must have seemed that their life could go on just as it was, for as long as they wanted. History—not in Wallington but in the world—would put an end to it all.

EIGHTEEN

STILL, FOR A WEEK OR TWO, EVEN A FEW MONTHS LONGER —until work on the book was nearly done—the world and its events hardly impinged upon Eric and Eileen in Wallington. For the time being, history was elsewhere. Yet if their life at The Stores had its idyllic aspect, it was very much an idyll in the tradition of the writer at work and his wife attending to his wants. For both of them, in their different ways, the book came first. Even the Spanish Civil War—which broke out in mid-July and which before another year was over would have such transformative and traumatic effect upon him, as a man, a writer, and a Socialist—could not distract him from the road to Wigan he had followed that winter and was traveling again, as best he knew how, on the typewriter that summer.

Only once did he allow a brief pause—two days—in the task he had imposed upon himself, and that was in early August, when he agreed to give a talk at the Summer School of the Adelphi Centre. The School was the most conspicuous and successful offshoot of the spiritual *communitas* and Socialist *universitas* that Middleton Murry had brought into being three years before. The Centre, though less influential, was as much a phenomenon of the 1930's as the Left Book Club, but its pedigree, mixing utopian and messianic strains, extended back as far as Coleridge and his Pantisocracy, and reflected too the yearnings of D. H. Lawrence, Murry's sometime idol, for a colony of kindred spirits (or disciples) with himself as Master (or leader).

In the Centre's three-year history, inseparable from Murry's own restless history and his continually evolving position vis-à-vis the world and himself—variously Communist, Socialist, Christian, and Pacifist—it had already been twice uprooted, as Murry would uproot himself and his household from one setting to the next, as Lawrence himself had done, always in search of his right place. The Centre was now situated where Murry, with his third wife and her child, and his two children by his second wife, had come temporarily to rest: in The Oaks, a large house in Langham, Essex, near Colchester. (The house had once belonged to a successful Edwardian courtesan in her years of opulent retirement. After the Murrys moved on, as inevitably they did, it became a temporary home for Basque children, orphaned victims of the Spanish Civil War.)

In the summer of 1936, the Centre was a meeting and holiday place for several hundred believers in self-education and -improvement, readers and contributors of the *Adelphi*, ardent Socialists, doctrinaire Communists, passionate Pacifists, along with such diversified celebrities (who came to speak) as the Marxist popularizer John Strachey and the theologian Reinhold Niebuhr. The greater number of those in attendance were Comrades of the middle class, but there was a smattering of the genuine working class—usually male and unmarried—and if a male Comrade of the working class found himself in due course in the arms of a female Comrade of the middle class, that was one of the unadvertised but undoubted rewards of attending the Centre's Summer School.

It was all very high-minded and yearnfully "matey," Bohemia looking Leftward in a way that Orwell thought contemptible, but a target ready-made for his use just then. He came, he observed, and he went home to vilify. Meanwhile, as against the displeasure of seeing and listening to Murry, whom he thought a "creeping Jesus," as master of his self-created *communitas*—and if ever a man was born not to be anyone's disciple it was Orwell—there was the pleasure of meeting with Rees for the first time since his return from the North. Also, unexpectedly, and more enjoyably than either might have anticipated, there was a reunion with Rayner Heppenstall, whose quest for money to live on while writing his book on the ballet—he had used up a meager advance from a publisher—had led him to Langham. Murry, with a certain logic, engaged him as his secretary, and with no logic whatever, as cook for the Centre. (It will be remembered that in Lawford Road all the cooking had been done by Orwell.) Neither job proved of long duration, and the most lasting consequence for Heppenstall of his stay at The Oaks was that it was there that he met the young woman he would presently marry.

Murry (who in his relation with Lawrence had cast himself in the role of Judas) decided that Heppenstall should be in the chair at Orwell's talk, a decision that cannot have been entirely free of malice and that must have made for a certain tension: this, after all, was the first time the two would have seen each other since the breakup of the ménage in Lawford Road. All went smoothly, however. Orwell spoke on poverty in the North, impromptu with a dry assurance, reinforcing his firsthand impressions with a formidable battery of statistics, and (especially surprising to Rees, who was in the audience) introducing, as though it were second nature to him, the occasional appropriate Marxist allusion. In effect, he was making a public declaration of his newfound Socialism, but since everybody there, more or less, had already found it before him, the impact (except upon Rees) was negligible. Indeed, Heppenstall, in his memoir of the event, didn't even feel the subject of the talk worth mentioning, but resumed his account with its sequel, when he and Orwell adjourned for an hour of amiable conversation in a nearby pub. Neither of them mentioned the shooting-stick debacle, and it is fair to say that their friendship, in its truest sense, began that evening at the Shepherd and Dog in Langham, and would continue thereafter, unmarred, until the end of Orwell's life.

In retrospect, it seemed odd to Heppenstall, or at least noteworthy, that Orwell should have said nothing to him during their conversation about the Spanish Civil War, in which, by the end of the year, he would be so deeply engaged. But it was not all that odd: it was early in August, and the Civil War had yet to reveal itself beyond Spain as the great anti-Fascist cause it was presently to become. A dedicated young English Communist like John Cornford, going off in August to fight for the Republic (one of the first English volunteers), was truly an exceptional figure. The only evidence to suggest that Orwell was more than mildly interested in the war from its very beginning, and immediately responsive to its significance, is to be found in the "autobiographical" Introduction he provided for the Ukrainian edition of *Animal Farm* in 1945. It was there he revealed to his Ukrainian readers that he got married "in the same week almost" that the Civil War "broke out in Spain. Both I and my wife expressed the wish to go to Spain and fight on the side of the Spanish government. We were ready within half a year. . . ." No doubt such an Introduction was not the proper place for the finer shadings and discriminations: even so, if one did not know the piece was Orwell's, one might reasonably assign it to some hard-pressed hack in a Ministry of Misinformation. (The actual manuscript, as written by Orwell, has disappeared. Translated into Ukrainian, it was retranslated back into English, in which form it appears in the *Collected Essays, Journalism and Letters*. In the movement from version to version, it may well have lost something, not least a style that is recognizably Orwell's.)

All the *contemporary* evidence would seem to agree that at the time of his visit to the Adelphi Summer School, and well into the autumn of 1936, Orwell's principal concern was his book. Even had it not been, the Summer School would not have served as an ideal testing ground for the question of Spain. Murry had undergone one of his deeply felt conversions, this time to Pacifism—presently he would make the facilities of the school available to the Peace Pledge Union—and Pacifism, as orchestrated by Murry, was the dominant theme, stirring up a good deal of unease among the Adelphians gathered there. Especially was this true for those among them—Rees, for example, who would soon break with the magazine altogether—who recognized the anomalous position history was forcing upon them. Until the summer of 1936, it was possible as a dedicated young man or woman of the Left to declare oneself a Socialist, an anti-Fascist, and a Pacifist, and not be troubled by a sense of inconsistency in any of these particulars. But Spain changed things. Suddenly reality caught up with one's idealism: it became possible (perhaps necessary) to bear arms against Fascism. And by so doing, did not one bring that much closer the nightmare of war that had haunted the European imagination since 1918, and shaped the generation in England that only three years earlier had sworn never to bear arms for King and Country?

In the September *Adelphi,* Murry made his commitment
to Pacifism public; in the February 1937 number his co-
editor, Max Plowman, a Pacifist of long standing, sought to
grapple more specifically with the troublesome question
history had thrust upon them. "Go Not to Spain," he argued,
pointing out that there were "more ways of winning a
fight than by rushing upon the enemy's bayonets." In
March, however, Murry allowed a reply to Plowman by
N. A. Holdaway, a Marxian theorist and a director of the
Centre, which he entitled "Go Not to Pacifism." But for
Orwell, and for thousands of other young men like him,
such questions had become academic. By the time the
February *Adelphi* appeared with its adjuration "Go Not to
Spain," he had already taken the road to Barcelona and
beyond, and was fighting on the Aragon front.

HE RETURNED FROM HIS HOLIDAY AT THE SUMMER SCHOOL
eager to hurry the book to its conclusion. Early in October
he had his first draft done, and immediately began work
on the revision. He had set a timetable for himself: the
final version to be in Gollancz's hands by mid-December.

As to what the first draft actually was, we can only
speculate. He himself described it to Jack Common as "a
sort of book of essays," which says rather less than it suggests: certainly, after the revision was done, no one would
ever resort to so diffident or reductive a description of
The Road to Wigan Pier. The two-part form he had chosen
ought to have served him well, with the first part setting
forth the problem, and the second its solution. The problem, of course, was poverty; the solution, Socialism. But
the neatness of the formal design was undone by the en-

croachments of history. The problem of poverty, looming so large in the first part of the book (as he intended), begins to recede in the second—displaced, so to speak, by a further problem, whose urgency, whose emotional claim upon him, he could not have anticipated: "the onslaught of Fascism" in Spain. In the eleventh chapter (only two from the end), events at the very moment they are happening in the world enter the book like bulletins of disaster: "As I write this, the Spanish Fascist forces are bombarding Madrid. . . ." We know this could not have been written before the end of October, for, as Hugh Thomas writes in *The Spanish Civil War*, "A heavy bombing campaign against Madrid was mounted from 29 October onwards, partly to satisfy the German advisers who were curious to see the civilian reaction."

It seems fair to say that from this time forward, Orwell was increasingly preoccupied with events in Spain and determined to go there to see them for himself as soon as he had finished his book. Uncertainty added a special urgency to the task: "It is quite likely that before the book is printed we shall have another Fascist country to add to the list. . . ."

The problem of poverty—which had called the book into being—is subordinated in these final chapters to the problem of Fascism, though the answer to both remains, as he intended, the same: the Socialism to which he had been converted after his journey North only six months before, and for which, only a few months in the future, he would be willing to risk his life—not simply in the rhetorical but even in the literal sense.

"Everyone who knows the meaning of poverty"—as he did—"everyone who has a genuine hatred of tyranny and war"—as he did—"is on the Socialist side"—as he was. "Socialism is the only real enemy that Fascism has to face," he wrote as he hurried to the end of his book and the beginning of his next journey. But such a formulation can be exactly reversed: *Fascism is the only real enemy.* . . .

Until now, until the book was done, this could not be other than what it was: the rhetoric of "the struggle," bravely phrased; the time was almost at hand, however, to close the book, to get beyond rhetoric, to discover its reality.

NINETEEN

OUTWARDLY, AT LEAST, THE DECISION TO GO TO SPAIN
—which he had reached by mid-November and presented
to Eileen, not for her advice nor conditional upon her
approval but as a *fait accompli*—was free of rhetorical
flourishes. How, one wonders, Orwell being Orwell, could
it have been otherwise? The "struggle"—that word of the
decade that sounds with such resonance, like a bell tolling
in Auden's "Spain" ("Today the struggle") and in count-
less other poems, fiction, and varieties of agitprop—hardly
entered into it. Sensible, practical, realistic—and from his
point of view the decision was all of these—it could be
made to seem (and quite possibly it was) as much an act of
literary professionalism as of political idealism. One book
was by now virtually finished, another would have to be
started: that was how he lived. A novel, perhaps? But he
had no compelling idea or experience that lent itself to
fictionalization; besides, he had found he was much more
at ease with the reportage of *Wigan Pier* than with the
invention and role-playing demanded of him in the two
novels that preceded it. It was more congenial, certainly, to
write about what one saw and felt and knew in one's own
person, whether as observer or participant, than trans-
muted, say, through a clergyman's spinster daughter, or a

self-pitying mini-poet at war with the Money God. Spain and its Civil War offered a great and logical subject for a writer such as himself, eager to see and know what was going on. And it coincided with his simple, straightforward, bourgeoning anti-Fascism: it was a subject to which he felt himself already deeply committed.

Then, too, it had the special virtue of answering Eileen's misgivings before she could even express them: how could she object if her husband carried out in practice the anti-Fascism her beloved brother had introduced to him, and to which Laurence was firmly, fatalistically dedicated? There might be some slight risk involved, Eric acknowledged in his offhand way—and her friends were quick to point the danger out to Eileen and to each other a good deal more emphatically, for they disapproved of Eric's going, thought it selfish of him to set out for Spain as though he had only himself to consider, and leave her isolated in Wallington, a mere six months after they were married, with the responsibility of The Stores and so little money—how would she manage? (Evidently the possibility of her going back to live with the O'Shaughnessys in Greenwich while he was away was never considered.) But the risks and dangers would be appreciably lessened, since he had decided to go as a journalist, a writer gathering materials for a few articles on the war, or perhaps with luck a new book. After all, he was not going as a soldier. That, at least, was what he told her, and what she told her friends when they expressed their concern; and it was very like her, whatever she might have felt, to pretend to believe him: it would make the parting that much easier. Yet she must have suspected, even as he himself must have understood at the back of his mind, that once he was there, he would do precisely what he did do two days after his arrival in Barcelona—volunteer to serve in the militia. His own subsequent explanation was a marvelous example of deflationary rhetoric in action: "It seemed the only conceivable thing to do."

At the end of November the writing was finished and Eileen had set to work, as she had used to do for Laurence, to type the final manuscript. On the eleventh of December, Orwell acquainted Leonard Moore with the no doubt welcome news that the book was finished—exactly on schedule —and the no doubt surprising news that he would be going to Spain at the earliest moment: while he was there, his wife would be empowered to act on his behalf. We can only conjecture as to what Moore made of this double announcement. No doubt as a sensible man of business, accustomed to the peculiarities of his authors, he glided over the Spanish venture and fixed upon the book—his legitimate concern—raising the possibility that Gollancz would make it a selection of the Left Book Club. Orwell was not so sanguine, however. On the fifteenth of December, when he sent off the manuscript, he was doubtful that it would be chosen for the Club: "Too fragmentary and, on the surface, not very left-wing." In any event, he hoped it would be possible for Gollancz to look at the book as early as possible, since he would be leaving for Spain within a week.

Sheila Hodges, in *Gollancz: The Story of a Publishing House 1928–1978*, tells us that "Victor read the manuscript in a couple of days, and afterwards he and Orwell had one of their rare meetings to discuss it." But what author and publisher said to each other at this rare meeting—which must have occurred sometime shortly before Christmas— she cannot tell us. Working back from what ultimately was to happen—*The Road* would become the Left Book Club selection for March 1937, and the special club edition in its

standard limp orange binding would include a foreword
by Victor Gollancz—one is free to speculate as to what
might have been said. Gollancz, predictably, and like many
readers of the book to this day, was divided in his reactions:
impressed by Part I and distressed by Part II. But on balance, whatever its defects, he felt they were far outweighed
by its virtues: "It is a long time since I have read so *living*
a book, or one so full of a burning indignation against
poverty and oppression." Very likely he had already made
up his mind that he would urge the book, defects and all,
upon his fellow selectors, John Strachey and Harold Laski,
confident that they would share his enthusiasm (and no
doubt also, his reservations). Very likely, too, he mentioned the possibility of its being chosen for the Club, and
stipulated that he would, in that case, want to write a
foreword, replying to certain debatable points in Part II.
Orwell agreed. One has the impression that, in his haste
to be off to Spain, he would have agreed to any condition,
short of rewriting a single sentence, or allowing a single
sentence to be tampered with. In fact there was no rewriting and no tampering. Author and publisher parted ami-
cably. (Theirs would always be an amicable if not especially
warm or confiding relationship, with more than a little
skepticism on both sides. When Orwell finally saw Gollancz's foreword—in May 1937 in Barcelona—he wrote to
thank him, saying that it was "the kind of discussion . . .
that one always wants and never seems to get from the
professional reviewers." This may, of course, have been no
more than an instance of Orwell's inbred courtesy—a tribute equally to his mother and to Mrs. Vaughan Wilkes—
or it may have represented irony of the most subtle sort.
In which case it seems worth noticing that when Orwell
decided to sever all ties with Victor Gollancz Ltd. in 1945

and to move for good to Martin Secker and Warburg, who had already published *Homage to Catalonia* and *Animal Farm,* he wrote to Moore about Gollancz: "I have no quarrel with him personally, he has treated me generously and published my work when no one else would but it is obviously unsatisfactory to be tied to a publisher who accepts or refuses books partly on political grounds [as Gollancz had done with *Homage,* refusing it before a word was written, and with *Animal Farm*] and whose political views were constantly changing . . .")

So Orwell set out for Spain, and Gollancz set out to launch what Franklin D. Roosevelt might have called his "hot potato," and what Frederic Warburg later described as a "lemon in an orange jacket."

The publication of *The Road* would make Orwell famous, it would win him more readers than he had ever had before—close to 50,000—and an equal measure of praise and abuse, and all this (it seems fair to say) was a consequence of the book's being made a selection of the Left Book Club. It is a part of Orwell's myth, though not of his history, that the book had been commissioned by the Club; in fact, the Club did not even exist in January of 1936 when he received his commission for the book from Gollancz. The first public announcement of the formation of the Club appeared as a two-page advertisement in the *New Statesman and Nation* for February 29, 1936. Its first selection appeared in May of that year. But because Gollancz was Orwell's publisher, and also the progenitor and leading spirit of the Club, it is understandable that some confusion should have arisen as to which came first. The truth, not the legend, is that *The Road* would have been written by Orwell and been published by Gollancz whether or not there had been a Left Book Club. It was the Club, however, that made the book a success (of a sort Orwell would not have again until *Animal Farm*) and among a number of its members a *succès de scandale*.

By March 1937, when *The Road* was sent out to its more than 40,000 members, the Club was already a resounding success—yet another coup for Gollancz, who had refused previously, in his style of advertising and in other ways, to conform to the taboos which were inherent in the "profession for gentlemen" which English publishing considered itself. But quite apart from its value as a way of distributing large quantities of Gollancz books, the Club fitted into his increasingly intense political interests, which moved ever more to the Left: a mix of Socialism, anti-Fascism, and Popular-Frontism. A shrewd publisher who was also something of a guru figure, Gollancz can be seen as a very accurate reflector of fellow-traveling trends in Britain in the 1930's. Shocked by the Nazi-Soviet pact—which seemed to him the embodiment of evil—he turned against Russia. Nonetheless, when the decisive *volte-face* occurred and the Soviets transformed themselves into Britain's gallant ally, he would not hesitate in his support of the alliance or allow anything to jeopardize it—hence, like so many other wartime publishers in Britain, he refused *Animal Farm,* fearing it might cause offense: politically unwise.

There is little question that in its early years the Club was at no great remove from the Communist "line." Strachey, though not officially a party member, was notably subservient or contributory to it, and both Laski and Gollancz tended to be cooperative: to the degree that one was committed to the cause of militant Socialism and anti-Fascism, cooperation with the party that shared those objectives had its logic. But too much can be made of this. The thinking of the three selectors was not as monolithic and undeviating as has sometimes been suggested. *The Road to Wigan Pier* was not designed to give aid and comfort to the party; and in due course it received a vitriolic review in the *Daily Worker* from Harry Pollitt, the general secretary of the party. That was to be expected, perhaps was even welcomed as showing that the Club was an independent agent. The "hot potato" aspect of sending out *The Road* as a Club selection was not the inevitable negative reception by Harry Pollitt, but its effect upon the majority of Club members who might imagine, not without cause, that they were pilloried in the second part of the book. It is very much to the credit of Gollancz, Strachey, and Laski that they decided to go ahead anyhow, and the choice was announced in the February issue of the *Left News*.

The book would be distributed to Club members, as usual, through bookstores and news agents at the ordinary members' price of 2/6 (the price for nonmembers was 10/6), and 43,690 copies were printed. Both the Club and trade editions contained thirty-two photographic illustrations and the Foreword by Victor Gollancz. The latter, however, was "addressed to members of the Left Book Club . . . and to them alone; members of the general public are asked to ignore it. But for technical considerations, it would have been deleted from the ordinary edition."

Gollancz's Foreword, interesting as a response to Orwell, is of equal interest as a "period" document. Why, he asks, should the selectors have thought a Foreword desirable? "Because," he answers

we find that many members . . . have the idea that in some sort of way a Left Book Club choice, first, represents the view of the three selectors, and secondly, in-

corporates the Left Book Club "policy." A moment's
thought should show that the first suggestion could be
true only in the worst kind of Fascist state, and that the
second is a contradiction in terms. . . . The Left Book
Club has no "policy": or rather it has no policy other
than that of equipping people to fight against war and
Fascism. . . . it would not even be true to say that the
People's Front is the "policy" of the Left Book Club,
though all three selectors are enthusiastically in favour
of it. What we rather feel is that by giving a wide dis-
tribution to books which represent many shades of Left
opinion . . . we are creating a mass basis without which
a genuine People's Front is impossible. In other words
the People's Front is not the policy of the Left Book
Club but the very existence of the Left Book Club tends
towards a People's Front.

All this was by way of prelude, and suggests a certain
uneasiness in approaching the subject: "We feel that a
Foreword to *The Road to Wigan Pier* . . . is desirable
. . . because we believe that the value of the book, for some
members, can be greatly increased if just a hint is given of
certain vital considerations that arise from a reading of it.
The value can be *increased:* as to the positive value itself,
no one of us has the smallest doubt."

Gollancz's Foreword runs to fourteen pages; of those, less
than one page is given to Part I—"a terrible record of evil
conditions, foul housing, wretched pay, hopeless unemployment and the villainies of the Means Test: it is also a
tribute to courage and patience—patience far too great. We
cannot imagine anything more likely to rouse the 'un-
converted' from their apathy than a reading of this part of
the book. . . . These chapters really are the kind of things
that make converts."

But most of the Foreword is concerned with that trouble-some Part II, with its crank speaking crankily, and its embarrassing admission that "in the opinion of the middle class in general, the working class smells," and its out-spokenness and wrongheadedness at so many points that Gollancz "marked well over a hundred passages about which I thought I should like to argue with Mr. Or-well. . . ." But that would have diverted him from his serious purpose: to point out the elements of anti-intel-lectualism in a man who is an intellectual in spite of himself, his romanticism, his refusal to accept industrialism, his dislike of Russia (most unusual in a Left Book Club book), and his failure to explain what he meant by those thrilling abstractions, Socialism, Justice, and Liberty. The last point is the most telling, and it catches the chief failing of Orwell's positive thought. He was a brilliant "against figure," and he could puncture pretensions and cant, but he could not envision an alternative society that one would want to live in other than to define it as decent and honor-able. (He was of course a master at describing an alterna-tive society in which one would rather die—or be dehumanized—and gave us a classic example of that sort in *1984.*) Gollancz's point is made decently and honorably:

It is indeed significant that so far as I can remember (he must forgive me if I am mistaken), Mr. Orwell does not once define what he means by Socialism; nor does he explain how the oppressors oppress, nor even what he understands by "liberty" and "justice." . . . What is indeed essential, once that first appeal has been made to "liberty" and "justice," is a careful and patient study of how the thing works: of *why* capitalism inevitably means oppression and injustice and the horrible class society which Mr. Orwell so brilliantly depicts; of the means

of transition to a Socialist society in which there will be
neither oppressor nor oppressed. In other words, *emotional* Socialism must become scientific Socialism. . . .

"A careful and patient study." The phrase sums up as
well as any precisely what Part II was not, nor would Orwell have claimed it to be. And Harold Laski, who reported
on the book in the March issue of *Left News,* would ask
for something similar: there was more to be learned, to
be studied, to be understood. Laski's review was favorable
and sympathetic. He compared the first part of the book
with *Hard Times,* as well as to Zola and Balzac. But when
he arrived at the second part, doubts rose to the surface.
"Having, very ably, depicted a disease, Mr. Orwell does
what so many well-meaning people do: needing a remedy
(he knows it is Socialism) he offers an incantation instead." Much in the manner of a teacher ticking off inadequacies on the part of a bright but insufficiently
prepared pupil, Laski complained that Orwell's concep-
tion of Socialism "ignores all that is implied in the urgent
reality of class antagonism. It refuses to confront the grave
problem of the State. It has no sense of the historic movement of the economic process. At bottom, in fact, it is an
emotional plea for Socialism addressed to comfortable
people." Of course, as Laski probably realized, most of
the members of the Left Book Club were "comfortable
people," and probably Orwell's appeal to them—to be
Socialists—perverse though it might be in some particulars,
was one to which they could respond in an emotional if
not a scientific way.

While the press, generally, received *The Road* with a
good deal more enthusiasm (despite some strictures) than
had been the case with *A Clergyman's Daughter* or *Keep*

the Aspidistra Flying, there seems to have been an almost missionary response on the part of the Club membership. In the April number of the *Left News,* Gollancz reported that the book had produced

> both more, and more interesting, letters than any other Club Choice. The book has done, perhaps in a greater degree than any previous book, what the Club is meant to do—it has provoked thought and discussion of the keenest kind. While members with a training in scientific socialism have been surprised at the naïveté of the second part, they have for this very reason found it valuable, as showing how much education they still have to do before the mass of vague humanitarianism can be turned into truly constructive channels: and middle class members have been so profoundly shocked by the conditions revealed in the first part of the book—a revelation which they have been all the more ready to accept precisely because Orwell's attitude in the second part is largely their own—that they have written to us, not one or two, by the hundreds, saying "Tell us, please, what can we *do.*"

Indeed, so powerful was the response that Gollancz decided to issue the first part separately, along with its illustrations, for a shilling. Announcing it in the *Left News,* he felt that it would "prove one of the best weapons in rousing the public conscience about the ghastly conditions of so many people in England today."

Essential to the whole notion of the Left Book Club was a belief in education: careful and patient study leading no doubt to a better world. But Gollancz and Laski, believing in a scientific rather than an emotional Socialism, believing (in 1937) that it was still possible to equip people to fight against war and Fascism, were caught in a time warp: history was leaving them behind. Orwell in Spain was continuing his education—in a real war against Fascism—and it was very different from anything envisioned by the selectors of the Left Book Club. What he was learning had less to do with scientific Socialism than with the morality of politics, and it would change his life.

PART FOUR

AN EDUCATION
IN SPAIN

TWENTY

HIS SIX MONTHS IN SPAIN PROVED THE MOST DECISIVE
experience of his life, and released within him the energy
and insight—the transformation—to accomplish the work
by which he is best remembered: the two most significant
(and popular) of his novels, *Animal Farm* and *1984;* the
greater number of his literary and political essays; and of
course, his memoir-analysis of his war experience and the
war itself, *Homage to Catalonia.*

Once having made up his mind to go, he recognized that
he would need official auspices of some sort or other to get
into Spain—he didn't much care which, so long as they
served his immediate purpose. As one logically would in
the circumstances, he turned to the Communist party, who
were well known as intermediaries. More specifically, he
turned first to the Old Etonian network, and asked his
friend Richard Rees to arrange for him to meet *his* friend
John Strachey, who had been at Eton with him—so, for
that matter, had Orwell, but he and Strachey had never
met. Rees took care of things with a telephone call, and
Strachey brought Orwell round to headquarters in King
Street to talk to Harry Pollitt, the general secretary of the
party. Pollitt had his virtues, but tact was not among them,
and he had a way of dealing with writers that some of them
tended to find grating. Stephen Spender, for example,

during his brief membership in the party, was taken aback when Pollitt suggested that he go out to Spain and get himself killed—"The Lord Byron of the Spanish Civil War!" —that would be a distinction; but Spender demurred. Pollitt's meeting with Orwell was less dramatic, but equally unproductive. Pollitt quizzed him, and Orwell's answers weren't satisfactory. He admitted to a sympathy for the Anarchists, who were already in the party's black books, so to speak, and when Pollitt asked if he would agree to join the International Brigade, he replied that he would make no agreement until he had seen what was going on. So that was that, as far as Pollitt was concerned, although he recommended that if Orwell was determined to go that he should get a safe-conduct at the Spanish Embassy in Paris.

With King Street behind him, he turned to another left-wing political group, the Independent Labour Party, whose Summer Institute at Letchworth he had briefly attended, and with whose weekly paper, the *New Leader*, he was not unfamiliar. It was typical of Orwell's luck (or fate) that he should have turned to a group that was in a state of declining influence and membership, and that would also, thanks to its special connections, determine the unpremeditated but formative course his experiences in Spain would take. The ILP had once been an important force in English politics—among the leading progenitors of the Labour party—but in the 1920's it had become increasingly sectarian and had disaffiliated from the Labour party in 1932. Fairly or not, it was regarded as the "crankiest" of the Labour groups, and it is a nice irony that Orwell, the anti-crank crank, should have become associated with it, even if for no other reason than to facilitate his trip to Spain. The party was more ideological than the newly politicized, independent-minded Socialist Orwell would have liked—it was more militantly Marxist and much more willing to co-operate with the Communists than with the Labour party. Its policies had cost it members, and it now had only slightly more than 4,000. But the party was willing to accredit Orwell as a correspondent for the *New Leader* and thus provided the means for him to go legitimately to Spain.

He was further equipped with a letter of introduction to John McNair, the ILP representative in Barcelona, from H. N. Brailsford, a well-known author, figure on the Left, and political journalist, who had edited the *New Leader* from 1922 to 1926. Orwell himself did not actually become a member of the ILP until June 1938, a year after he returned from Spain, and remained in the party only briefly —there is no indication that he paid more than one annual subscription. But in 1936, with his useful political introduction, his political press card, and a nonpolitical reading knowledge of Spanish, he departed for the war after Christmas, in order to report and perhaps to fight on the side of the Republic.

En route, he stopped off in Paris, and after collecting his safe-conduct pass at the Spanish Embassy, paid a visit to Henry Miller. Orwell, one of the earliest admirers of Miller's work at a time when it was banned from England and the United States, had, as we have seen, written an admiring and discerning review of *Tropic of Cancer* in the *New English Weekly* in 1935. The two men had corresponded, and Miller managed to get hold of a copy of *Down and Out*, long since out of print; later he would say it was the book of Orwell's he liked best. Their meeting, in the sort of bistro-Paris each knew and enjoyed to the dregs, went very well. Miller, completely apolitical and predictably outspoken, did not hesitate to tell Blair he thought him a fool to be going to Spain for any reason other than curiosity—certainly not any sense of political commitment. Nevertheless, he gave him a corduroy jacket of his own to help him keep warm, and Orwell was off, arriving in Barcelona on December 30.

In a somewhat belated, convoluted way, Orwell was beginning to achieve that identification with and recognition by the proletariat he had earlier yearned for. Perhaps in a foreign country, in the midst of a civil war, it might be possible, even for an Englishman of the lower-upper-middle, to declass himself. In Paris, on his way to Miller's in a taxi, he had had an argument with the driver and come away angry. The memory of that altercation rankled. But now, on the journey to Spain with his fellow recruits—and what a mixed bag they were, proletarians and honorary proletarians all jumbled together—he noticed as the train passed on its way through the countryside the peasants coming to attention and giving the Communist "raised-fist" salute: a "guard of honor." Retrospectively, he felt himself in sympathy with that Parisian taxi driver, who naturally would have regarded him as a rich Englishman rather than as a potential comrade. It is indicative of Orwell's excited state that he should have seen himself, the pugnacious taxi driver, the brave recruits on the train, and the cheering peasants in the fields as all united in the struggle against Fascism. He was prepared to be overwhelmed by his experience in Spain.

On his arrival, Barcelona seemed to him to be a socialist paradise. He could not have known that such a world was not to be found elsewhere in Spain, except perhaps in certain other Catalan towns and parts of Aragon. Barcelona appeared to his dazzled eyes as a city where the workers were triumphant—hats and ties had vanished, rents had been reduced by half, churches, convents, and monasteries had either been burned or taken over for use of the army, hotels had been commandeered by the people, tipping abolished, shops and cafes collectivized, not to mention 70 percent of all industry. It would strike a sympathetic newcomer from gray, class-ridden Britain that here equality and freedom had triumphed.

In fact there was already developing a power struggle between the great Anarcho-Syndicalist organization, the CNT, which was dominant in Catalonia, and the party of the Socialists, the PSUC, supported by the Communists. But Orwell, in the first flush of enthusiasm, was unaware of such tensions. Here was a world that he felt he had no choice but to fight for. It was the moment which T. R. Fyvel, his close friend and professional associate after 1940, labeled as "the starting-point for the ideas of a new humanist English left movement which he [Orwell] tried later to express." Certainly it was the moment that Orwell's particular dream of democratic Socialism began to take its mature form. The mood—not the maneuvering of the various factions and counter-factions within the government—was what counted, and propelled him forward.

In fact, although Orwell had too recently arrived and was too briefly on the scene to know, the "revolutionary" period was just about over, and the participation in the government of the Anarcho-Syndicalists and even the splinter Marxist party, the POUM, meant that the halcyon stage of the revolution—the tail-end of which Orwell had arrived to experience and which so fascinated him—had virtually run its course. But the hope and possibility it represented still lingered on to be responded to, especially by the unsuspecting and untutored observer who did not detect what lay beneath the surface.

Starting in October 1936, with Russia's decision to send the Republic arms, the only one of the great powers to do so, the balance of power in the government had begun to shift, and the preconditions that would be so important in forming Orwell's later thought were taking shape. In the exhilarated mood that transformed him from an observer to a participant, Orwell wished to fight for common decency and against Fascism—objectives no civilized soul could take objection to. He had no desire to be involved with, and at that time certainly hadn't the knowledge to understand, the complicated and "tiresome" details of Spanish political life. In some senses he did not mind depicting himself in the role of the political naïf and would consciously do so in *Homage to Catalonia*. But even if he had been preternaturally wise in the intricacies of the situation as it was, it is unlikely that it would have modified his exhilaration and commitment to the cause. (Still, it is ironic to contrast the "devil's advocate" tone he adopted in the second part of *The Road*, putting down an English Socialism still in its theoretical, larval stage, with his "born-again" tone in the early chapters of *Homage*, seeing, as it were, the Socialist Light of a newborn society.)

Shortly after his arrival in Barcelona, he presented his introduction from Brailsford to John McNair. McNair, a Newcastle man in his late forties, a self-taught workingman and dedicated Socialist, had spent twenty-five years in the leather trade in France. He came back to England in 1936, and attended the ILP Summer Conference at Letchworth. There, James Maxton, leader of the party, and Fenner Brockway, then the party secretary, had asked him to go to Spain as the party's representative. Quite apart from his dedication as a Socialist, his fluency in French and Spanish would be of inestimable value. Early in December he was in Barcelona and had established an ILP office on the Ramblas, one of the great avenues of the city, bustling with activity and famous for its central promenade. There, on a morning in January, Orwell came to see McNair in his office, and, according to McNair, that first meeting was not a success: he was put off by what he took to be Orwell's Etonian manner, and apart from this initial social chill, which the *pro forma* "Salud" on both sides did little to dispel, there was a misunderstanding of intent. McNair, understandably, thought that Orwell had come out as a journalist, and his mind leapt forward thinking of useful introductions to political leaders, possible interviews with ILP volunteers from England—that sort of thing. But no, Orwell, it turned out, rather thought he wanted to join one of the militias—he had had, which was more than could be said of most of the volunteers, actual military experience—and he wanted to go up to the front and fight. McNair had only some hazy familiarity with Orwell's literary reputation, such as it was: it was not as though an André Malraux or an Ernest Hemingway had appeared in the office. (Recollecting these events many years later, he thought it more than likely that he would not yet have read anything Orwell had written.) But he was also blessed with a mix of good-humored cynicism and common sense: Barcelona was swarming with writers from abroad who were sympathetic to the cause of the Republic; one writer more or less hardly made a significant difference. Whereas a man with military experience was not to be valued lightly. If this tall Englishman with his rasping, rather high-pitched voice and his diffident yet confident manner wanted to join the militia as a fighting man, McNair would do what he could to assist him; and it was settled that Orwell would come back to the office the next day.

The ILP's sister party in Spain was the POUM, the self-styled Party of Marxist Unification, though its very existence suggested the extent of disunity among Spanish Marxists. At the risk of offending or confusing readers with a plethora of all those initials that are endemic to a discussion, even a simple discussion, of Spanish Civil War politics, we must say that the POUM, that Marxist splinter party, was somewhat within the orbit of the CNT, the principal Anarcho-Syndicalist party, which was opposed by the PSUC, the Socialist party, which was increasingly influenced by its Communist members.

Now, it was the particular fate, one might say the fatality, of the POUM that it should have been caught up in the ever more bitter struggle, and in the end the bloody struggle to the death, between the CNT and the PSUC. And as a further aspect of its ultimately fatal history, that the POUM should have incurred the particular hostility of the Communists because of its alleged Trotskyist affiliations.

From the beginning of the Civil War in the previous July, virtually each of the many political parties had established a militia of its own, ranging along a broad spectrum of ideological "positions," and these "independent fighting units," taken together, comprised in the loosest sort of way the Army of the Republic. If this was not the most professional, or even the most sensible, method of waging a war, it was undoubtedly casual (which made joining up essentially a matter of choice or chance) and very much in the spirit of what has been called "the Bohemian period" of the Revolution. But the chief objection, which was already coming clear in the early winter of 1937, was that it did not seem to be leading to the defeat of Fascism.

Keeping in mind the situation as it was in December 1936, John McNair's advice and conduct is entirely understandable. As we have said, the ILP's sister party was the POUM, and ILP members coming out from England to fight in Spain automatically enlisted in the POUM militia. As arranged with McNair, Orwell came round to the ILP office in the Ramblas the day after their first meeting, and McNair conducted him to the Lenin Barracks. There were the headquarters of the POUM militia, and there Comrade Blair joined up. It could hardly have been more casually done, and very much in the spirit of the time; but it was a crucial step for Orwell himself, determining the shape of his Spanish experience, and of his commitment then and thereafter to the cause of human freedom.

2

HE RECEIVED VERY LITTLE TRAINING IN THE LENIN BARRACKS, but of course he had his considerable experience as a Burmese policeman and in the officer training corps at Eton to stand him in good stead as a soldier. Approximately a week after joining the militia, he set out with a contingent of very young and inexperienced volunteers for the front. They went by train from Barcelona to Barbastro, midway between Lérida and Huesca, then by truck to Siétamo, and then on to Alcubierre, on the Saragossa section of the Aragon front. The brigade was positioned a half-mile from the enemy. Orwell, eager for action, volunteered for patrols, and was soon promoted to corporal. But of action he saw little: Aragon, now, was "a quiet front." Danger, hardship, the risks of death, the chance of meeting in any significant way with the enemy—these were elsewhere. The reader of *Homage to Catalonia*, coming upon it for the first time and knowing its reputation as a classic of the

Spanish Civil War, may be surprised at how little intense, sustained, or large-scale military engagement it commemorates. But of course this is true of any number of other classics of war: genius (unfair though it should be so) can endow with equal intensity the long dull hours and days and nights when nothing important ever happens, and that incandescent moment of excitement and crisis when life itself seems to explode and is burnt out forever.

IT SEEMS USEFUL TO SAY SOMETHING FURTHER HERE ABOUT *Homage to Catalonia*. It has become, deservedly so, inseparable from the Spanish Civil War, as much a part of its literature as *Man's Hope* or *For Whom the Bell Tolls*. And yet, paradoxically, in its very permanence as something we all know and value and take for granted, it stands in the way of our seeing the transformation of Orwell as it happened, simple though it is to recognize the transformation after it occurred.

Part of the difficulty is inherent in the nature of the book itself: its sense of the present is so strong that one tends to forget that it was lived before it was written, and thought about after the events it describes. Then there is its peculiar formal organization: those contrasting sections of personal experience and of political-historical analysis—they are made to exist side by side in the text, as though happening together, or at the least as filtering through the same sensibility and in the same evocative process. But there is a difference that has to be kept in mind between writing that is lived and writing that has been worked up. As we will presently show, the actual composition of the book had its unusual aspect—it certainly was not written in its entirety in the traditional chronological fashion—and this too may account for the difficulty.

We have no wish here to devalue *Homage to Catalonia,* but if we seem to circumvent it, or to lay less than conventional emphasis upon it as a literary achievement or a compendium of celebrated quotations, it is simply that we think it more useful—for who has not yet read *Homage to Catalonia,* or will not someday read it?—to look behind the book for its author.

TOWARDS THE END OF JANUARY HE WAS TRANSFERRED FROM his largely Spanish group to join several English volunteers who had come out from the ILP under the leadership of Bob Edwards—members of the International Militia, as distinct from the International Brigade, by then predominantly under Communist control and fighting heroically on the crucial and very bloody Madrid front. This group of ILP volunteers, twenty-five strong, was assigned to the 3rd Regiment, Division Lenin, POUM, on the Aragon front at Alcubierre. For Orwell, and for Bob Williams, another English volunteer who had gone up with him earlier in the month to join the 3rd Regiment, it was essentially a matter of carrying one's rifle from one trench to another. Life became more interesting, not because the war showed any sign of hotting up—it was still very much a quiet front— but because, being among English-speaking comrades, one could talk a lot, and talk among soldiers tends to be engrossing, at least while it is going on, though elusive in memory.

The 3rd Regiment included some more than ordinarily interesting figures: the Comandante was Georges Kopp, a

Belgian who had been engaged in smuggling war matériel from France into Spain, until, on the verge of discovery, he simply crossed the border into Spain to take part in the fighting. He and Orwell became close friends—one of the few of Orwell's friendships from Spain that continued into the Second World War; in 1944, after an adventurous wartime history, Kopp made a second marriage: to a sister of Gwen O'Shaughnessy. Then there was Stafford Cottman, only seventeen, who looked up to Orwell, almost twice his age, as a model of wisdom and experience—he describes the English contingent as divided into Intellectuals, ready to argue issues, with whom he associated Orwell; Fundamentalists, who had a direct, uncomplicated commitment to winning the war; and Prolis (pronounced "proleys"), the ordinary "blokes," who complained, enjoyed themselves, and did what had to be done. Perhaps the best-known of the group was Bob Smillie—son of Bob Smillie, the Scottish Labour leader, one-time M.P., and a leading figure in the ILP—who would later die in prison in Valencia, possibly murdered by the Communists and certainly ill-treated by them.

Then, too, there was Bob Edwards, who still keeps a vivid memory of Orwell in battle dress: "corduroy riding breeches, khaki puttees and huge boots caked with mud, a yellow pigskin jerkin, a chocolate-colored balaclava helmet with a knitted khaki scarf of immeasurable length wrapped round and round his neck and face up to his ears." (Sybil Wingate, a nurse in Spain at the time, remembers Kopp telling her that Orwell was so tall "that one needed to climb up and talk to him.")

Adding up their glimpses and recollections—and there are others we shall be giving in due course—one comes away with an impression of an Orwell who was cheerful, agreeable, companionable, decent, interesting, uncomplaining—yes, even happy, and very different from the caustic, sardonic, dour figure one has encountered at most of the earlier stages in his life. Indeed, the Orwell evoked by those who knew him in Spain bears a strong likeness to Orwell in Wallington, with Eileen, tending to The Stores, the garden, the goats. So striking is the likeness that it does not seem unduly sentimental to suggest that the happiness that had its inception then, continued into Spain, sustaining itself under the most adverse and trying conditions.

Regrettably, the correspondence between Eileen and Eric has not survived. (A number of her letters to Jack Common, written from Morocco, are in the Berg Collection in New York, and they make for delightful reading.) But John McNair, who acted as postman for the ILP volunteers at the front, remembered a steady flow of letters between the two; beyond this, we have the quite extraordinary evidence of what happened.

Once Eileen heard from Eric that he had volunteered to serve in the POUM militia, she decided that she would go out to Spain too, not for political reasons (though her sympathies were entirely with the Republic) but simply because she wanted to be near him, and because she felt that there must be something useful she could do. What she proposed was not easy: the number of wives of foreign volunteers who got into Spain must have been few indeed. But Eileen was determined. Following the precedent set by Eric himself, she turned to the ILP for assistance. When she learned that John McNair needed a secretary who could type and deal with correspondence in English, she volunteered for the post, was accepted, and with a supply of Indian tea and Havana cigars in her suitcase was soon on her way. By mid-February she was at her desk in the office in the Ramblas.

Her arrival in Barcelona did not signal an immediate re-union. We know that she was at the front for two days early in March; conceivably Eric went into Barcelona to be with her before that. But, in the phrase that would become popular in the next war against Fascism, "there was a war on," Orwell was a soldier who took his duties seriously, and with his unwavering belief in "fairness," it is hard to think he would have requested a leave to which he was not entitled. In any event, the correspondence between them continued more regularly than before, and with a significant difference. Letters sent abroad from Spain were opened by the censors, and one put things in and left things out accordingly. But letters carried by hand and delivered at either end of the route by John McNair were a different matter.

From this time on, Eric wrote a kind of journal-letter for Eileen, reporting the day's events as they happened. Hastily scrawled in pencil on scraps of paper, crammed with abbreviations, jottings, initials, and fragmentary phrases, they would certainly prove useful as "raw material" for the book about Spain that he intended eventually to write. But the letters themselves were in a fragile state—even unfolding a page for the first time one ran the risk of tearing it—and Eileen, who had had the experience of typing the manuscript of *The Road* and her brother Laurence's book on chest surgery, decided to prepare a continuing typescript of these journal-letters as they arrived. McNair, who helped her to decipher them, long afterwards described them as "first drafts" for *Homage to Catalonia*, but this would seem to be so only in the loosest and most optimistic manner of speaking. "Raw material," as we have suggested, better describes the typescript that Eric and Eileen brought away with them in their hasty departure from Spain in June 1937, and a lot of writing would have to be done before the raw was cooked. On the thirty-first of July, back home in Wallington, he wrote to Rayner Heppenstall, "I have started my book but of course my fingers are all thumbs at present."

3

HIS EXPERIENCE AT HIS SECOND POSTING WAS AS UNEVENTFUL as his first: he went out on patrols; he tried to keep warm; the trenches stank of shit; he talked knowingly about politics, about which he knew less than he claimed, improvising from point to point, and prompting Bob Edwards to scoff at him as "a bloody scribbler." Most important, of course, he stored up for future use the "incidents" of military life at the front: a battle by megaphone, where each side tried to convert the other—which he regarded as improper—and a small engagement in February, when the Fascists were celebrating the victory of their army at Málaga, and he came under fire seriously for the first time— he was at pains to record how scared he was.

One incident that he failed to record—rather surprisingly, given its latent political implication—is included in Bob Edwards's introduction to a deluxe edition of *Homage to Catalonia* published in 1970. A friend of Orwell's was wounded, and he and Edwards strapped him to a donkey to take him to a first-aid post in the darkness. "We were new to this territory but mutually agreed that if we followed the valley immediately behind our lines we were bound to arrive at the small village in which the first-aid post was situated. Leading the donkey, we groped our way through the darkness and reached the village as dawn was breaking. We were both wearing at this time huge all-covering

Spanish cloaks, and as we trooped up the only road in the village we were saluted at frequent intervals by small groups of patrolling soldiers. As we reached the village square, however, the gold and red flag of the Fascists was flying from a large building, and both Orwell and I instantly realized that we had entered a Fascist-held village. We retraced our steps as quickly as we dared. . . ."

This incident may have been one origin of an accusation made by Frank Frankfort the following September in the *Daily Worker*. Frankfort, who had been one of the English volunteers in the 3rd Regiment, now accused the POUM of having been Fascist spies. He claimed, among other things, that a cart carrying food had crossed each night from the POUM lines to the Fascists—he himself had heard the rattle of the cartwheels; that a mysterious light (presumably a signal?) had been seen between the lines; and that Georges Kopp had been observed visiting the enemy. In the September 24 *New Leader*, Orwell wrote a rebuttal to these charges, and had it signed by as many members of his group as he could find on short notice—fourteen in all.

Frankfort's letter, of no consequence in itself, was symptomatic of the campaign to blacken the POUM after the May events in Barcelona, and a good deal of Orwell's time when he returned to England was used up in attempting to refute such charges. It was the price exacted by his "political education."

He came an extraordinary distance in an extraordinarily short time—but, of course, the circumstances were extraordinary. The original impetus that led Orwell to fight with the POUM militia—and if his meeting with Harry Pollitt at Communist party headquarters in King Street had been less grating, he would just as certainly have fought with the International Brigade—was a fundamental innocence that was easy to ridicule and difficult not to honor. He believed simply that it was a matter of fighting against Fascism and for common decency. Measured by Stafford Cottman's standard, Orwell began as a Fundamentalist and became an Intellectual. Bob Edwards, more experienced in such things, was startled by his political naïveté. So too was Harry Milton, a young American dissident of the far Left, a union organizer and a Trotskyite who came to Spain to fight against Fascism, and gravitated to the POUM militia (a logical place for someone of his political disposition), ending up beside Orwell in the 3rd Regiment. After only an hour of conversation with the very tall Englishman, the very short New Yorker felt that Orwell's political education would have to begin at "square one."

Orwell's attitude, in the abstract and divorced from events, was utterly logical and sensible, and if it had been more widely held (especially by Spaniards) and if it had prevailed, the end of the war might possibly have been different: since all of the various political parties under the Republican government umbrella were in the war together, and since all of them had everything to lose in a Fascist victory, it followed that they should cooperate and work to ensure the defeat of Fascism. This did not happen; that it did not happen is a matter of history. Logic and common sense, those virtues beloved of the English, measured in the scale, do not weigh much against passion, and irrationalism, and hatred, and envy, and greed, and all those other toxins that poison the human spirit. A major reason Orwell became so disillusioned about the war—which brought out the best and the worst in many of the people who were involved in it—was that his expectations were so high. His previous actual experience with the dirty deals of politics—as opposed, say, to what he had read of them in the *New Statesman*—had been nonexistent. It was easier to be the young cynic at a fashionable English Public School, or sampling life at the bottom in Paris and London, than to be in Spain in the winter of 1937, believing in the cause of the Spanish Republic, at a time when Nazi Germany and Fascist Italy were blatantly intervening on behalf of the insurrectionary government of General Franco, when the United States, Great Britain, and France were cravenly non-intervening on anyone's behalf, and only Soviet Russia and Mexico were intervening on behalf of the Republic. Spain revealed to him the heights and depths of human experience; ultimately, Spain transformed him.

But he was, or so it would appear, a political innocent. It seems hard to grasp to what extent this was so, although he testifies to it himself in *Homage to Catalonia,* and it is in this context that one should read Bob Edwards's account of his part in Orwell's political education: "I found it very difficult to convince Orwell that the civil war in Spain was essentially a political conflict—a conflict of ideas—and that without the willing support of the overwhelming majority of the Spanish people the war could not be won against Franco, and this involved social changes based on social equality and a democratic structure of Government." From Harry Milton he would have heard a more sophisticated line of argument, emphasizing and sorting out the divagations among the parties of the Left. But it is permissible to wonder how much influence either of these would-be educators had upon him at this time. Orwell's contradictory and argumentative nature was such that while he enjoyed (and may even have profited from) a good political discussion, he equally enjoyed a good disagreement with prevailing orthodoxy—in this case, the POUM/ILP line, which put winning the revolution ahead of winning the war, for only the right sort of revolutionary government would ensure the right sort of victory. And there can be no doubt that, at this stage of things—in the spring of 1937—such a line did not deeply appeal to him. It was a case of actions speaking louder than dialectic.

Orwell was too much the experienced police officer and old public schoolboy not to be appalled at the inefficiency of the POUM's military activities. In spite of being rebuffed by Harry Pollitt, he was still drawn to the International Brigade and the drama of the active fighting in defense of Madrid. Early in April he had mentioned the possibility to John McNair, when he came up to the front, and in a letter to Eileen at this time he suggested that she too might say something to McNair "abt my wanting to go to Madrid etc." When he came on leave to Barcelona less than a month later—that is, immediately prior to the May "events"—he had every intention of resigning from the POUM and signing up with the International Brigade. A German whom he met upon his arrival in Barcelona remembers that they "argued quite vociferously about political matters. At the time he [Orwell] was serving in the militia of the POUM, but he sharply criticized the politics of the party and demonstrated great sympathy for the politics of the Communists and for the popular front." Orwell himself recorded this preference in the pages of *Homage to Catalonia*. There seems no question but that the "winning of the war" was more important to him than the "winning of the revolution." In the circumstances, joining the International Brigade would have been a logical next step.

But history arranged things differently.

Whatever his dissatisfactions—and they were, as we have seen, essentially on a pragmatic level, the urgency of a man determined to get on with it and get things done—Orwell was increasingly aware of the ways in which the POUM was being misrepresented as a counterrevolutionary party of the Fascists in disguise. The Stalinists, and those who supported them, were intensifying their campaign, as part of the purges going on in the Soviet Union, against all those who called themselves Marxists but were unwilling to follow the line from Moscow.

Ironically, POUM had the reputation of being the most unrelentingly doctrinaire of the Spanish Marxist parties. Formed in September 1935, it argued that the workers and not the bourgeoisie must lead the coming revolution. Andrés Nin, formerly Trotsky's secretary (but now broken with him), was its present leader. Although believing that the great Anarchist party, the CNT, was weak on doctrine (however full of revolutionary ardor), the POUM had no choice but to become an ally of the CNT if it wished to have any influence at all.

It is not inconceivable that (as its enemies claimed) there were some spies and agents provocateurs in the POUM, as it was perhaps the easiest party to join at a time when it was dangerous not to belong to a political party. But why secret supporters of the Right would want to join a small party increasingly under attack by other parties on the Left and clearly in some state of disarray is not at all obvious. It hardly offered much in the way of cover.

POUM had only seven to eight thousand men at the Aragon front. It had little trade-union support. Nin had for a time been Minister of Justice in the Catalan government, but had been eased out in December at the insistence of the PSUC. Franz Borkenau, whose book *The Spanish Cockpit* Orwell greatly admired, there describes the December crisis, a foretelling of the far more traumatic interparty struggle still five months in the future:

It is difficult to say whether [the POUM] was more hateful to the PSUC on account of its anti-Stalinism in Russian affairs or its extreme Leftist tendencies in Spanish questions. . . . As a matter of fact the POUM was liked by nobody, being overbearing and claiming with its small forces leadership over the old established mass organizations, both anarchist and socialist. All through the time of their supremacy the anarchists had handled the POUM rather rudely, but this time they felt they were themselves concerned in the attack. The PSUC claimed the exclusion of the POUM from the Catalan Government on the ground of their alleged "counterrevolutionary activities," meaning by that the pretended collaboration of Trotsky with the Gestapo. The anarchists resisted, and a ministerial crisis of four days ensued. But the Russians withheld important arms they had promised, and finally the anarchists had to give in.

This December crisis had, of course, occurred before Orwell's arrival in Barcelona, and very likely McNair would have thought it too complicated to explain it to him at their first meeting: the departure of Nin, the one POUM man in the government, would hardly suggest the party as wielding much power. But the war of words between POUM and other parties of the Left continued unabated. POUM attacked the Communists as "the Mensheviks of the Revolution"; the Communists counterattacked: the POUM were "demagogic Bukharinites." Such slanging might stir the passions in Barcelona, but even assuming that Orwell caught the reference (and Harry Milton's recollections suggest that he didn't), their potency would be appreciably diminished in the trenches of Alcubierre. There is nothing like a whiff of gunpowder to clear the mind of questions of doctrinal purity.

In mid-April, when the subterranean tensions in Barcelona were moving closer to the surface, Orwell had a night of military action of the sort for which he yearned and too seldom got. At 1:45 a.m. he led out a party of fifteen men in a surprise raid. The result was a gain of several thousand yards, which forced the enemy to retreat from its advance position. Orwell's account, familiar to all readers of *Homage,* is in the clear, exact style we now think of as Orwellian. Kopp's account, immediately after the raid, is in the manner of a front-line dispatch during the First World War: "We have had a complete success, which is largely due to the courage of the English comrades who were in charge of assaulting the principal of the enemy's parapets. Among them I feel it is my duty to give a particular mention of the splendid action of Eric Blair, Bob Smillie and Paddy Donovan." And the account of the raid in the *New Leader* for April 30 is in a style pleasantly reminiscent of all those adventure stories for boys that used to be written under the influence of G. A. Henty: " 'Charge' shouted Blair. . . . In front of the parapet was Eric Blair's tall figure, coolly strolling forward through the storm of fire. He leapt at the parapet, then stumbled. Hell, had they got him? No, he was over, closely followed by Gross, of Hammersmith, Frankfort, of Hackney, and Bob Smillie, with the others right after them."

Whether as a consequence of this rare taste of military action, or the coming of spring and the end of the cold from which he particularly suffered, or, more likely his approaching leave and reunion with Eileen—"what a rest we will have, and go fishing too if it is in any way possible"— Orwell's spirits noticeably lifted in these last weeks on the quiet front. One of Stafford Cottman's recollections of this time is of Orwell asking him to whistle the "Eton Boating Song" for him.

He had spent some hundred and fifteen days at the front. They represented an accumulation of boredom and impatience and the sort of physical hardship and discomfort that went with being in the trenches, of long days of inaction, of patrols at night with nothing to show for them . . . earthbound, commonplace. Yet he valued this period, when it was happening and afterwards when he came to write about it. It was imbued for him with a sense of comradeship, freely and generously given, and which had been prefigured on his first day at the Lenin Barracks when he had met and clasped hands, exchanging hardly five words (in Italian and Spanish) with an Italian volunteer like himself. Better than any political slogan, it explained and justified his being there.

On April 25 the group was relieved and went down the line quickly to Barcelona. His impressions of the city, in the first weeks in January, had made it seem paradisal; now, in the first weeks of May, he was to experience his expulsion from Paradise.

4

THE POLITICAL SITUATION IN REPUBLICAN SPAIN HAD changed in the early months of 1937, had become more complex in its aims, more openly disharmonious in its notions of how to achieve them, and more fatally polarized between Anarchists on the Left and Communists on the Right. Orwell, acutely responsive to the situation in which he found himself on the Aragon front, had only the vaguest notion of what was happening away from it. He seems to have had no inkling—and indeed, why should he have had? —of the Communists' determination that Largo Caballero, the Premier of the Republic—too independent-minded, and a Socialist whom they thought to be too favorably disposed to the Anarchists—must be ousted from office. This was the prime motive in a complex of motives that would set off the events of May.

The mood of Barcelona to which Orwell returned late in April was very different from what it had been when he arrived there at the end of 1936. Month by month it was becoming steadily less expressive of a revolutionary workers' state (which Orwell had found so attractive), dominated from the Left of the spectrum by the Anarchists of the CNT. Instead, it showed more overtly the influence of the progressive/democratic/bourgeois government of the Republic, in which, odd as it might seem, the Socialists and their Communist allies were on the Right. The hope, of course, was that the Republic, in its evolution rightward, might prove itself so respectable a member of the Popular Front, and so unrevolutionary under the moderating influence of the Soviet Union, that it would win the approval and support of the middle classes without whom it could not survive.

Underlying the immediate disagreements of the various parties as they wrangled for control of the government (and hence the direction of the war) were two crucial questions that had yet to be resolved. In the words of Raymond Carr, in his *Spain 1808–1939*, "Was the Civil War part of a social revolution, set off prematurely by a generals' revolt . . . ? Or was it a war to defend an advanced form of democracy, a war whose successful prosecution was incompatible with radical social revolution which would alienate support abroad and drive out of the Republic those very classes whose skills and loyalty could best organize victory?"

Through the winter and early spring of 1937 there was a succession of provocative incidents: the relations between the two great parties of the state, the Anarchists and the Socialists (and within the latter, between the Socialists and the Communists), became potentially explosive—all that was needed was a final provocation.

Towards the end of April the pace quickened.

On the twenty-fifth, the day before Orwell's return to Barcelona, the Anarchist paper *Solidaridad Obrera* attacked the Communist commissar for public order in Madrid, José Carzorla, who had shut down an Anarchist paper in the capital which charged the Communists with maintaining a secret prison for their enemies.

Also on the twenty-fifth, the Socialist premier, Largo Caballero, dissolved the defense committee in Madrid, which was dominated by Communists.

Also on the twenty-fifth, in the border town of Puigcerdá in Catalonia, there was an armed clash between government carabineros and Anarchists who had taken over the operation of the frontier post there. Also on the twenty-fifth, the body of Roldán Cortada, a leading Communist in Barcelona, was found shot—it was assumed he had been slain by Anarchists.

On April 26, the day Orwell arrived in Barcelona, Cortada's funeral was made the excuse for a huge Socialist demonstration.

Also on the twenty-sixth, the police chief of Barcelona authorized a punitive expedition to the suburb where Cortada's body had been found, and a number of Anarchists were rounded up and arrested.

Also on the twenty-sixth, the mayor of Puigcerdá, an Anarchist, was shot when the Anarchists tried to regain command of the frontier post from which they had been driven the day before.

The various headquarters of the parties in Barcelona—

CNT, PSUC, and POUM—began to prepare for the next and fatal stage in the power struggle: the point at which slogans would give way to bullets.

It was against this extraordinarily explosive background that Orwell returned from the front, and in the joy of his reunion with Eileen, in his rediscovery of those small-scale pleasures that loom so large in the mind of a returning soldier—a hot bath, clean clothes, dinner in a restaurant, a night between sheets—he was able to defuse the situation of its urgency. For a few days longer, even another week, it was possible to pretend that life was going on as usual, that at the end of his second week of leave he would be returning to the front.

In fact, if life *had* gone on as usual, when his leave was up he would have served on a very different front. He had come back to Barcelona firmly decided to withdraw from the POUM. He would have preferred to join the troops of the Anarchists, with whom he was politically and temperamentally in sympathy, but this would not have resulted in the difference he wanted: above all, he was anxious to get to Madrid, the heart of the struggle, and for that the practical, positive answer was to serve with the International Brigade.

Shortly after his arrival in Barcelona, he got in touch with a friend in Spanish Medical Aid who was able to make arrangements for him to go to Albacete, where the Brigade had its headquarters, and enlist—the first stop, as it were, on the road to Madrid.

His friend, an English Communist, urged him to move promptly, the sooner the better, and to bring along with him, if he wanted, any other members of the ILP contingent who might welcome, as he would, the opportunity to be where the fire was hot—to take part in military action on a significant, even a decisive scale, and by so doing, play a more valuable role in the struggle against Fascism. Restless as he was, after three months of inactivity on the Aragon front, and dissatisfied as he was with the rather slipshod way things were done in the POUM, he might well have accepted the offer, gone to Albacete, joined the International Brigade, been assigned to the Madrid front. Had he done so, his history would have been very different. But he was determined to wait in Barcelona a bit longer: he was entitled to a second week of leave, not something a soldier would give up lightly, and he meant to enjoy it to the full—perhaps he and Eileen would go to the seaside for a few days. More than that, he had ordered a pair of boots that were in the process of being made for him—his feet were large, and the boots he had been issued in the Lenin Barracks were too small, and he had come to doubt that any boots in the Spanish army would be big enough for him— therefore he couldn't think of leaving until he had his new, specially fitted boots, that was understood, and it was unlikely they would be ready for him (to judge from the experience of soldiers from here to eternity) until the last or next-to-last day of his leave.

Staying on in Barcelona, he missed the opportunity to participate significantly in the actual fighting against the Fascist forces; instead, he witnessed and participated in the war within the war within the Republic—the struggle on the Left—in that first week of May 1937, as the contending parties and splinter parties warred among themselves to take control of the government, and so determine the course of the "revolution" and the conduct of the war against Franco and his German and Italian allies.

Orwell, coming straight from the front, was unprepared for the changed atmosphere of Barcelona. The idealism of

December, to which he had responded with such excitement, was virtually dissipated; the working class was no longer the one class in a classless society; the bourgeoisie were reemerging. As against the earlier promise of a "revolution" that would fulfill the dream of Socialism, now there was the disillusioning prospect of sectarian wrangling, Socialism betrayed, and the emergence of a capitalist Republic. Before the year was out, Orwell would be looking back nostalgically to that time when people believed in the "revolution": for him it had been a strange and moving experience, and the memory of it would prove ineffaceable.

That, of course, was the retrospective view. In May, one saw a city where the hateful signs of class differences were in evidence again. One felt a great rise in tension. At the headquarters of the three parties, preparations went forward, fatalistically and combatively, for the explosion everyone felt was bound to occur. (The PSUC launched a prophetic slogan—"Before we capture Saragossa, we have to take Barcelona"—which would be fulfilled only in the latter condition: Saragossa, to the end of the war, remained in Nationalist control.)

Determined though Orwell was to enjoy his leave, he couldn't help being aware of the "situation," which he saw, perhaps too simply, as the struggle between those who wanted the "revolution" to go forward (CNT and POUM) and those who did not (PSUC). Despite his educative political discussions at the front, starting at "square one," there were nuances of the situation in Barcelona he failed to recognize, complexities he oversimplified. Perhaps, in some sense, he still saw the war, and the war within the war, too firmly in terms of black and white, even though not the black and white he had originally expected. If, on the government side, there was a power struggle coming to a climax in Barcelona, he may have recognized it without recognizing sufficiently that the question of "revolution" in Spain (which had such considerable implications for Russian foreign policy, which in turn had such effect upon Spanish domestic policy) was precisely the issue upon which the fate of the Republic depended. And this may explain, better than totting up a list of omissions, errors of fact, and misinterpretations, why the historian Hugh Thomas should conclude that *Homage to Catalonia*, "marvellously written though it is, is a better book about war itself than about the Spanish War."

The troubles, the May Days, had their beginning—and a comic beginning it was for events that were to have so tragic an ending—on the second of May in the Telephone Exchange Building on the Plaza de Cataluña, the huge square at the top of the Ramblas, and a center for demonstrations. The Exchange, taken over from the American Telephone and Telegraph Company, was run by a joint committee of the UGT, the union arm of the Socialist party, and the CNT, but it was dominated by the latter. The Anarchist operators tended to harass members of the PSUC making telephone calls. On the second, when a high official of the Republic, in Valencia, telephoned the government of Catalonia, the Generalidad, in Barcelona, he was told by the operator that "there was no such thing as a government in Barcelona, only a 'defence committee.'" Later on the same day, a conversation between Azaña, the president of the Republic, and Companys, president of the Generalidad, was interrupted by the Anarchist operator, remarking that the lines were needed for more important purposes than a talk between the two presidents! This was to take Anarchy past the point of anarchy, and the central governments in both Valencia and Barcelona decided to assert their authority. On the third of May, Rodriguez Salas, the chief of police in Barcelona, arrived at the Telephone Exchange, and established himself in the Censor's Department on the first floor, with the declared intent of taking over the building. But the Anarchists, legally there, refused to be dislodged and took up their rifles. From the second floor, they began firing down the great staircase in the general direction of the Censor's office. Rodriguez was not to be drawn; he remained out of sight and out of reach behind closed doors, and summoned help. Within minutes a truckload of civil guards, armed and ready to follow his orders, arrived at the building; and in their wake came two of the Anarchist leaders (themselves highly placed in the police) who persuaded their comrades to put down their arms and return to their switchboards. But in a final burst of high spirits the indignant telephonists fired their remaining ammunition out the windows, into the crowded square. Whether anyone was hit is not known; what is certain is that the unmistakable sound of gunfire racketing through the square (and the shouting that followed upon it) was misunderstood. It was taken to signal the beginning of something—whether unplanned violence, a deliberate *coup*, or a long-smoldering rivalry bursting into flame. Within hours, in their separate headquarters the various political parties had mobilized their followers, brought stored-up weapons out of hiding, and begun building barricades, in anticipation of a siege, guerrilla stratagems, the random fatalities that are inseparable from fighting in the streets. (Actually, by the eighth of May, when the riots were over and "peace" was restored to the streets of Barcelona, more than four hundred people had been killed, more than a thousand wounded.)

Orwell's firsthand experience of the events of May (the

uprising, the troubles, the riots?—one has difficulty in choosing the term most appropriate to what actually occurred in that week in Barcelona) was oddly unsatisfactory: a mix of tension, uncertainty, excitement, fatigue, and anticlimax. And oddly similar in those respects to his experience at the Aragon front. He devotes a chapter to it in *Homage to Catalonia,* "marvellously"—as Hugh Thomas says—and also so clearly written that for anyone interested in following Orwell through the week, not simply on the page but (as the present authors have done) in Barcelona itself, step by step as it were, it proves as efficient as a guidebook.

There, on the left-hand side of the Ramblas, a short walk down from the Plaza de Cataluña, is the Hotel Continental, where Eileen had been living since coming out in February; there, on the same side, further along, is the Hotel Falcon, which had been taken over by the POUM as a combination of dormitory and offices; and a few doors further, the Café Moka, where a group of Civil Guards had holed up, the only visible "enemy" but singularly peaceful and unthreatening. From the sidewalk in front of the Moka —continuing our "Orwell tour"—one crosses the three strips of the Ramblas: the road for cars; the broad, tree-lined central walkway, with its kiosks and stalls, each with its special items for sale (canaries in wicker cages; goat cheese and sausages; newspapers); and the parallel road for cars. Safely on the other side, one starts up the Ramblas towards the Plaza de Cataluña; midway, one arrives at the sometime Poliorama Cinema (still a cinema, but renamed), where for three nights Orwell was on the roof on sentry duty, waiting for action that never came: the predictable anticlimax.

It seems emblematic of the deflationary way in which he chooses to tell the tale—and which makes it all the more credible, therefore—that when, at midday on the third, a friend whom he encountered in the lounge of the Continental told him there had been trouble at the Telephone Exchange he shrugged the news aside. Perhaps he had only been half-listening. Later in the afternoon, however, as he was coming down the Ramblas, he heard gunfire behind him, turned, saw some Anarchist youths, carrying rifles, edging along a side street: they had been exchanging shots with a sniper high up in a neighboring church tower. Now the reaction that he might have had earlier in the day occurred: "It's started." But what had started he would not precisely know throughout the week it was happening: rumors, conjectures, guesses, and speculations figured importantly in the absence of concrete news. (And when he came to write of it, several months later, he followed the chapter of personal history with a chapter of political analysis, though even then he knew less than he would have liked, and apologized in advance for the mistakes he would almost certainly be making.)

He and an American friend hurried down to the Falcon: there, presumably, something was to be learned. But all was confusion, and he went out, and crossed the Ramblas to the Comité Local of the POUM, which had been set up in the dusty remains of an abandoned nightclub and theater. In one of the rooms weapons were being distributed, and Orwell was issued a rifle and a small supply of ammunition. What next? No news, of course; confusion, of course. Rumors and speculation: "a vague idea" that they would be attacked momentarily (by whom?); "a general impression that the Civil Guards were after the CNT and the working class generally," and if that was the case, there was no question as to which side he was on.

Time passed; and passed; and nothing seemed to be happening: no attack was made in the next moment (or any time during the week) on the Comité Local or the other POUM buildings. But out of sight and out of earshot, who could say? Barcelona is an immense city, and the bird's-eye view is not given to the ordinary participant in great events. One is reminded, as much by Orwell's predicament as his prose, of Stendhal's Fabrice looking for the battle of Waterloo. Outside in the streets there would be sporadic bursts of gunfire. In the Comité Local, the younger members of the POUM, boy soldiers, thought it all a kind of picnic; one of them even made off deftly with Orwell's rifle.

He had taken it for granted that the telephones would be out of service; in fact, the operators had long since gone back to their switchboards. Once he had tracked down the number of the Continental, he had no difficulty in reaching the hotel, but Eileen wasn't to be found. He had better luck with John McNair, who was standing close by in the lobby, and who took the message for Eileen that he would be spending the night at the Comité Local in case there should be an attack.

McNair asked him if he needed anything.

"Only cigarettes," Orwell replied jokingly.

But McNair was willing to oblige. He set out with two packs of Lucky Strikes, down the pitch-dark Ramblas, getting past two armed patrols, as he later recalled, by whistling alternately the Anarchist and Communist anthems.

THAT NIGHT, WRAPPED IN A CURTAIN HE'D CUT DOWN FROM the stage of the cabaret, Orwell slept fitfully until three a.m., when he was awakened by the man who seemed to be in charge, handed a rifle, and put on guard duty at a

window. At dawn he was relieved of his post and his rifle—
rifles were in much too short supply to be given out indis-
criminately. Armed only with two primitive grenades, he
went downstairs and outside. Barricades were being constructed of cobblestones, in front of the Comité Local, and
across the Ramblas in front of the Hotel Falcon: for Orwell,
a "strange and wonderful" sight. Surely today something
was going to happen . . . where *he* was. (What he had
no way of knowing was that attempts were already being
made to end the fighting, both the PSUC and the CNT
trying to contain their extremists as the party leaders got
ready, not, as the innocent builders of the barricades might
imagine, to battle, but to bargain.) He walked up the
Ramblas, exposing himself in his great height to the stray
sniper's bullet, paused for a cup of coffee and to buy a
wedge of cheese at one of the few stalls opened for business, continued on to the Continental, where he had a brief
reunion with Eileen, then back to the POUM Executive
Building, in search of orders. From all over Barcelona came
the din of street fighting, the roar of gunfire in a gathering
crescendo: surely today something was going to happen
. . . where *he* was. He was talking to Kopp in an office on
the second floor, asking the usual question—what were
they supposed to do?—when there was a terrific booming
below, as though a field-gun were being fired.

Very calmly, as always, Kopp led the way downstairs to
investigate what was going on.

POUM shock troopers, in the doorway of the building,
were lobbing grenades along the pavement towards the
Café Moka next door. There, some twenty or so Civil
Guards had been barricaded since midafternoon of the day
before. In the early morning they had emerged long
enough for an exchange of gunfire—one POUMista badly

wounded; one Civil Guard killed—then hastily drew back into the safety of the café. Now they had come out again to fire at an unarmed POUM militiaman dodging his way down the central walk; he had found temporary shelter behind a kiosk.

Kopp ordered the shock troopers to stop their game of skittles. In Spanish, French, German, Italian, and English, he repeated that there must not be bloodshed, no provocations. Then, in full view of the "enemy," he stepped forward and put his pistol down on the pavement. Accompanied by two Spanish militiamen, who also made a great show of taking off their weapons, he started slowly toward the entrance of the café, where the Guards, unnerved by the exploding grenades, huddled in terror. One of them came forward to negotiate with Kopp. The unarmed militiaman, crouching behind the kiosk, was no longer a worry to them; their concern was with two of the grenades that hadn't exploded and lay there on the pavement in front of the café, ready to go off at any moment . . .

Kopp returned to the group clustered around the POUM building and decreed that the grenades should be touched off. One of the troopers took up his rifle, aimed, fired, on target—the first grenade disposed of. But his next shot was a miss. Orwell asked for the rifle. He got down on one knee, aimed, fired, and missed.

A pity, really; for it was the only shot he fired during the eight days of the riots. As it turned out, no other opportunity was presented to him.

After the incident, Kopp resumed their interrupted conversation. Their role had been decided on by the POUM leaders; they were simply and exclusively to defend their buildings; unless it proved unavoidable, they were not to open fire. To Orwell's earlier question, "What are we supposed to do?" Kopp replied in a practical way by assigning him to guard duty on the roof of the building opposite. Above the Poliorama Cinema was the Science Club of Barcelona with a two-domed observatory on its roof. From the observatory one may well have had a splendid view of the stars above Barcelona; from the parapet, looking down, one had a wide-range, supervisory view of the Hotel Falcon and the POUM Executive Building, which would have to be defended if attacked, and the "enemy" stronghold, the Café Moka, in the ground floor of a building whose upper floors housed a hotel, and whose roof was now being used as a sentry point by Civil Guards from the café.

Orwell spent the next three days on duty at the observatory, but nothing happened to disturb the long hours of loafing: he grew used to the racket of gunfire rising up from different areas of the city, a kind of accompaniment to his reading (he'd brought a lot of Penguins with him), and he used to go across to the Continental for his meals. From his aerie he tried to puzzle out what was happening, but on the rooftop with all the city spread out before him, he found he was in no better position to answer the question than he had been on the ground. The newspapers, which continued to publish through the week, added to his confusion, since each adhered to its own party's line. Thus, on Tuesday the fourth, Solidaridad Obrera, the paper of the CNT, was outraged by the attack on the Telephone Exchange; on Wednesday the fifth (as the negotiations about which Orwell had no knowledge got under way) it was urging that the riots be ended and that people return to their jobs. La Batalla, the paper of the POUM, which managed to publish in spite of police harassment, took the contrary view: the riots must go on, the barricades be maintained. Orwell, summing up the mood of the first three days, tells us that, although people were still at the barricades, "everyone was sick of the meaningless fighting, which could obviously lead to no real decision, because no one wanted this to develop into a full-sized civil war which might mean losing the war against Franco."

But "meaningless fighting" can be made the pretext for real decisions, as Orwell himself was presently to discover; and even as he thought that "nothing was happening," accords were being reached, decisions arrived at, that allow historians to conclude, as Raymond Carr has done, that "As a consequence of the May events both the revolutionary forces in Barcelona and Catalan independence of the central government were destroyed."

On May 5 there had been a broadcast of an accord between the Government and the CNT leadership, but the barricades continued to be manned. Kopp warned Orwell that there might be more serious fighting, particularly if the POUM was outlawed. He had had "information" that that was going to happen; the Government might be moving against them that very evening. Feverishly they set to work to fortify the Executive Building, and drew up plans to seize the Civil Guards in the Café Moka as soon as word came that the news was definite. "Our only chance was to attack them first." There is an excitement at this point in Orwell's narrative that is unmistakable: at last something is going to happen, here, to him. Eileen, too, came over from the Continental, ready to act as a nurse should it be necessary, though there was a lamentable absence of supplies: not even iodine or bandages. Orwell lay down on a sofa for a half-hour nap before the start of the fighting in which he presumed he would be killed. Uncomfortable though he was with his pistol sticking into his back, he slept a long time. When he woke up in the morning, Eileen told

him nothing had happened: the Government hadn't
attacked, the POUM hadn't been outlawed. Evidently
Kopp's information was false; in fact, it was merely pre-
mature.

The familiar sense of anticlimax—so much a part of his
Spanish experience—added to the depression he felt going
back to his post on the roof of the observatory. Nor did it
lighten when news came in the afternoon that there had
been some sort of truce arranged . . . short-lived in the
event, but it was clear by now that the end was in sight
. . . and clear, too, what at first he perceived only dimly,
that when the disturbances were over, a scapegoat would
have to be found, and who would be more likely than the
POUM, the smallest, weakest, most uncompromising and
revolutionary of the parties of the Left?

On the sixth of May, ships dispatched by the Government
in Valencia—two destroyers and a battleship—arrived in
the harbor. They brought four thousand Assault Guards,
picked Government troops, impressive in their conventional uniforms and new, standardized equipment—a far
cry from the ragtag "people's army" of the POUM. Soon
they were everywhere in the streets, restoring "law and
order," and the irony of their being there, rather than at
the front, fighting against Franco, was not lost upon Orwell.
On the seventh of May, the CNT asked for a return to
"normality"; on the eighth, the last sporadic fighting
ceased, and Barcelona was at peace again. The "May Days"
entered into history, an extraordinary and tragic event to
have taken place in the middle of a civil war. The consequences would be far-reaching: the suppression of a
political party, the deposition and replacement of a prime
minister, an end to the autonomy of Catalonia, an end to
the hopes of a workers' revolution, the strengthening and

bourgeoisification of the central government of the Republic. And among the minor consequences—but of crucial importance to the man himself, and to his work, and so ultimately to the millions of people who would become familiar with it and his name in succeeding generations— was the effect upon Orwell. His experience of the May Days completed the transformation that had begun in Wigan: henceforth he was a writer passionate in his political interests, sympathies, and convictions. For him it was no longer possible to separate art and politics; thanks to Spain, they had become inextricable.

On the ninth of May, as the semblance of peace and normality returned and the flags of the Republic were flying over Barcelona, the campaign of vilification began.

The POUM had been, all along, more provocative than Orwell may have recognized. It was disliked by the CNT and hated by the PSUC. Its continual exposures of the Moscow trials, its uncompromising denunciations of Stalinism as a betrayal of the Revolution had driven the Communists to a state of fury. It seems almost certain that the price of Russian military aid to the Republic would ultimately have included the suppression of the POUM; the May Days provided the necessary pretext. Hardly had the last gun been fired than the papers of the PSUC were describing the POUM as a Fascist party in disguise and demanding that it be outlawed. The widest possible circulation was given to a cartoon that depicted the POUM as "a figure slipping off a mask marked with the hammer and sickle and revealing a hideous, maniacal face marked with the swastika." For Orwell this was evidence enough that "the official version of the Barcelona fighting was already fixed upon: it was to be represented as a 'fifth column' Fascist rising engineered solely by the POUM."

He suffered a profound revulsion. At the heart of his Socialism, as we have seen, was a belief in honor and decency. And the ways in which the POUM was being misrepresented by its enemies seemed to him indecent and dishonorable: the politics of lying, the malignant distortions of language. (Here, surely, were the seeds of *Animal Farm* and *1984*.) He was not blind to the POUM's defects —only two weeks earlier he had come back to Barcelona intending to join the International Brigade. After the May Days, such a move was unthinkable. When his friend in Medical Aid, the English Communist to whom he'd originally broached the possibility, came to the Continental to ask if he was now ready to make the transfer, he replied, "Your papers are saying I'm a Fascist. Surely I should be politically suspect coming from the POUM." And he went on to say that he could never join any "Communist-controlled unit" for fear that it might be used against the Spanish working class.

The apparent peculiarity, not to say perversity, of his statement—especially for those who think of Communism and working-class revolution as synonymous—takes on a different aspect when set in context with the Spanish Communist party. For this, as Hugh Thomas writes,

was no ordinary communist party. If its propaganda harked back to the Russian revolution, its practice suited, and reflected the desires of, the small shopkeepers, small farmers, taxi drivers, minor officials and junior officers who joined it between July 1936 and the end of the year, without reading much Marx or knowing much of Russia, in the hope of finding protection against anarchism and lawlessness. The communists stood for a disciplined, left-of-Centre, bourgeois régime, capable of winning the war, with private industry limited by some nationalization, but not by collectivization, or workers' control.

This was a program that would not be likely to have offended a left-of-center Democrat in the United States or Labourite in Great Britain; certainly it would not have appealed to a militant Socialist such as Orwell had become.

In any event, his commitment to the POUM had now become a matter of principle: it would have been dishonorable and indecent to desert it when it was so palpably the underdog in a struggle it could not possibly win. Before the end of June the Government would suppress this gadfly of a party, but in May it still had its enfeebled legal existence, as well as its militia on the Huesca front, to which on May 10 Orwell returned, as a lieutenant, commanding about thirty men, English and Spanish. It was, as before, a quiet front. Action, such as it was, consisted mainly of going out on patrols. There was a good deal of sniping on both sides, but nothing that could count as even a minor engagement. There was ample time accordingly for political discussions, and, as Harry Milton observed, the old naïve Orwell had been utterly transformed by his experience in Barcelona. Such discussions would go on for hours, and it was at five A.M. one morning, some ten days after his return to the front, while talking about politics, that Orwell was found out and brought down by a sniper's bullet. Georges Kopp, in a letter to Orwell's brother-in-law, Laurence O'Shaughnessy, described the wound so precisely that one can safely assume he was transcribing a medical report: "The bullet entered the neck just under the larynx, slightly at the left side of its vertical axis, and went out at the dorsal right side of the neck's base. It was a normal 7 mm. bore, copper-plated Spanish mauser bullet, shot from a distance of some 175 yards. At this gauge, it still had the velocity of some 600 feet per second and a cauterising temperature. . . . The hemorrhaging was insignificant."

For Orwell it was as though he had been "*at the centre of an explosion.*" Lying on the ground, dazed, he knew that he had been wounded, but did not yet realize where. When he heard someone remark he had been shot through the neck, he assumed he would die, for a minute or two wondered if he might already have been killed: he did not feel any pain, only resentment that his life should end so pointlessly. He thought first of Eileen, and then, in logical sequence, of this world he had come to value and which he was leaving, not heroically in battle, but stupidly, picked off by a sniper. On the stretcher, he began to feel pain, so strong as to convince him that he was alive, and his thoughts now were of the four men who were carrying the stretcher, no easy burden, a mile and a half over slippery terrain to the ambulance. Then he was moved down the line, pausing for rudimentary care at a succession of primitive military hospitals that were little more than first-aid stations, in a slow, eight-day progress towards professional diagnosis and treatment: five miles to Siétamo, a further twenty-seven miles to Barbastro, then to Lérida, where Eileen and Kopp came to see him. (The doctor took Kopp aside and told him that no essential organ had been damaged, already Orwell was stronger, he would survive, in a day or two he would be able to get out of bed and walk about—but when he attempted to talk, the best he could manage was a whisper; his voice was gone.) He spent five or six days at Lérida; then he was sent on to the hospital at Tarragona, where there were sufficient doctors and nurses and equipment to care for the wounded as they deserved.

There, eight days after leaving the front, he was given a careful examination, and it was determined that one of his vocal chords was paralyzed. This meant, the doctor told him cheerfully, he would never recover the use of his voice. (In fact, he would speak in a whisper for the next two months; then his voice did begin to come back; after another four months he spoke quite normally, though with an occasional squeak.)

On May 27, Kopp and Eileen drove the sixty-one miles to Tarragona to pick him up and bring him back to Barcelona. He was being released from the hospital with the recommendation that he report for further treatment at the POUM's Sanitorium Maurin, on the outskirts of the city. It seemed to Kopp that he was not quite as "voiceless" as he had been at Lérida. In his letter to Laurence O'Shaughnessy, he writes that "Eric was able to utter any articulate sound but feebly and with the characteristic grinding noise of the brakes of a Model T, very antiquated Ford. His speech was inaudible outside a range of two yards."

He spent the next three days with Eileen at the Continental, and on May 31, the day before he was to enter the Sanitorium Maurin, they had cocktails and lunch with Kopp in a restaurant near the hotel, an event so agreeable (and proof of Eric's progress) that Kopp mentioned it in his letters to Laurence O'Shaughnessy.

On June 1, he entered the sanitorium, and would spend much of the next two weeks there, receiving treatment, not for the "incomplete semi-paralysis of the larynx" which was apparently untreatable, but for the extreme pain he was suffering in his arm and shoulder. There was a good deal of time, however, when he was free to come and go as he pleased, and then he and Eileen would start out from the Continental to wander about the city, sightseeing, adding

up all the obvious, sensible reasons why they should leave
as soon as it was feasible. Obviously the sooner he was at
home, the sooner he would regain his health. Obviously
he could be of no further use as a soldier. Obviously there
was nothing left for him to do for the POUM, *here:* its
story would have to be told, and he had already made up
his mind to tell it in his next book. But above all—however
many sensible and obvious reasons he could call upon to
justify leaving now—he was prey to an immense despair and
revulsion: "I had an overwhelming desire to get away from
it all; away from the horrible atmosphere of political suspicion and hatred, from streets thronged by armed men,
from air-raids, trenches, machine-guns, screaming trams,
milkless tea, oil cookery and shortage of cigarettes—from
almost everything I had learnt to associate with Spain."

They would leave as soon as it was feasible—and honor-
able. It was the latter condition that led to the melodrama
of Orwell's last days in Barcelona. If he had wanted, he
might have been able to leave Spain on his British passport
and as a journalist—it would have been entirely legal. But
to do so would have been at odds with his concept of
honor. He had served as a soldier, he would leave as a
soldier, honorably discharged. When he had come out to
Spain six months before, he had joined a voluntary group,
formed in the first fervor of revolutionary action, and he
had had great faith in the power of its enthusiasm. But the
army was now being formally organized and unified, gathering in the militias, and depended on conscripts. Weapons
would be needed to replace enthusiasm, and he was very
doubtful whether they would arrive in sufficient numbers
to bring about an ultimate, convincing victory. (Events
were to justify his skepticism. Russian military aid to the
Republic—the principal military aid from abroad—was gen-

erous up to a point, but was never allowed past the point where it might have outweighed the generosity of Hitler and Mussolini to Franco.) The change in the character of the army made his own position equivocal: one could no longer resign; and could one, having served with the POUM militia (now so open to question), count on being honorably discharged? Mightn't one just as likely be tossed into prison as a Fascist sympathizer? One heard such stories in Barcelona, but Orwell had also heard that he might be able to receive a proper discharge at the front: it would be worth the journey to find out, he thought, even though each day's delay added to the difficulty of getting safely out.

The doctors in the hospital in Tarragona had already determined that he was medically unfit. Regulations required that the diagnosis be confirmed by a hospital at the front. It was also necessary to have his papers stamped at the POUM militia headquarters. (No matter that he had been warned not to show his party card at the numerous paper checks that were taking place in Barcelona.) On June 15, he set out for Siétamo, just a few miles from Huesca, arriving there at midnight, in a truck bringing up troops for the new attack about to be launched against the city. Before he could explain why he was there, he was issued a rifle and ammunition, and ordered to stand by. That night he slept on the ground, fearing the worst but unwilling to be treated differently from the other soldiers with whom he'd come up to the front. Still, he was in a rather different situation from theirs, and he might, without apology, have pointed this out. In the morning, when it became evident that the attack would not be getting under way for some time—the inevitable anticlimax—he did show his hospital paper and set about to find the right place to be examined, going from Siétamo to Barbastro and Monzón and back to

Siétamo, which proved to be the right place after all: he was declared "useless," his papers were stamped, the discharge issued, and he started back to Barcelona. He arrived late on the night of the twentieth, and went straight to the Continental.

EARLIER THAT DAY EILEEN HAD WRITTEN TO HER BELOVED brother Laurence:

Eric is I think much better, though he cannot be brought to admit any improvement. His voice certainly improves very *slowly*, but he uses his arm much more freely though it is still very painful at times. He eats as much as anyone else and can walk about and do ordinary things quite effectively for a short time. He is *violently* depressed, which I think encouraging. I have now agreed to spend two or three days on the Mediterranean (in France) on the way home—probably at Port-Vendres. In any case we shall probably have to wait somewhere for money. The discharge is not through but I think we can leave next week, wire you for money when we arrive at Port-Vendres or other resting place, go on to Paris and spend there the nights and the day between, and then get the morning train to England. I do not altogether like this protracted travel, but no urgent complication seems possible now and he has an overwhelming desire to follow this programme—anyway, it has overwhelmed me.

As he came into the lounge, Eileen hurried up to embrace him, smiled affectionately, and whispered "Get out," meanwhile moving with him to the door, whispering "You can't stay here, someone may call the police." Out on the pavement, she slipped her arm through his, and they strolled along the Ramblas, to the casual eye another pair of lovers —in fact, it was only now that she explained that the Government had finally taken the long-awaited action: the POUM had been suppressed on the fifteenth, the day he left for Siétamo. Since then there had been widespread arrests—more than a thousand, it was said, among them forty members of the central committee of the party. And Georges Kopp! The headquarters at the Hotel Falcon was closed: the hotel itself was "immediately turned into a prison."

For Orwell, out of Barcelona and on the move since the fifteenth, the news came less as a surprise than as a confirmation of his deepest fears: the suppression of the POUM put the seal on his Spanish experience.

He led her into a nearby café—you never could tell who might be following—and listened grimly as she related what she knew to be fact: that the police had burst into her room at the Continental in the early morning when she was still in bed, in search of "evidence." They had taken everything of his from the sanitorium, even his dirty laundry, and everything they could lay hands on in the way of papers. Only their passports and checkbooks, which were hidden under the mattress, went undiscovered: the police had apologized for disturbing her (the touch of Spanish gallantry) and did not ask her to get out of the bed. (John McNair was later to say that he preserved the notes and an early "manuscript version" of what became *Homage to Catalonia* by placing the folder in which they were contained on the sill outside the window when the police arrived to search the office of the ILP.)

The question was no longer, When would they leave? but, How could they avoid arrest while they waited to leave? They decided that Eileen would remain at the hotel, and he himself would go into hiding; his POUM card he tore up at her insistence.

There followed three days and nights of tension and a curious bravado. Although he slept "out"—in the crypt of a ruined church, on a park bench—he did not conduct himself as a "fugitive." By day he would meet with Eileen and McNair; he and Eileen would eat in "fancy" restaurants, as unlikely haunts for former members of POUM, and would revenge himself afterwards by scrawling the graffito "Visca POUM" in the hallways of the restaurant.

The scheme finally devised was that he, McNair, and Stafford Cottman, the very young English member of the group, would meet at the British consulate to enlist the consul's help in getting the three necessary stamps in their passports: from the French consul, so they could travel through France; from the Catalan immigration authorities; and from the chief of police. The last was the potential danger, for he might put Orwell under arrest if he recognized that the 29th Division, as indicated on Orwell's papers, was part of the POUM.

The consul proved helpful; telephone calls were made; late on the second day they would have the stamps they needed. But Orwell also was determined to do all he could to help Kopp. That afternoon he and Eileen visited him in prison. Kopp wanted them to retrieve a letter of his in the Ministry of War that might be a valuable credential; without it he was simply another Fascist-Trotskyist wrecker from POUM and, as he said with a lightheartedness that did not mask the seriousness of his situation, he might end up in front of a firing squad.

Going to visit the prison, going to the Ministry of War (which he did next), Orwell did not hesitate to put himself

in a dangerous position—perhaps at such moments he sub-
scribed to the traditional belief of the Englishman that
somehow he was protected by a higher power when he
was among foreigners, and that he couldn't be arrested
unless he had broken a law. His confidence would seem
to have been justified: not only did he secure the letter,
but the officer who gave it to him shook hands with him
when they parted—an action that Orwell would compare,
in *Homage,* to an Englishman shaking hands with a German during the First World War. But the letter, duly
delivered to Kopp, failed to serve its purpose; he would
be held in that Spanish prison for another eighteen months,
when he managed to escape and crossed into France to
fight with the Resistance: he and Orwell would not meet
again until the middle of the Second World War.

On the evening of the second day, with their passports
and visas in order, they held back until the last possible
moment before entering the railway station: their destina-
tion was Port Bou. But the train left forty minutes *early,* so
they had to wait until the next morning. That night, their
last in Spain, they spent in a cheap hotel run by a member
of the CNT, who did not register them with the police.

For their second attempt, they decided to run the risk of
interception by the police, and arrived in the station early.
The train was already there, and they boarded separately:
first Eileen, who had come from the Continental, then Orwell, then Cottman, then McNair, and they crossed the
frontier without incident. Detectives did come through the
train taking some names, but didn't bother with the four
English, who were in the dining car and hence bourgeois
and respectable. Looking bourgeois would have endan-
gered them in Barcelona the previous December; now it
was a passport to safety. At the frontier their names were

checked against various lists, from which they were absent, and the police at the border seemed not to know that the 29th was the POUM division. Orwell felt they were lucky to get out alive.

At the border the quartet divided: McNair and Cottman would go straight on to England, Eileen and Orwell would spend a few days at Banyuls—not Port-Vendres—six miles into France, and the world at peace. Unexpectedly he felt a terrible urge to return to Spain: that was where real life was. He had experienced nobility and baseness, courage and betrayal, but his faith in the human, the crystal spirit, remained undimmed.

5

THERE IS A MEMORABLE SENTENCE BY V. S. PRITCHETT THAT portrays the legendary Orwell: "Tall and bony, the face lined with pain, eyes that stared out of their caves, he looked far away over one's head, as if seeking more discomfort and new indignations." But this is only a partial portrait, and like the legend itself somewhat misleading: in fact, he was looking (at and into and beyond) the subject about which he meant to write, and searching for the words that would allow him to bring it as precisely and powerfully alive as possible. His life was dedicated to his art as he understood it. He had his intense political and personal concerns: he was not abstracted, as the legend would have it, into a kind of saintliness. The difficulties and pleasures of ordinary life were important to him. But for the man who wrote—as a self-aware, protesting middle-class figure in twentieth-century England, heir to a great intellectual tradition of dissent—what he wrote was his overriding concern.

He had come to Spain with his politics untried and his ideals untested. As Harry Milton remarked of him after their first meeting: "He was a political innocent." Spain educated him in the complexities, ambiguities, compromises, and betrayals of politics. It cost him his innocence, but not, as might have seemed inevitable, his idealism.

Early in June, four weeks after the uprising in Barcelona —the decisive event in his political education—he wrote to Cyril Connolly from the sanitarium where he was slowly recovering from the wound in his throat: "I have seen wonderful things and at last really believe in Socialism, which I never did before." A decade later he would write: "Every line of serious work that I have written since 1936 has been written, directly or indirectly, *against* totalitarianism and *for* democratic Socialism, as I understand it." His seekings came to their resolution in Spain, and he was able to make peace with himself as a man, and find his way as an artist. And it was for this that he became George Orwell.

NOTES
INDEX

NOTES

Notes are given when it is not clear from the text where the sources are to be found, except in those few instances when the source of information did not wish to be identified. Letters from Orwell to Leonard Moore in the text which are not in *The Collected Essays, Journalism and Letters of George Orwell: An Age Like This, 1920–1940,* edited by Sonia Orwell and Ian Angus (New York, 1968), are in the Berg Collection, the New York Public Library.

p. 5 "In Communion with Reality," *The Times Literary Supplement* 21 December 1973, pp. 1153–5.

p. 15 Reviews the dates for which are not clear from the text: *Tatler* 11 January 1933, p. 52; *New Clarion* 21 January 1933, p. 139; *Adelphi* February 1933, pp. 381–2; *The Times Literary Supplement* 12 January 1933, p. 22; correspondence with Possenti and others in *The Times* 31 January, 11, 17, 21 February 1933.

p. 24 Details on printings and information on sales for *Down and Out* and other Orwell books are from the invaluable I. R. Willison, "George Orwell: Some Materials for a Bibliography," School of Librarianship, London University, 1953. Copies available in the British Library and the Stanford University Library.

p. 30 *New York Times Book Review* 6 August 1933, p. 4.

p. 40 Evelyn's and Frays: correspondence with John Bennett and C. A. Pratt, Chief Education Office, London Borough of Hillingdon; and interviews, Mr. and Mrs. H. S. K. Stapley and Graham Bennett.

p. 46   Rayner Heppenstall, *Four Absentees* (London, 1960), p. 58; T. R. Fyvel, "A Case for George Orwell," *Twentieth Century* September 1956.

p. 47   Avril Dunn, "My Brother, George Orwell," *Twentieth Century* March 1961, p. 257.

p. 53   American reviews of *Burmese Days*: *Herald Tribune Books* 28 October 1934, p. 3; *New York Times Book Review* 28 October 1934, p. 7; *Boston Evening Transcript* 1 December 1934, p. 3.

p. 86   Reviews of *A Clergyman's Daughter*: Compton Mackenzie, *Daily Mail* 21 March 1935, p. 4; Bonamy Dobrée, *Morning Post* 12 March 1935, p. 14; V. S. Pritchett, *Spectator* 22 March 1935, p. 504; Peter Quennell, *New Statesman and Nation* 23 March 1935, pp. 421–2; L. P. Hartley, *Sketch* 27 March 1935, p. xviii.

p. 89   Vincent McHugh, *Herald Tribune Books* 16 August 1936, p. 8.

p. 98   Heppenstall, p. 51.

p. 105   Frederick L. Gwynn, *Sturge Moore and the Life of the Arts* (London, 1952), p. 66.

p. 109   See Elizaveta Fen, "George Orwell's First Wife," *Twentieth Century* August 1960, pp. 115–26. Also interview.

p. 125   Isaac Rosenfeld, *Commentary* July 1955.

p. 128   Reviews of *Burmese Days*: *The Times Literary Supplement* 19 July 1935, p. 462; Sean O'Faolain, *Spectator* 28 June 1935, p. 1118; Compton Mackenzie, *Daily Mail*; Cyril Connolly, *New Statesman and Nation* 6 July 1935, p. 18.

p. 174   Reviews of *Keep the Aspidistra Flying*: Douglas West, *Daily Mail*; *The Times Literary Supplement* 3 May 1936, p. 376; Richard Church, *John O'London's Weekly* 2 May 1936, p. 164.

p. 188   Quoted in John Lehmann, *A Nest of Tigers* (Boston, 1968), p. 188.

p. 204   Fen, p. 117.

p. 206   Anthony Powell, *Infants of the Spring* (London, 1976), p. 136.

p. 213   We are particularly grateful to Mary Deiner, Richard
          Middletown Murry, Rayner Heppenstall, and Lawrence
          Bradshaw for talking to us about the Centre and other
          aspects of Orwell.

p. 236   Robert E. Dowse, *Left in the Centre* (London, 1966),
          p. 200.

p. 239   *Twentieth Century* September 1956, p. 256.

p. 241   Interview. See also John McNair, *James Maxton* (Lon-
          don, 1955), pp. 255–6.

p. 246   Bob Edwards, Introduction to *Homage to Catalonia*
          (London, 1970), pp. 7–11, for all quotations from Ed-
          wards. Also interview with him.

p. 246   Sybil Wingate to authors, 13 November 1967.

p. 250   *Daily Worker* 14 September 1937, p. 2.

p. 253   Peter Blackstein to authors, 8 January 1968.

p. 255   Franz Borkenau, *The Spanish Cockpit* (Ann Arbor,
          1963), p. 183 (first edition, 1937).

p. 256   Dan MacArthur, *We Carry On: Our Tribute to Bob
          Smillie* (London, n.d.), p. 4.

p. 258   Raymond Carr, *Spain 1808–1939* (Oxford, 1966), p.
          657.

p. 263   Hugh Thomas, *The Spanish Civil War*, 3rd ed., rev.
          and enl. (Harmondsworth, 1977), p. 653.

p. 271   Raymond Carr, *The Spanish Tragedy* (London, 1977),
          p. 174.

p. 274   Thomas, p. 646.

p. 275   British Library 49, 384 Georges Kopp to Laurence
          O'Shaughnessy, 10 June 1937, f. 5. Copy of lost 31
          May–1 June letter.

p. 280   British Library 49, 384 Eileen Blair to Laurence
          O'Shaughnessy, 20 June 1937, ff. 14–15.

p. 284   V. S. Pritchett, *New York Review of Books* 15 Decem-
          ber 1966, p. 6.

p. 284   8 June 1937, *Collected* I, p. 269.

p. 284   "Why I Write" (1946), *Collected* I, p. 5.

INDEX

Adam, (Aunt) Nellie, 8, 11, 49
Adelphi Centre summer school,
    158, 213–14, 217
Adelphi magazine, 5, 8, 71–3,
    75, 100, 103, 124, 138, 154,
    158, 164, 166; Blair/Orwell
    contributions to, 5, 8, 17, 49,
    68, 122, 124, 143–5, 218; re-
    views of Orwell books in,
    18–19, 131–2
Anarchists, Orwell's sympathy
    with, 236; *see also* CNT
Anarcho-Syndicalists (CNT),
    see CNT
Animal Farm, 8 *n.*, 14, 19, 60,
    63, 225, 226, 235, 274; Amer-
    ican publication of, 89;
    Ukrainian edition of, 153,
    216–17
Anzaña (president of Spanish
    Republic), 263
Auden, W. H., 19, 181, 202,
    221
"Auden & Co.," 181, 182

Balzac, Honoré de, 230
Barcelona: Eileen Orwell in,

247–8, 260–1; George Or-
    well in, 238–43, 258–61; May
    1937 troubles in, 263–75
Batalla, La, newspaper, 270
Bates, H. E., 18
Bates, Ralph, 202
Beadon, Roger, 44, 50; *see also*
    Indian Imperial Police
Bedales School, 95
Belloc, Hilaire, 19
Bennet-Coles (Doctor), 47, 49
Bennett, John, and family, 40,
    42, 45–7; *see also* Frays Col-
    lege
Berg Collection, New York, 247
Bertorelli's restaurant, 75
Best Poems of 1934, The, 138
Blair, Avril, 9, 11, 41, 47, 49,
    71, 178
Blair, Eileen O'Shaughnessy, 37,
    38, 79, 99–100, 107–11, 114–
    15, 117–18, 171–2, 176–80;
    death of, 110, 204; descrip-
    tions of, 117, 134, 140, 205,
    206; educational background
    of, 113, 116–18, 127, 177; in-
    fluence of, on husband, 110,
    184; social status of family of,
    112–13; in Spain, 247–9, 253,

A NOTE ON THE TYPE

This book was set in Caledonia, a Linotype face designed by W. A. Dwiggins. It belongs to the family of printing types called "modern face" by printers—a term used to mark the change in style of type letters that occurred about 1800. Caledonia borders on the general design of Scotch Modern, but is more freely drawn than that letter.

The book was composed, printed, and bound by American Book–Stratford Press, Brattleboro, Vermont and Saddle Brook, New Jersey.

Typography and binding based on a design by Clint Anglin.